POLITICAL ECONOMIES OF THE MIDDLE EAST AND NORTH AFRICA

POLITICAL ECONOMIES OF THE MIDDLE EAST AND NORTH AFRICA

ROBERT SPRINGBORG

polity

First published in 2020 by Polity Press

Polity Press
65 Bridge Street
Cambridge CB2 1UR, UK

Polity Press
101 Station Landing
Suite 300
Medford, MA 02155, USA

ISBN-13: 978-1-5095-3559-0
ISBN-13: 978-1-5095-3560-6(pb)

A catalogue record for this book is available from the British Library.

Library of Congress Cataloging-in-Publication Data
Names: Springborg, Robert, author.
Title: Political economies of the Middle East and North Africa / Robert Springborg.
Description: Cambridge, UK ; Medford, MA : Polity Press, 2020. | Includes bibliographical references and index. | Summary: "Despite its oil wealth, the Middle East and North Africa is economically stagnating. In this book leading Middle East scholar Robert Springborg discusses the economic future of this region by examining the national and regional political causes of its contemporary underperformance"-- Provided by publisher.
Identifiers: LCCN 2019023998 (print) | LCCN 2019023999 (ebook) | ISBN 9781509535590 (hardback) | ISBN 9781509535606 (paperback) | ISBN 9781509535613 (epub)
Subjects: LCSH: Middle East--Economic policy. | Africa, North--Economic policy. | Middle East--Economic conditions. | Africa, North--Economic conditions.
Classification: LCC HC415.15 .S67 2020 (print) | LCC HC415.15 (ebook) | DDC 330.956--dc23
LC record available at https://lccn.loc.gov/2019023998
LC ebook record available at https://lccn.loc.gov/2019023999

Typeset in 10.5 on 12pt Sabon
by Fakenham Prepress Solutions, Fakenham, Norfolk, NR21 8NL
Printed and bound in Great Britain by CPI Group (UK) Ltd, Croydon

For further information on Polity, visit our website: politybooks.com

CONTENTS

PREFACE AND ACKNOWLEDGMENTS

When approached by Polity Press editor Louise Knight to write what could be used as a textbook in courses on the political economy of the Middle East, I was hesitant. Having taught such courses over the years, I was aware of existing texts, most prominent of which is that initially written by my old friends Alan Richards and John Waterbury, then revised and updated by my newer friends Melani Cammett and Ishac Diwan. On reflection, however, I realized there was a need for a book complementary to rather than competitive with others in the field. If the new book were to focus on the state and its relative capacities to guide economic development, it would facilitate understanding of the economic outcomes on which other books concentrate.

My ensuing exploration of the origins and natures of Middle East and North Africa (MENA) states and assessments of their capacities to manage economies convinced me of two fundamental propositions. The first is the power of path dependency. These states and their effectiveness are products of their histories, hence reasonably fixed and unlikely to change swiftly or substantially. Linking histories to current forms and behavior is thus a central feature of the book and one that connects the past not only to the present, but also to the future. The second proposition is that MENA states have not well served the interests of their citizens, an assessment given empirical weight by the extensive comparative data made available in the last decade or so. The book draws upon this data to evaluate the performance of states and economies cross-nationally and longitudinally, thus adding comparative dimensions not typically addressed. This volume, in sum, is an old-fashioned political economy, in that it constitutes a return to an analysis of the political causes of economic outcomes, the original focus of that historically grounded discipline.

While developing these ideas and writing them up I have become indebted to many institutions, friends, colleagues and even relatives. As just indicated, I have long been an admirer of and learned from Alan, John, Melani and Ishac, not only from their jointly produced book but from their voluminous other writings as well. Ishac kindly shared with me papers delivered to the conference he organized in Paris in 2018. More recent interactions with colleagues at Harvard, Sciences Po and the Naval Postgraduate School, among whom I would like to single out Tom Bruneau, Philippe Droz-Vincent and Davide Luca, have enhanced my understandings of both MENA and other states, their origins, the roles played within them by coercive agencies, and their developmental impacts. Amr Adly, a pioneer explorer of the Egyptian and Turkish states, has informed my thinking while providing numerous empirical insights. Readers of the manuscript whose suggestions substantially improved it include Guilain Denoeux, Glenn Robinson, Sarah Smierciak, my son, Ziyad Springborg, and two anonymous readers recruited by Polity Press. Louise Knight not only inspired the volume but provided invaluable advice throughout. Tim Clark copy-edited the manuscript in record time and with his usual professionalism. My sincere thanks are extended to all, none of whom bears any responsibility for the final product.

I appreciate permission being granted by editors to include herein portions of material that initially appeared in different forms in their publications. These include Roel Meijer and Nils Butenschon, in whose *The Crisis of Citizenship in the Arab World*, published by Brill in 2017, my chapter, "The Effects of Patronage Systems and Clientelism on Citizenship in the Middle East" appeared; Anne Joyce, editor of *Middle East Policy*, in the Spring 2018 issue of which my "Deep States in MENA" was published; Benedikt van den Woldenberg, co-head of the editorial office of *Orient*, in the January 2019 issue of which my "Globalisation and Contentious Politics in the MENA," appeared; and Jacob Passel, editor of *The Middle East Journal*, which published my "Arab Armed Forces: State Makers or State Breakers?" in its Summer issue, 2015. Finally, I would like to thank Rashid Chaker, Division Chief for the Near East and South Asia of the Office of Opinion Research for the US Department of State, for assisting my understanding of results from public opinion polling in the MENA.

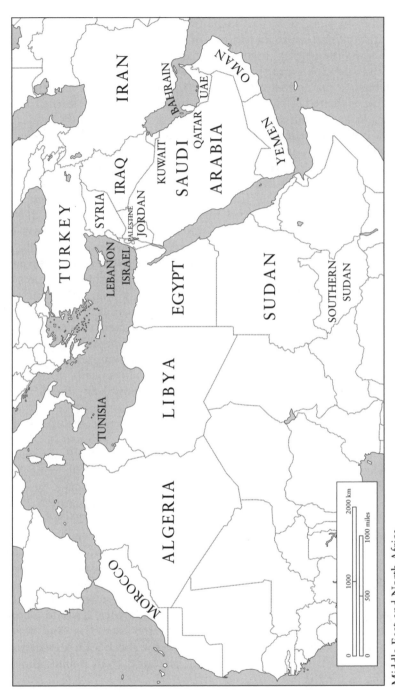

Middle East and North Africa

INTRODUCTION

The national economies of the Middle East and North Africa (MENA), and the region's economy as a whole, are today in a disorder that is deeply rooted historically and structurally and therefore not susceptible to rapid resolution. MENA nation states have been profoundly shaped by their respective pre-colonial histories, their encounters with colonialism, and the subsequent interaction between them, their region, and the world beyond. Variation in nation-state capacities—the means through which they govern—result from those historical legacies. Although the differences in national capacities are substantial, none of the Muslim Middle Eastern states is capable of managing its economy at a globally competitive level, as selected performance evidence will demonstrate. This raises the question of why these overgrown but weak states have been unable to escape their historical legacies, so still lack adequate governing capacities. The answer will be sought through investigations of how so-called "limited access orders," typically long established, are defended by deep states, the behavior of which in turn undermines the capacities of government as well as civil and political societies.

MENA economies, with the partial exception of Israel, face challenges of varying magnitude. In the Arab states that have dissolved into civil war—Syria, Yemen and Libya—national economies no longer exist. In the other Arab republics—Algeria, Tunisia, Egypt, Sudan, Lebanon and Iraq—per capita GDP growth has flattened at below 2% annually, a low rate by the standards of developing and emerging economies. Rates of unemployment and poverty, driven by comparatively high population growth unsupported by adequate job creation, have risen above those of comparator countries in other developing regions. A "30/30 rule" provides a rough estimate of

1

those rates—30% of youths unemployed and 30% of the population impoverished. Arab monarchies of the Gulf Cooperation Council (GCC), which are the MENA states most heavily dependent upon oil and gas revenues, have stagnated economically since the dramatic downturn in hydrocarbon prices from June 2014. They face the daunting challenge of urgently diversifying non-sustainable rentier political economies away from dependence on energy revenues. Jordan and Morocco, the other two Arab monarchies, present more mixed pictures. The former's economy depends ever more precariously on its regional security role, as its production of tradeable goods, exports and even remittances have failed to keep pace with population growth. Morocco's exports of agricultural commodities and manufactures, along with phosphates, have been increasing, but this bright spot among Arab economies is dimmed by relatively slow per capita growth, poor human resource development, and unequal distribution of national income.

Non-Arab Turkey and Iran are faring better, but no longer remarkably so. The former's "economic miracle" that commenced with the new millennium has now ended, as indicated by per capita income hovering at $10,000 for a decade. The combination of rising debt, stagnating productivity and political insecurity have subdued foreign investment, previously the main driver propelling rapid growth. The "peace dividend" Iran anticipated from agreeing in 2015 to the Joint Comprehensive Plan of Action (JCPOA) to temporarily suspend its nuclear program did not materialize in the hoped-for magnitude and, in any event, the JCPOA was unilaterally abrogated by the Trump Administration in 2018. Low oil and gas prices combined with stagnating exports of those hydrocarbons have eroded hopes for a dramatic increase in foreign currency earnings that might have driven more rapid economic growth. Only Israel in the MENA has managed to achieve high rates of economic growth and to graduate its economy to OECD levels of output, export diversification and overall sophistication. But Israel's is the economy least interconnected within the region, having very few backward or forward linkages that might pull along the broader MENA economy. Israel's very success as an outlier appears to attest to the region's dead weight, drag effect on its "inliers," a hypothesis that receives further support from Morocco's comparative economic success. It is the Arab state most connected to the European and least connected to the Arab economy.

As for the regional economy, its relative underperformance both results from and contributes to its comparative lack of integration.

2

Low rates of intra-regional trade, especially of an intra-industry nature that arises from production integrated across borders, reflect persisting tariff and increasingly non-tariff trade barriers. Service sectors, especially that of finance, continue to enjoy substantial protection, so are comparatively inefficient and non-competitive internationally. Regional physical infrastructure is deficient, providing inadequate transportation and communication linkages, to say nothing of failing to adequately capitalize on possible synergies from energy sharing. The region-wide oil economy that was predicted in the mid-1970s and early 1980s to emerge from connecting petrodollars, surplus Arab labor and imported technology to diversify and industrialize, failed to materialize. Oil-rich Arab states, out of political and economic motives, have chosen instead to substitute non-Arab for Arab migrant labor. Public and private capital transfers from GCC to other Arab countries have declined as a proportion of total GCC investments and expenditures, which have increasingly been directed toward the West and East Asia. The MENA economy has not moved up value-added ladders other than in downstream hydrocarbon processing. Its share of global manufacturing has been in steady decline since the oil boom of the 1970s. The MENA economy is not being driven forward by infusions of technology, capital and managerial expertise in a manner analogous to the "flying goose" model of East Asia, where Japan and now China have led the way for emulators such as Taiwan and South Korea. Potential MENA "lead geese," which could be non-Arab Israel, Turkey and/ or Iran, are precluded from playing that role for both political and economic reasons, while Saudi Arabia's economy is too oil-centric, Dubai's too service-centric, and both too expatriate-dependent, to be widely emulated.

The political deficiencies of MENA nation states result primarily from the combination of their previous histories followed by their encounters with colonialism. Historically "embedded" countries whose pedigrees as virtual nation states extend over centuries or millennia, including Egypt, Iran, Morocco, Tunisia and Turkey, had better prospects for developing what the historical sociologist Michael Mann has referred to as infrastructural power than those with shallower historical roots, such as Libya, Algeria, Sudan, Lebanon, Syria, Yemen or Iraq. The colonial dialectics which drove nationalism and ultimately independence varied from country to country, reinforcing or undermining pre-existing potential state capacities. As a whole, however, MENA post-colonial states were relatively brittle, depending more upon Mann's "despotic" than his infrastructural power, incapable as they were of truly penetrating the heterogeneous societies over which most ruled. Repression or patronage were thus inevitably the primary means of ruling, neither of which was compatible with sustainable economic development. Both approaches depended upon states that would exercise power arbitrarily and carefully select the few to whom it would grant political and economic access. Republics and, to a lesser degree, monarchies created "deep states" to defend their limited access orders. Those deep states in turn undermined the nominal, visible governmental institutions upon which effective governance and the rule of law must rest. Erosion of nationalist legitimacy through the sheer passage of time since the end of colonial rule, combined with economic stagnation resulting from the structural deficiencies of the political economies of these post-colonial states, has eroded the legitimacy of incumbent elites and caused ever increasing mass political disaffection. That in turn has necessitated yet more repression and/or patronage, reinforcing the downward economic spiral in which these states are trapped.

This book will elaborate these ideas theoretically and empirically in the following chapters. It will do so within the discipline of political economy as it was originally articulated, which is to say, with a primary focus on political factors driving economic outcomes.

Chapter 1 will review explanations of the MENA's cross-national and longitudinal comparative underperformance offered by scholars of political economy and related disciplines. The common theme of these explanations is that weak institutions have failed to provide adequate governance, including that to support efficient political and economic markets. While inadequate contemporary institutions are so because they are "path dependent," in the sense that they have evolved historically as subsequent actions have been conditioned by previous ones, today's institutions in the MENA are also the result of contemporary contextual factors, key of which is economic dependence on hydrocarbon exports.

Chapter 2 will discuss pre-colonial legacies of state formation in the MENA and how varying degrees of "stateness" prior to the imposition of colonial rule impacted subsequent development of state effectiveness. Measured by governance capacities, degree of societal cohesion and quality of political leadership, MENA countries are less effective than comparators and face greater obstacles to enhancing that effectiveness, which varies substantially between countries. Those with historical roots with capitals and borders pre-dating the colonial era (Morocco, Tunisia, Egypt, Iran and Turkey) display greater effectiveness than those with "artificial borders" fabricated and managed by colonial powers and, in some cases, the settlers and national leaders chosen by them, which include Algeria, Libya, Lebanon, Syria, Sudan, Iraq, Israel/Palestine and South Yemen, as well as the Arabian Peninsula states that were shaped by interactions between locals and imperial powers, but with no colonial settlement (GCC countries plus North Yemen). The principal exception to this general rule consists of the small Arab oil exporters, which essentially imported their states and the personnel to run them from the West, and Great Britain in particular.

Chapter 3 traces the further historical development of MENA stateness through the colonial and post-colonial eras and that of today's globalization. The colonial encounter and the nationalist elites it generated substantially impacted contemporary MENA states. Those that went through a full dialectical confrontation, resulting finally in independence led by civilians informed by the political practices and beliefs of their colonial antagonists, developed the most cohesive institutions, as best exemplified by Tunisia. The military cut short that dialectical process in several other countries with anti-monarchial coups. In still other countries monarchs remained in place, either legitimated by nationalist struggles or external combat (Morocco and Saudi Arabia), or simply backed by the British. Neither militaries nor monarchs have developed state capacities as effectively as have civilian political leaders, such as those in Tunisia, Turkey, Israel and, to a lesser extent, Iran.

Globalization's take-off from the mid-1980s, combined with the end of the Cold War and a reduction in the geo-strategic rents it had generated for the MENA, induced the region's states to undertake the political and economic reforms required to ride the globalization wave and extract benefits from it, including capturing more foreign direct investment (FDI). Two decades of rapid globalization, however, did not produce a new liberal age in the MENA. Most if not all reforms of MENA political economies came to an abrupt halt with the Arab uprisings of 2011, which themselves followed the global economic crisis of 2008–9 and which presaged several years of stagnating globalization and slower economic growth. As globalization has slowed to a crawl, MENA states have scrambled to meet intensifying domestic and regional economic and political challenges. Just as they turned in unison in a liberal direction in the late 1980s as globalization intensified, so they then turned en bloc in a conservative one, shoring up state authority over the polity in their search for ways and means to confront intensifying economic problems. Commonly accused in the MENA of being a false flag for neo-colonialism, globalization has paradoxically been more beneficial than harmful for the region. It is the slowing of globalization that poses the greater threat to the MENA's political economies because it puts downward pressure on oil and gas prices, renders more difficult the challenge of diversifying economies away from hydrocarbons, and reduces support for liberalization.

Chapter 4 explores the root cause of the general weakness in the MENA of infrastructural power, which is the capacity of a state to interact effectively with civil society in the formation and implementation of policies as regards provision of order, the formation of a coherent national outlook or ideology, and management of the economy. That root cause lies in the domination of the region's political economies by what institutional economists, led by Douglass North, have called "limited access orders." These are systems in which order is based on political elites appropriating for themselves privileged control over the economy and the rents accrued therefrom, barring access to "outsiders." The chapter discusses how the MENA's limited access orders operate, the political and economic consequences of limited inclusion due to curtailment of citizenship rights, and the dependence of these orders on gate-keeping by deep states, contending interpretations of the historical origins of which are reviewed.

Deep states in the republics are analyzed and their possible existence in monarchies assessed in Chapter 5. Typically comprised of militaries, security/intelligence services, ruler's "households," and legal/judicial systems, republican deep states vary in their degree of institutionalization, their rootedness in social forces, and whether they have been constructed from the top down or the bottom up. These characteristics in turn impact the ways and means by which they acquire resources, and hence impact economies. While deep states are to be found in one form or another in all the republics, only in one monarchy, Jordan, is one clearly present. But in the other monarchies deep states appear to be emerging as the level of internal coercion and external conflict rises, coupled with intra-elite tensions due in part to declining resources.

Chapter 6 is concerned with the degree to which MENA states have succeeded in including their populations in the making and implementation of public policies, in providing them with health and educational services, and in ensuring public security and order. Measures of state capacity to effect inclusion include the institutional performances of bureaucracies and representative bodies, such as local governments and national legislatures. The World Bank's comparative assessment of the engagement of stakeholders in rulemaking processes in such bodies reveals that "the Middle East and North Africa stands out as the region with the least inclusive rulemaking."[1] MENA bureaucracies are centralized and stove-piped, thus providing neither access to citizens nor adequate administration. MENA parliaments rank exceedingly low on the "parliamentary powers index."

Human capital growth is produced by health and educational services. By virtually all standard measures other than proportion of age cohorts in school, MENA education is underperforming. Equivalent years of schooling based on standardized, globalized tests indicate that MENA students are not learning at globally competitive rates. In the initial iteration of the Human Capital Index based on 2018 data, only one MENA country ranked in the top 50 of the 157 countries included. According to these and other global comparisons, the MENA is not producing the levels of human capital predicted by its GDP per capita and essential if it is to become more competitive in the coming generation.

MENA states are also deficient in power, measured by their provision of public security. Development requires domestic law and order and military defense against external enemies. Although MENA states invest disproportionately in security, they generally fail adequately to deliver it to their populations. In 2018 countries in the MENA were the world's least peaceful. Of the world's ten most dangerous countries in that year, five were in the region. About 90% of the MENA population lives in countries more dangerous than the world average, while almost 100 million live in five of the most dangerous. MENA residents, in other words, experience comparatively little security, are exposed to high levels of domestic and international conflict, and are compelled to support costly militarization which militates against order and security rather than providing it.

Chapter 7 assesses MENA state capacities to manage the economy, of which the most longstanding, vital measure is revenue extraction. Heavily dependent upon direct or indirect revenue from hydrocarbon exports and public foreign assistance, MENA countries extract less revenue from direct taxation than any other global region or comparator lower-middle and middle-income countries. On other measures of state economic management, including fiscal responsibility, prevention of capital flight and corruption, and containing informalism, MENA states perform below levels predicted by their

GDPs per capita. Of these various measures, fiscal responsibility is the most crucial and is typically measured by budget deficit and public debt as a percentage of GDP. Of the 19 MENA countries for which data is available, only four had budget deficits that were below the average of all listed countries. In 2018, the average deficit for all MENA countries was 7.9% of GDP, a figure almost four times the maximum deficit permitted in the EU. Not surprisingly, with budget deficits of this magnitude MENA governments have accumulated substantial debt, the median level of which in 2019 was about 50% of GDP. If one excludes the major MENA oil exporters, however, the median debt is 88% of GDP, more than double the proportion considered safe by the IMF for developing economies.

Chapter 8 investigates the causes and consequences of regionalization, meaning socio-political interaction, without regionalism, which is the formation of effective transnational, regional institutions and organizations. The most important cause is that national governments form limited access orders closed not only to their own citizens, but to mutually beneficial, institutionalized relationships with other regional states. Unlike in other regions and most notably the EU, where independent economic actors, key of which have been the bourgeoisie and their economic enterprises, have been strong advocates of regionalism, in the MENA such actors are comparatively few, weak and more dependent upon government. MENA regionalism is also rendered more difficult by dependence on hydrocarbon exports and the associated lack of product diversification, hence limited complementarity. Intense regionalization and its implied threat to incumbent regimes has long militated against institutionalizing regional inter-state relations. The intensification of that regionalization into virtual regional civil war renders the prospects for effective regionalism ever more distant.

Chapters 9 and 10 review the survival strategies of the weaker and stronger MENA states, respectively. With the partial exception of Israel, all MENA states are under serious and sustained political and economic threat. Survival strategies are remarkably similar within categories of states determined by their capacity levels, which are in turn reflective of their histories. The MENA states with significant pre-colonial histories as national entities, including Egypt, Morocco, Tunisia, Iran and Turkey, have sustained governmental coherence in the face of various challenges, but as they rely ever more heavily on repression, so do their economic development prospects recede. Many of the MENA countries that lack significant pre-colonial histories of stateness are either failed or fragile states, now facing the most basic of challenges to states, which is to maintain order within their territory. Prospects for economic development in these states are dismal.

The MENA monarchies are seeking to diversify their economies but, under sustained pressure from rising populations and stagnant "rental" income, are in effect in races against time. The monarchy with the lowest GDP per capita, Morocco, is diversifying at least as successfully, if not more so, than its fellow monarchies. Finally, both Tunisia and Israel are outliers in that their survival strategies hold out greater promise for long-term economic development. But they too face substantial challenges, whether mobilizing economic resources while sustaining national political coherence in Tunisia's case, or devising a strategy to peacefully integrate into the MENA in Israel's.

This book, in sum, represents a return to the origins of political economy by exploring the political causes of economic outcomes. It argues that those causes are deeply embedded in historical and contemporary structural factors, so the prospects for dramatic improvements in the MENA's economic performance are slim.

1

ACCOUNTING FOR DEVELOPMENT IN THE MENA

Polities and economies in the Middle East and North Africa are dramatically underperforming. As a group those polities are the world's most authoritarian and violence prone. The Arab world alone contributes 11 times the number of global refugees, almost ten times the number of internally displaced persons, ten times the number of terrorist attacks and 14 times the battle deaths predicted by its population, while spending triple the global average on militaries. The MENA accounts for two-thirds of the world's known executions. MENA economies have, according to the World Bank, "stayed below potential for at least 40 years."[1] GDP growth has been moderate and misshapen, resulting almost entirely from demographic and structural change, not from productivity growth, which has lagged behind all other developing regions.[2] As a consequence, the MENA has the world's highest rate of youth unemployment, with about a third of its youths overall and over half of young women seeking employment in several of its countries unable to find jobs.[3]

Political and economic underperformance are interrelated, as the nexus between inadequate economic growth, youth unemployment, authoritarianism, radicalization and violence suggests. The Human Freedom Index, which measures both political and economic freedom, ranks the MENA as the least free of the 17 regions it compares. Of the bottom ten on the index of 159 countries, seven are in the MENA.[4] The effort to understand dual political and economic under-performance should, therefore, be grounded in political economy, which was "the old name of economics ... or the study of the *political* management of the economy."[5] As the italicized emphasis suggests, politics were deemed by the founders of the discipline of economics to be *a* if not *the* prime cause of economic outcomes.

As that discipline became more "scientific," so did the primacy of politics become obscured behind allegedly "apolitical" technical economic considerations and calculations.[6] This obfuscation has been reflected in much contemporary academic analysis of MENA economies, including especially that supported by the international financial institutions, in which politics are commonly downplayed in accounting for economic performance. The approach of this book is to draw upon the intellectual origins of economics in emphasizing the primacy of politics in understanding why most MENA economies— those that stretch from Morocco across North Africa, through the Levant and on to Iran, therefore including both Turkey and Israel— have not lived up to their potential.

MENA Endowments

That potential is both historical and in the form of economic endowments. If long-established historical patterns, so-called "path dependency," were the sole determinant of a region's contemporary economy, the MENA would be richer than it is. Two of its states, Egypt and Iran, are virtually unique in being modern countries based geographically on traditional empires, the only other in the world being China, which has drawn upon indigenous historical models to guide its dramatic economic growth over the past 30 years.[7] Turkey is the inheritor of the core of the once mighty Ottoman Empire, still capable at its demise in WWI of defeating Allied forces, as it did at Gallipoli in 1915–16. In the ancient world, areas controlled then or subsequently by these three empires were among the world's most developed and prosperous, serving as breadbaskets for the Greek and Roman Empires and as conduits for trade between the Mediterranean and China. Morocco from medieval times was the principal corridor of trade between West Africa and Europe. The MENA was the core of the Islamic world, which in the medieval era was at least the equal of the West in economic prowess, the size and sophistication of its cities, the accomplishments of its intellectuals, the development of its legal/judicial systems, and in military power.

From the early nineteenth century, imperialism and colonialism began to reshape MENA political economies, both for the better and for the worse, as it did throughout the world. The region became more closely integrated with Europe and various of its economies became richer and more developed than most others in Africa, Asia and Latin America. By the 1860s, for example, Egypt was the world's largest cotton exporter, its railways more extensive than Japan's and its GDP per capita higher. Some two generations later Morocco was being touted as the California of North Africa, as intensive irrigation made possible a surge of horticultural crops for export. Beirut came to serve as a principal entrepot for the region, being dubbed the Switzerland of the Middle East. When decolonization began in earnest after WWII, several MENA states came to lead that global movement because of their relative political and economic sophistication, to say nothing of their military capacities. In the 1950s and into the 1960s much of the MENA was wealthier than East Asia and seemed poised to emerge as a global economic center. Syria, for example, despite political instability, had one of the world's most rapidly growing economies in the early 1950s as more of its Jazeera, or central steppe land south of the Euphrates River, was brought under irrigated cultivation. Their streets choked with large American cars, Damascus and Aleppo appeared to mimic Havana, but with economies more broadly based and less corrupt. So, if path dependency established by long if discontinuous historical precedent is truly determinative, it is hard to explain the region's political and economic deterioration that commenced in earnest some two generations ago, just as its enormous oil resources were brought under national control and began to generate huge increases in export earnings.

The path-dependency explanation of the MENA's current travails has more purchase regarding the region's politics. None of the pre-colonial empires or states were democratic, although some had competent institutions of governance as well as civil societies that shared with government some responsibilities for the administration of justice as well as economic regulation and management. Colonialism and indigenous attempts to Westernize, such as that by Egypt's Muhammad Ali in the first half of the nineteenth century, destroyed much of this pre-existing political infrastructure, substituting in its place models imported from Europe, most of which never gained the traction they had in their lands of origin.[8] But other countries and regions in the developing world with even poorer initial endowments of governance capacities emerged from their colonial encounters with stronger governmental institutions and political organizations. Any investigation of the path dependency of MENA political development, therefore, must carefully consider whether the particulars of its colonial encounter had especially negative consequences.

If economic endowments were more determinative than the political management of them, the contemporary MENA should be wealthier.

Of those endowments, three stand out—fossil fuels, geographical position and a youthful population. The MENA holds far and away the biggest share of the world's oil and gas reserves and is the largest exporter of them. Since the outset of the twentieth century, "black gold" and subsequently natural gas have propelled rapid economic development in a host of settings, from Texas and California to Norway, Russia and Indonesia.

The relative value of MENA hydrocarbons, as well as its overall economies, is enhanced by the region's strategic global location straddling the Asian and African continents and adjoining Europe. For millennia the region has served as the trade crossroads linking those continents, while in modern times its proximity to markets for oil and gas, whether by pipeline or tanker, combined with the easy accessibility of major MENA oil and gas fields, have provided it with substantial economic advantages.

Finally, the MENA's "youth bulge," which began to swell a generation ago, is at least demographically if not economically analogous to that which two generations ago was a key driving force behind the Asian "economic miracle." At present the MENA is enjoying the same "demographic gift" of an increasingly favorable ratio between those of working age, on the one hand, and dependents either too young or too old to work, on the other. Indeed, this potential boost to development is now more pronounced in the MENA than in any other region. Yet, as noted above, this hypothetical demographic gift has been, as to some extent has oil, more curse than blessing. Instead of contributing to economic growth by working in productive jobs, a remarkably high proportion of MENA youths have joined the very young and the old as unemployed or underemployed dependents.

Whether by virtue of at least some its historical inheritance or its present factor endowment, the MENA should be enjoying more rapid economic growth than it is. The mystery of why it is not has generated considerable interest among historians and social scientists, who have offered various explanations.

Explanations of Inadequate Growth

The "father" of the field of economic history of the Middle East, Charles Issawi, spent much of his career investigating why economic growth in the region failed from the thirteenth century to keep pace with more rapid development in Europe.[9] He identified a range of socio-cultural, geo-political and economic contributing factors. In the first category he focused on the ideational context within which Middle Eastern political economies operated, noting that "by the beginning of the Twelfth Century the scientific and intellectual life of Islamic society was already showing signs of fatigue and rigidity, and its religion becoming more dogmatic and intolerant."[10] The hypothesized relationship between religion and development has subsequently been extensively investigated, as we shall discuss below.

The key geo-political force Issawi identified was that of "prolonged warfare with Mongols, Crusaders and Tatars," the consequence of which was that Arab countries "transformed themselves into militaristic, 'feudalistic' societies whose institutions were much less conducive to economic and social development."[11] In this assessment he also presaged contemporary analyses, both of why warfare in Europe stimulated development of state capacities whereas it did not in the Middle East, and of the vital economic role of governance.[12] On this latter point Issawi himself went on to argue that the decay of central Ottoman institutions of government from the seventeenth century onwards exacerbated the rate of economic decline by creating "petty dynasties and quasi-independent governors."[13] Another geo-political factor was the loss of control of maritime transport in the Mediterranean and the Indian Ocean by the Muslim Middle East, initially to the Byzantines and Venetians, subsequently to the Portuguese, Dutch and English. Trade, a key contributor to the wealth of the Muslim Middle East for centuries, thus passed out of Muslim hands not only with other regions, but within the Middle Eastern Muslim world itself, where non-Muslim minority protected communities, chief of which were Christian and Jewish, assumed preponderant commercial roles.

The third category of factors listed by Issawi—so presumably those he considered least important in explaining the Middle East's decline—were of a more direct economic nature. He noted that the region's resource endowment did not include sufficient forests, minerals and rivers, among the consequences being overdependence on land as opposed to water-borne transport, and inadequate development of watermills, the key source of inanimate energy in Europe.[14] The Middle East thus depended much more heavily on human than machine-generated energy. Both Issawi and Richard Bulliet emphasized the significance of camels rather than wheeled vehicles being the primary bearers of freight, a factor that further disadvantaged the Middle East vis-à-vis Europe.[15]

Issawi's emphasis of the roles of ideas and institutions in accounting for the Middle East's underperformance since the early modern era has had a substantial impact on subsequent scholarship. Timur Kuran, for example, notes that capitalism failed to develop in the Middle East, as evidenced by the fact that in Cairo and Istanbul, credit, investment and trading practices remained unchanged for 800 years from the tenth century.[16] This failure was not due to geography, colonialism or strictly economic factors, nor to a fundamental incompatibility between Islam and capitalism. Instead it was due to static Islamic legal provisions which became increasingly incompatible with modern economies, preventing private exchange and capital accumulation, the emergence of corporations, and large-scale production. The limiting features of Islamic law and practice included inheritance that fragmented wealth; the lack of the concept of a corporation so that organizational development, including that of civil society, was impeded; and the *waqf*, or religious endowment, which froze capital within poorly managed, typically jointly owned legal entities. With this negative path dependency propelling the contemporary Middle East, Kuran concludes that there is no quick fix: the "low trust, rampant corruption, and weak civil societies all characteristic of the region's economies today and all legacies of its economic history ... will take generations to overcome."[17]

Although not explicitly focused on the Middle East, Daron Acemoglu and James A. Robinson's *Why Nations Fail: The Origins of Power, Prosperity, and Poverty*, both cites examples from the region and is informed by the emphasis on political institutions embodied in Issawi's work.[18] Their thesis is that economic prosperity depends primarily on the inclusiveness of political and economic institutions. Inclusive institutions, which provide access to decision making for relatively large numbers of people, support economic growth by guaranteeing the rule of law and by providing appropriate incentive structures that reward talent and creativity. By contrast, extractive institutions, according to Acemoglu and Robinson, permit an elite to dominate and exploit others, extracting resources from non-elites, thereby discouraging investment and innovation. This view of open institutions as being key to development and closed ones as inimical to it is reflective of the larger school of institutional economics, led by Douglass North, whose terms for those two types of institutional systems are open as opposed to limited access orders. All Muslim majority countries in the Middle East, according to North and his colleagues, fall into the latter category.

In this book we shall draw upon the argument of the centrality of institutions in explaining economic outcomes, which now has a comparatively venerable history in the study of Middle Eastern economies. Indeed, even the World Bank, whose mandate prevents it from directly analyzing the political systems of its member states, came up with the term "governance" in the mid-1990s, more or less as a synonym for politics, to enable it to investigate more systematically the impact of institutional capacities on development. Since then its work on the Middle East has become steadily more explicit in identifying political constraints on economic development in the region, although this work remains guarded in tone and focused more on individual institutions than on political systems as a whole.

Defining Characteristics of the MENA—Regional and Global Penetration

As with all economic theories, however, neo-institutional economics also has its limitations, key of which is that it discounts or ignores other important factors, partly because many such factors are specific to a particular region, so not of general theoretical interest. Middle East "exceptionalism" is thus shortchanged by a too narrow focus on its institutions that ignores its history, society and the particular features of its economy that interact with and therefore shape those institutions. Distilled out of this complexity are three vital characteristics of this region that operate both independently and through their impact on national political and economic institutions to shape the rate and nature of economic change.

The first is that the region's nation states are impacted to an unusual degree by their interactions with both regional neighbors and global actors. A central paradox of the region results from it—and especially its core Arab component—having an informally integrated, or more accurately, interpenetrated political system, but very little effective, structured, region-wide formal integration. In other words, it has regionalization without regionalism.[19] The former is a "spontaneous, bottom-up, endogenous process involving a variety of non-state actors organized in formal and informal networks," whereas "regionalism is a state-led process of integration, whereby formal regional institutions and organizations, mostly in the economic and security realms, are established and sustained."[20]

The phenomenon of mutual inter-state penetration was noted by Leon Carl Brown in the 1960s and, if anything, it has intensified since then, propelled by pan-regional electronic communications, human migration, the emergence of the regional oil economy, and the growth of sub- and super-state socio-political movements and organizations.[21] No other world region, for example, has

the equivalent of the Arab World's pan-Arab television broadcasting, which commenced in 1996 with Al Jazeera. Nor does any
other region have the equivalent of Islamists seeking to replace all
Muslim states with a single Caliphate. The MENA is the developing
world's most interpenetrated political subsystem, with cross-border
political engagements exceeding those on the African, Asian or
South American continents. Underlying this informal integration,
especially in the Arab core, is shared language and culture, combined
with political identities and aspirations at variance with national
borders. Among other consequences, these conditions impel the
region's relatively weak nation states, fearful of manipulation and
penetration by neighboring ones, to pre-empt, themselves interfering
in their neighbor's politics. Paradoxically, this informally integrated
but dysfunctional regional political system renders formal, especially
economic integration more difficult than in other global sub-regions.
The modern history of the MENA is littered with failed efforts to
create formal economic and political regional integration associations. A principal reason for their failure is the national insecurity,
especially of ruling elites, that results from the region's transnational
politics. The Hobbesian MENA engenders heightened political risk
awareness in all capitals of the region, thereby rendering very
problematical the task of building and sustaining regional associations, with or without centralized organizational structures, as the all
but moribund Arab League attests. Regionalization, in sum, undermines not only regionalism, but national political institutions as well.

The MENA is also characterized by an extraordinary degree of
interference from external actors. The world's and especially the
West's "fatal embrace" of the MENA has been driven by numerous
factors and extends over millennia. The Romans based much of the
economic weight of their empire in Egypt, North Africa and the
Levant, using the first as a transit point for the eastern trade, to say
nothing of providing Rome with basic foodstuffs. The Crusaders
were not driven primarily by the motive of economic conquest,
but their presence was nonetheless economically disruptive, to say
nothing of creating an historical analogy that remains alive and well
to this day, contributing in no small measure to perceived clashes
of civilizations. Extra-regional power struggles, such as that which
pitted Napoleonic France against Britain, have been played out in
the region, in part because the MENA sits astride arteries of empires.
Discovery of the world's largest fossil fuel reserves in the region vastly
increased its magnetism to foreign powers. The MENA was among if
not the most important venue for Cold War rivalries. More recently,

America's New World Order crumbled as a result of its ill-conceived invasion of Iraq and attendant policy failures, which have in turn now drawn Russia back into the region while luring China into becoming a new player, using its Belt and Road Initiative to pave the way into the MENA.

The economic legacies and continuing impacts of virtually perpetual foreign interference in the MENA take several forms. When fighting their battles in the region external actors have mobilized local support and in so doing have militarized political economies. The US-led War on Terror is but one of several recent manifestations of this phenomenon. The economic impacts of that militarization, ranging from procurement costs to the distortion of civilian economies, have long exceeded those in any other global region.

A second form of interference has been that of external actors seeking to mold local political economies in distorted images of their own, the distortions resulting primarily from the economic and political interests of the foreigner in question. Colonial economies were structured around the raw material needs of metropoles, as was much of the MENA oil economy that flowered after WWII. Economically dysfunctional Arab socialism was indebted in large measure to Soviet interventions, just as much of the region's present crony capitalism resulted from the imposition of neo-liberalism as embodied in the appropriately named Washington Consensus. Its "ten commandments" reflected the predilections and even possibly the interests of the international financial institutions headquartered there, to say nothing of the country whose capital it is. The net result of the region being jerked around by malignant or even benign interventions into its national political economies is that few of its countries have managed to create and sustain a successful development model, as compared for example to various Asian Tigers. Instead they have lurched from one ostensible economic model to another. Incumbent elite interests have been focused more on attracting economic and political support from foreign patrons, for example by appearing to emulate the models they advocate, than on forging independent development models resonant with indigenous traditions and capacities.

Foreign assistance is a third means of intervention into the region, the MENA being the world's largest recipient of it on a per capita basis. This has not only profoundly shaped regional political dynamics, ensuring the ascendancy of various countries and regimes, but has deeply impacted national economies from the top down and bottom up. It has reinforced incumbent elites by reducing the need to tax, and hence grant representation, thereby militating against the development of extractive capacities and the broader infrastructural power of which extraction of resources forms a vital component.[22] As for the bottom up, foreign assistance has favored some constituencies and sectors over others while also subsidizing the provision of imported goods and services, thereby undercutting local producers.

Similar to the distorting effects of foreign assistance have been the impacts of the EU's and most of its member countries' economic policies toward the MENA. They have reinforced the hub-and-spoke system through which MENA countries relate not just to Europe, but to much of the developed world, thereby further undermining regional integration. Moreover, key EU policies have been driven by protectionism, especially of the vital agricultural sector in which actual and aspiring MENA exporters enjoy potentially significant natural advantages. In recent years Europe has shifted its attention from economic relations with the MENA and half-hearted attempts to foster political liberalization, to combatting terrorism and, now most crucially, seeking to interdict the flow of potential migrants. The MENA's largest trading partner has essentially securitized its relationship with the region, relegating economic and political development to subsidiary concerns. A primary consequence has been to reinforce the powers of incumbent regimes which proclaim commitments to countering terrorism and interdicting the flow of migrants. By so doing these elites and their foreign backers render yet more difficult the emergence of autonomous political and economic actors. The same can be said about US policy toward the MENA, geared as it is to protecting Israel and the flow of oil, hence of regimes useful for those purposes. Russia and China have similarly become steadily more engaged in propping up "friendly" regimes, whatever their transgressions.

Warfare's Impacts on State Building

A second set of characteristics of the MENA that are not specifically economic in nature but have contributed to shaping the political institutions that manage its national economies include protracted warfare and the costs thereof, as well as the region's demography and the preponderant values and attitudes of its peoples. Of these three characteristics, warfare and political violence constitute the most distinctive, destructive force shaping the region's institutions.

19

Middle Eastern armed forces are the world's largest, as measured by size in proportion to population and by spending as a percentage of GDP.[23] Over the first decade of the twenty-first century, countries in the Middle East and North Africa spent more than twice as much on defense as a percentage of GDP than South Asia, the next highest spending region.[24] Elbadawi and Keefer summarize the relevant evidence linking warfare and institutional quality, noting that the frequency of "sustainable" democratic transitions is lowest in the Arab region; that the occurrence of external or civil wars there is surpassed only by Sub-Saharan Africa; and that other than the GCC states, Arab countries are on average the world's most repressive.[25] Transparency International's Government Defense Anti-Corruption Index, first issued in 2013, ranks 82 countries according to the measures in place to prevent corruption in their armed forces. Since these measures reflect specific aspects of institutionalized civilian control, this index is in effect a surrogate measure of civilian control of the armed forces, hence of institutional quality more generally. Of the five regions in the world assessed on the index, the Arab one scores the lowest, with 13 of its 19 countries receiving the scores of E or F, the bottom two grades on the scale. Of the ten countries out of the 82 evaluated that spent more than 4% of their GDP on their militaries, seven are in the Arab world.

Proliferation and intensification of coercive force in the Arab world since 2011, combined with decay of Arab states, seems at first glance to run counter to the implicit predictions of two relevant bodies of literature about the relationship between wars and militaries, on the one hand, and state institution building, on the other. The modernization school, which emerged as Arab states were becoming independent in the 1950s, held that Arab militaries were state builders—mobilizing, integrating and organizing their societies to face development challenges, including that of inter-state war. More or less simultaneously, European-focused historical sociology, led by Charles Tilly, made the case that war making, requiring as it does increased domestic extraction coupled with the subordination of internal rivals to central authority, was the engine of state making.[26] The historical trajectory of the Arab world for some half a century up until 2011 seemed at least superficially to substantiate both views, as militaries and states grew in tandem under the ever-present threat of war.

The near collapse of both militaries and states in Syria, Libya, Iraq and Yemen, however, calls into question the interpretation of the military as socio-economic modernizer and state maker, as does

Egypt's chronic underperformance since the military seized power in 1952. The monarchies have behaved ostensibly as the European historical model would predict, redoubling their efforts to further expand military capacities in the face of various threats. However, those efforts have not been coupled with intensified domestic extraction nor with effective state building, suggesting that these patrimonial political systems are becoming militarily top heavy, hence politically unbalanced. Arab militaries, in sum, whether in direct control or as agents of ruling monarchs, appear not to have fulfilled their promise as state builders, and four formerly military-dominated Arab states have already lost their monopoly over the legitimate use of coercion within their borders, the essential defining component of statehood. Why then has the hypothesized link between war, armed forces and state building broken down in the Arab world?

A closer look at the state-building literature reveals disagreement over the interpretation of Arab militaries as potential state builders. Tilly himself, for example, cautioned that "the extension of the Europe-based state-making process to the rest of the world ... did not result in the creation of states in the strict European image." The reason for this, he explained, lies in the nature of the respective militaries. In Europe, building strong militaries required a "forging of mutual constraints between rulers and ruled," whereas post-colonial states "acquired their military organization from outside," with those external providers continuing to "supply military goods and expertise in return for commodities, military alliance or both." As a result, these militaries "overshadow all other organizations within their territories," thereby creating enormous "incentives to seize power over the state as a whole." He concludes that "the old national states of Europe almost never experienced the great disproportion between military organization and all other forms of organization that seems the fate of client states throughout the contemporary world."[27] In short, militarization produces effective, participatory states only if it needs them to extract societal resources. If those resources are provided otherwise, say by internally or externally generated rents, such as foreign assistance or oil exports, militarization will produce states more analogous to "organized criminals," to use Tilly's term, than to the European state prototype.

Arab nation states fit into Tilly's paradigm of dependent, post-colonial states with overgrown militaries subsisting off "tribute" rather than generating and extracting economic surplus. These are

21

militaries at war with their own societies, not developers of them or of states that would serve societal interests. So when the balance of power between military and society was dramatically tipped in favor of the latter throughout much of the Arab world in 2011, the malformed states caught in the middle weakened yet further, as in the case of Egypt, or essentially disappeared, as in Libya, Syria, Yemen and, to a lesser extent, Iraq. As extensions of patrimonial monarchial rule, the states of the Gulf Cooperation Council, Jordan and Morocco were pulled yet tighter into the royal embrace and further militarized to counter perceived domestic and regional threats.

As states weakened, vanished or became more militarized, societal longing for "protection" increased, as Tilly also predicted. Such longing has manifested itself in at least two, contradictory ways. One has been that of desertion, metaphorically but also literally, from the state and its coercive forces, into the arms of opposing coercive forces typically based on organic social solidarities such as sect, tribe or locale. The other is the ultimately self-defeating strategy of seeking protection from the very institution responsible for state decay—the military. Public opinion polling worldwide consistently reveals higher levels of support for, and confidence in, militaries than in civilian institutions of government, including parliaments, executives and, frequently, legal-judicial systems. In the Arab world this disjunction has traditionally been even more pronounced, as suggested by a 2011 poll in 12 Arab countries in which 71% of respondents professed trust in their national armed forces, compared to 47% in the government and 36% in their legislatures. The subsequent "wave IV" of the Arab Barometer survey, conducted in 2016–17, revealed that enhanced militarism in the region had paradoxically stimulated yet greater public trust in Arab armies and increasing distrust of civilian governmental institutions; 88% of Arab respondents expressed trust in their nations' armed forces, compared to 38% who trusted their governments.[28] In Egypt, polls typically reveal that strongly positive images of the military are held by around 90% of respondents, a proportion only exceeded in the Arab world in Jordan. The lowest levels of trust in militaries in Arab countries are not surprisingly found where the "desertion" rates are highest, including Iraq and Yemen (there is no similar polling data for Libya and Syria). Left unprotected by malformed states long subordinate to militaries, Arab publics tend to seek shelter under either anti-state militias or their states' militaries, hoping for the best and having little confidence in civilian institutions of governance.

The MENA's Peoples: Demographics and Values

The MENA's youthful population and its potential, as yet unrealized "demographic gift" to the economy has already been mentioned. Youthfulness also appears to have an impact on political institutions. Recent research has revealed that democratic transitions are positively correlated with a national population's median age.[29] The threshold age for successful transitions appears to be 30. The median age in Arab countries, 22 years, is the second lowest in the world, with only Sub-Saharan African countries' populations being younger. The global median age is 28. Tunisia, whose prospects for a successful transition appear to be the brightest in the Arab world, is also the "oldest" Arab country, with a median age of 29. As with other demographic correlates of democratization, age may be a surrogate indicator of other phenomena, such as various attributes of economic development, including the positive correlation between average age and rate of economic growth. But age may also have an independent effect, with a youthful population being more volatile and difficult to integrate into participatory political institutions.

A second aspect of MENA demography with implications for the quality of its governance institutions is that it is relatively heterogeneous overall as well as within most of its countries. The magnitude of ethnic, religious, linguistic, tribal and other vertical divisions of populations is negatively correlated globally with both democratic consolidation and national rates of economic growth.[30] So in this sense the Middle East is triply cursed. The region as a whole is relatively factionalized, as are most of its countries, and many of the deepest ethnic, religious, linguistic and tribal divisions overlap borders, further accentuating the region-wide problem of national interpenetration.

The challenges MENA demography pose to institution building are paralleled by the prevailing attitudes and values of the region's populations. Economic historians have investigated the contemporary impacts of cultures and the histories and institutions by which they are shaped. Acemoglu and Robinson, for example, have posited that "fixed national effects" explain both economic development and democratization.[31] Operationalization of the culture variable has been attempted through longitudinal comparative survey research which measures variations in mass attitudes that in researchers' views reflect different cultural norms and values. The primary assumption underlying the research is the same as that of Acemoglu and Robinson and other economic historians, namely, that "a given society's institutional and cultural heritage is remarkably enduring..." and its "religious and historical heritage leaves a lasting imprint."[32]

Analyses of the World Value Survey (WVS) and associated, more focused attitudinal survey data suggest to the team of scholars working with Robert Inglehart that the most vital cross-cultural variation can be conceptualized along two major axes—traditional versus secular-rational values, and a survival versus self-expression value.[33] The survival value places a higher priority on material welfare than on free choice, as implied by the term "self-expression." Cross-national attitudinal studies have repeatedly produced clusters of societies reflecting distinctive mixes of these allegedly core cultural values. The cluster of societies in which traditional and survival values most predominate is the Muslim-majority one, most countries within which assessed in the WVS being those of the MENA. The conclusion drawn by these researchers is that cultural path dependence in these societies, as reflected in attitudes that value hierarchy and authority over autonomy, on the one hand, and access to resources over choices about public policies, on the other, comprises a major obstacle to their economic development and democratization.[34]

What this research does not directly address is the source of this configuration of values and attitudes. It is reasonable to conclude that this distinctive pattern reflects the socio-economic and political realities of the region. Individuals, after all, adjust their thinking to suit prevailing conditions, key elements of which in the MENA are material deprivation and the prevalence of political clientelism. Perceptions of the former, as evidenced by responses to the 2015 Arab Opinion Survey conducted in 12 Arab countries, are ubiquitous. Only 20% of respondents reported that their household incomes were sufficient for them to save; almost half said they managed on a day to day basis and had no savings; and 29% said they lived in need, without sufficient funds to meet daily expenses.[35] Small wonder that Arabs are concerned with "survival values."

Clientelism is a behavior that reflects such values and the conditions that give rise to them. The dense variety of overlapping social, economic and political transactions, noted as particularly common in the MENA, is based on unequal, deferential relations. These in turn structure role behavior and expectations in a manner consistent with the sub-dimensions of traditional thinking, key of which is acceptance of authority, especially that of status superiors, such as religious, tribal or clan leaders. As for the survival versus self-expression dimension, political clientelism is based on the exchange of material resources for political loyalty, thereby affirming in individual value systems the dominance of "survival" over independent decision making and, indeed, the lack of importance of the latter. Votes produced through clientelism are choices for material rewards, not decisions about policies. In the Muslim majority countries of the MENA, therefore, prevailing values appear more consonant with attitudes congruent with clientelism than appears to be the case for most if not all other global regions.

An explanation of the MENA's path dependence in the form of lagging economic and political development can thus be found in the mutually reinforcing roles played by clientelism and prevailing values. Rendered more potent by this synergy, "culture" in this setting poses significant obstacles to the development of effective, rational-legal and programmatic focused governmental institutions and civil-society organizations, both of which are vital to economic growth and democratization. In the absence of such organizations the exercise of citizenship is necessarily limited.

MENA Economic Exceptionalism

The final factor contributing to the relative weakness of MENA governing institutions is the region's and its states' profound economic dependence on rents, which is to say benefits received above normal profits that result from privileges generated by contrived exclusivity, such as monopolies. That the term "rentier state" was coined with reference to a MENA political economy, Iran, before then being generalized to non-MENA, primarily oil-dependent countries, reflects both the centrality of unearned income in the MENA and its profound impacts on economies, polities and societies. That income has been generated primarily by fossil fuel exports, secondarily by side payments from global actors for geo-strategic advantages in the MENA, and more incidentally by fees, such as for use of the Suez Canal or access to touristic facilities, or by remittances to home countries by their nationals working abroad. As just discussed with reference to the role of armies in state building, external support for these states reduced or altogether eliminated their need to extract resources from their populations, hence to create state infrastructural power in order to do so. The surge of hydrocarbon-generated wealth thus did not transform the nature of these states, it simply reinforced the primacy of external over internal resources for them, whether they were direct beneficiaries by virtue of domestic oil and gas production, or indirect beneficiaries as a result of side payments or the employment of their nationals by the major oil and gas exporting countries. A region-wide rentier economy thus emerged, causing all MENA states to fashion their own version of a "social contract" in which they would bestow on their citizens entitlements generated primarily from rents, in return for those citizens' acceptance of the regime, its policies and self-appointed privileges, including lack of accountability. The adjectives "distributive" or "allocative" were thus rightly applied to these states, which focused on obtaining rents from external sources to mollify their populations, rather than generating tax revenues from domestic economic activities. They thus had comparatively little interest in fostering economic growth as it did not constitute their primary resource base. The imposition of direct taxes to generate substantial revenues was also avoided out of the fear it could stimulate demands for accountability.

Rents not only militated against building effective, accountable institutions, they also impacted economies directly and negatively by making them comparatively expensive in two interrelated ways. One was through the region-wide affliction of the Dutch Disease, referring to the comparative overvaluation of national currencies driven by energy exports, thereby undermining the competitiveness of other tradeable goods and services. Whereas the East Asian economic miracle was driven in considerable measure by purposely under-valued currencies intended to stimulate exports of tradeable goods, the stagnation of MENA exports other than oil and gas resulted partly from overvalued currencies.[36] Fiscal measures to combat the Dutch Disease were theoretically possible but were not taken mainly because overvalued currencies reduced the direct costs to governments of providing entitlements to citizens stemming from implicit social contracts.

The second negative economic impact of overreliance on rents was on the labor market. Salaries and wages were inflated so became non-competitive globally. The government's share of total employment is higher in the MENA than in any other region, both because of governments' need to service social contracts, and because relatively favorable terms of public employment raise labor costs to potential private employers, all too frequently beyond comparative global rates. Labor markets in the MENA are thus trifurcated between a large share in government employment; a small share in formal private employment in reasonably capitalized, modern firms; and a large and growing third share in informal employment, principally in small, underfunded enterprises, which now absorb the bulk of youth seeking jobs in all but the wealthiest oil exporting MENA countries.

MENA rentier economies have thus become ever more dependent upon rents as their global competitiveness outside the energy sector has steadily declined. All of the major MENA oil and gas exporters are more dependent on revenues from hydrocarbon exports now than they were a generation ago. At least as troubling as the failure to diversify economies is the fact that the rent to population ratios in all MENA countries have become less favorable as fossil fuel prices have slumped and populations have continued to grow. The economic diversification necessary to expand exports and increase national income depends upon state institutions fashioning and implementing policies that transform rentier into productive economies. For this to happen, however, those states must be reconfigured so that they eliminate the Dutch Disease, extract resources from their populations, and provide a suitable policy framework to nurture economic diversification. The shift from allocation to extraction requires not only enhanced infrastructural state capacities, but the consent of citizens being asked to forgo entitlements and pay new imposts, the politically most challenging component of the potential transformation. Whether that consent is obtained through repression or by exchange of representation for taxation is the vital political question facing all MENA governments. None so far has demonstrated a commitment to trading its privileges and power for public compliance based on participation and accountability, suggesting that all governments are likely to try to continue to rely primarily on repression as they are forced by the relative and per capita declines of rents to seek to extract more resources from their citizens.

Facing a Perfect Storm

The once bright prospects of the MENA have been clouded over by an intensifying storm that threatens the entire region. From the end of WWII until 1971, when the last of the MENA states gained independence, the era of decolonization stimulated optimism about the political and economic futures of the region. The belief that imperialism and colonialism had retarded the region's potential economic development and that its newly independent states could do better, was virtually canonical. Military rule was interpreted as expressing the will of the nation and its long-subordinated peoples, rather than as an obstacle to the development of effective institutions of governance.

Surviving monarchies in Jordan, Morocco and the GCC states seemed reasonably benign, popular and capable of belying the global trend toward republicanism. Resources left behind by departing colonialists or provided by newly exploited oilfields contributed to globally respectable, even leading rates of economic growth. Population expansion in most countries was about average for the developing world, having typically only doubled by the 1960s from comparatively small bases at the beginning of the twentieth century. The population explosion that tripled the size of most MENA countries from that time had yet to occur, so civil services could absorb virtually all graduate job seekers. Hopes for effective Arab unity ran high, while the days of external manipulation by foreign powers seemed to be coming to an end if not having already reached it. In sum, everything seemed to be in place for the MENA to prosper. The gathering storm was ignored.

At the eye of that storm are the inadequate national institutions which have failed to provide effective, accountable governance for their citizens, or indeed even to recognize the basic rights of citizenship. In no MENA country are the rights and duties of citizens fully enshrined in law and practice in a manner consonant with the meaning of the term. In the MENA as a whole the quality of governance as measured by the World Bank has deteriorated since first assessed in 1996, such that it now shares the dubious distinction, along with Sub-Saharan Africa, of being the world's worst-governed region. State institutions in the MENA were simply not equipped to deal with the domestic, regional and global challenges that began to mount from the 1970s. The globalization that accelerated dramatically at the end of the Cold War in 1989–90 intensified those challenges as the MENA began to fall ever further behind comparator regions and countries. Increasing economic and political pressures stemming from poor governance have resulted in a dramatic upsurge in coercion of all sorts, whether in the form of governmental repression, terrorism, dissolution into civil war, or internecine tribal/ethnic/religious violence. A steadily larger proportion of national resources in every MENA country is devoted to coercive capacities, ranging from ballistic missiles and satellites to Kalashnikovs. Instead of instituting wide-ranging reforms to open up political economies, MENA governments are battening down the political hatches as the economic storm surrounding them intensifies. The reasons they are doing so, rather than opening their political economies to new ideas, participants and practices, lie in the very nature of those political economies and that of the region's as a whole. The focus of this book is to clarify that nature and explain why it poses such an obstacle to effective development.

2

THE ORIGINS OF STATE EFFECTIVENESS

Economic performance is influenced by "world economic conditions, resource endowments, differing starting points, and demographic factors," according to Atul Kohli. But of greatest importance in his view is the role "of institutions, especially the role of government." He goes on to observe that "patterns of state authority ... often exhibit long-term continuities."[1] Institutionalists such as Kohli seek to understand why some governments, invariably referred to as states, perform better than others in facilitating economic growth. They have generally analyzed state performance along two dimensions, capacity and politics. By the former they mean "the bureaucratic, managerial, and organizational ability to process information, implement policies, and maintain governing systems."[2] The four dimensions along which state capacity is typically measured include the abilities to generate resources; to penetrate the broader society—which is what Michael Mann has referred to as infrastructural power; to deploy a trained and professional civil service; and to ensure the coherence of policy mandates "across and within institutions," coupled with oversight to assure that civil servants pursue those mandates.[3]

By politics the institutionalists are referring to decisions by political actors to deploy state capacities. In other words, state capacity is "just a tool and can deliver only if deployed in the right direction and insulated from interference. So competent leadership is vital."[4] Effective states are those in which leaders make appropriate political decisions and have the organizational capacity to implement them. State effectiveness also depends on society's response to those decisions and their implementation. "Some societies are harder to manage than others," with difficult ones forcing states and their leaders to choose between coercing those they rule or generating support from them by accommodating at least some of their demands.[5] State effectiveness is thus the result of capacity, politics and the nature of the society being ruled. That effectiveness or performance is typically measured by the delivery of three types of public goods—order, economic development and social/political/economic inclusion.

Because the key defining characteristic of statehood is physical control of territory, without which a state cannot be said to exist, the imposition of order has received the greatest attention from institutionalists. But they also argue that coercion alone, even when coupled with citizens' self-interest, is insufficient for a state to be effective or even to survive over the long term. Effective governance and sustained order also depend upon the regulation and enforcement of contracts as well as protection of citizenship rights. Order is the product not just of coercion, but of institutions in which interests are represented and conflicts resolved. In other words, state endurance depends on legitimacy in addition to force or material reward. That legitimacy rests heavily on the state's ability to incorporate as much of the population as possible through social well-being and by avoiding capture of the state by a particular group or sector. The principal means through which these objectives are achieved are either by provision of universal, effective citizenship rights, or by clientelism. Finally, institutionalists contend that the reach of states is typically geographically uneven, deeper in capital cities and urban centers and shallower on rural peripheries. In sum, the challenges facing all states are to maintain order and to facilitate economic growth as well as socio-political and economic inclusion. In this chapter we shall investigate how MENA states have discharged these tasks and why in almost all cases they have emphasized order at the expense of both effective economic management and inclusion.

Governance

Since 1996 the World Bank's Worldwide Governance Indicators have provided comparative assessments of state capacities along six dimensions: Voice and Accountability, Political Stability and Absence of Violence, Government Effectiveness, Regulatory Quality, Rule of Law, and Control of Corruption. According to the Bank, "Governance consists of the ... process by which governments are selected, monitored and replaced; the capacity of the government to effectively formulate and implement sound policies; and the respect of citizens and the state for the institutions that govern economic and social interactions among them."[6] In other words, governance for the Bank is an aggregate concept that integrates all three dimensions identified by institutionalists as critical to state performance—capacity, politics, and the nature of society—albeit with each of the six indicators being more pertinent to one or another dimension, with considerable overlap. The literature that has emerged on the relationships between scores on these governance indicators and the performance of states in providing order, economic growth and inclusion generally supports the proposition that they are all positively correlated, although with some exceptions.[7] These World Bank governance indicators can thus serve as rough approximations of the MENA's standings in regional rankings of state capacities, as well as of differences between MENA states.

The data reveal two major findings about the MENA's performance over time and by comparison to other regions. Between 1996 and 2017 the MENA's score deteriorated on five of the six indicators, remaining unchanged on "regulatory quality." Not surprisingly, the most pronounced deterioration was on the "political stability and absence of violence" indicator, on which the MENA's percentile rank out of 100 dropped from 41 to 26. For all lower-middle-income countries, by comparison, the ranking remained unchanged at 39, while it improved from 47 to 50 for upper-middle-income countries. In no other global region did performance deteriorate over these two decades so deeply or across so many indicators. It is worth noting that of the 19 MENA countries ranked, five are lower-middle-income, seven are upper-middle-income, and another seven are high-income countries, suggesting that the MENA's performance is substantially worse if controlled by relative national wealth.

The MENA was the world's worst performing region in 1996 and 2017 on "voice and accountability," and in the latter year on "political stability and absence of violence." On the other four indicators in both years the MENA outperformed only South Asia and Sub-Saharan Africa, while falling behind all the world's developed regions as well as East Asia and the Pacific, East Europe and Central Asia, and Latin America and the Caribbean.[8] The MENA thus outperformed only the world's two poorest regions while substantially underperforming its closer comparators by GNI per capita, including Latin America and the Caribbean, in which GNI per capita of slightly less than $8,000 annually is almost identical to that in the MENA. In sum, longitudinal comparisons of governance performance indicate deterioration of state capacity in the MENA over the last some 20 years, while cross-regional comparisons suggest it is weaker than comparator regions.

Governance indicators also provide insight into the MENA's relative provision of the three key public goods of order, economic development and inclusion. The indicators most relevant to inclusion, "voice and accountability" and "political stability and absence of violence," show the steepest decline between 1996 and 2017. The implication is that the region's states failed during that period to reach out to their own populations, either by extending full citizenship rights to them or ensuring their inclusion through robust clientelist networks, lending support to the institutionalists' contention that state coercion alone is insufficient to sustain order. The other four indicators are more relevant to state capacity to promote economic growth. Of these four, only "regulatory quality" remained unchanged, while "government effectiveness," "rule of law" and "control of corruption" all deteriorated, with the last declining the most. The MENA thus appears for some two decades to have suffered from declining state capacities to promote inclusion and economic development, falling ever further behind comparator regions. These trends are suggestive of the causes of underlying popular discontent that drove the "Arab Spring" that erupted in 2011 and of the inability of coercion alone to contain that discontent.

Governance indicators reflect the existence of sub-categories of MENA states. Assigning each country a 0 or 1 for a score below or above, respectively, the MENA composite score on each of the six indicators, and then averaging the scores for each country, produces three country clusters. The first and largest is composed of the authoritarian Arab republics presently or previously under military rule, including Algeria, Egypt, Iraq, Libya, Syria, Sudan and Yemen, all of which score zero because they are below MENA composite scores on all indicators. The second cluster, composed of Iran and Lebanon with scores of 1, West Bank/Gaza with a score of 2, and Turkey with a score of 4, groups the two large non-Arab MENA republics along with the Arab mini-"republics" that have never been under direct military rule. The third cluster includes all of the Arab monarchies, with non-GCC states Jordan and Morocco both scoring 6 and the GCC states arrayed from Kuwait, also with 6, down to Saudi Arabia and Bahrain at 4, with the UAE, Oman and Qatar at 5. For those five GCC states which obtained less than the "perfect" score of 6, all lost one or both points on the two indicators that reflect state–society interactions, which are "voice and accountability" and "political stability and the absence of violence." By contrast, all had perfect scores on indicators that pertain exclusively to their state's internal as opposed to societal relationship capacities. Israel, with a score of 5, scores below the MENA composite only on "political stability and the absence of violence."

The tripartite division of MENA states along the combined governance dimensions points to several characteristics of those states. As for the delivery of the public goods of order, economic growth and inclusion, the region's pervasive authoritarianism appears to undermine state capacities to provide order and inclusion, as indicated by double and four times the number of states scoring below as opposed to above the MENA composite score on "voice and accountability" and "political stability and absence of violence." On all the other indicators the balance of those above and below the composite score is much more even. The MENA states, in other words, have uneasy relations with the societies they govern, hence those states fall well below global averages on providing order and inclusion, at least as suggested by these World Bank indicators.

As for economic growth, it is only the Arab monarchies, Turkey and Israel that score above average on all indicators reflecting state capacities to manage the economy through overall effectiveness, regulation, rule of law and control of corruption. A strong correlation thus exists between performance on the indicators related to economic growth and actual rates of growth, which on average are higher for these ten countries than for the rest of the MENA. This in turn suggests that many of these states, most notably the Arab monarchies, are pursuing strategies based on economic growth and top down distribution through clientele networks as substitutes for political inclusion.

Finally, there is a strong, negative relationship between population size and quality of governance. Countries with larger populations, such as Egypt, Iraq, Sudan, Syria and Yemen, are governed less well than those with smaller populations, including all the monarchies with the exceptions of Morocco and Saudi Arabia, whose populations are slightly below the average of the larger Arab states just mentioned. The great majority of Middle Easterners thus live in comparatively poorly governed countries, outnumbering those living in relatively well governed ones by a factor of four or five to one.

Societal Characteristics Impact State Effectiveness

One determinant of state effectiveness is state capacity, of which the governance indicators just reviewed provide a measure. A second determinant is the nature of the societies being governed, with the relevant literature suggesting that the more heterogeneous the society, the more difficult it is to govern. While measurement of social homogeneity/heterogeneity is notoriously difficult, complicated by varying findings along different sub-dimensions such as ethnic, religious, linguistic or tribal heterogeneity, the MENA at first glance appears to be neither significantly more nor less socially fragmented than other regions. According to James Fearon, for example, the MENA is substantially more "culturally fractionalized" than the West or Latin America, about the same as Eastern Europe and the former Soviet Union, slightly less than Asia and substantially less than Sub-Saharan Africa. On the more limited measure of "ethnic fractionalization," however, the MENA is the world's second most divided society after Sub-Saharan Africa.[9] Within the MENA, Fearon's ranking of countries on the broader "cultural fractionalization" dimension reveals that the GCC countries are the least fractionalized, while the most are Jordan, Lebanon and the authoritarian Arab republics except Iraq. Turkey and Iran are less fractionalized than those Arab republics, but more than the Arab monarchies.

The results, in sum, tend to parallel those of the governance rankings. Governance in the MENA lags behind that in much of the world, while Middle Eastern society is more ethnically fractionalized than most other regions. Within the region, the best governed states preside over societies that are the least fractionalized, while the worst governed ones prevail over relatively highly fractionalized societies. These measures of state capacities and of the nature of societies, in other words, suggest that MENA states have relatively weak capacities to confront the challenges that inevitably arise from comparatively fractionalized societies.

Political Leadership

The third determinant of state effectiveness is the quality of political leadership as reflected by its policies. This dimension is more subjective than that of state capacity or societal coherence, for both of which there are commonly agreed indicators that have been subjected to empirical measurement. By contrast, assessment of politics tends more to mix normative and empirical measures, or at least to shape the latter by assumptions about relative qualities of different types of political systems. Democratic systems, for example, benefit from the assumption that their institutionalized checks and balances produce higher quality decisions, although in recent years a countervailing view has emerged that attributes authoritarianism with producing equal or even superior political decisions.[10] There is nevertheless an abundant literature relevant to the assessment of quality of political decision making, but it tends to focus on process rather than product. The mechanisms through which representative bodies formulate and oversee budgets, hold executives accountable, supervise coercive institutions, and represent different constituencies and viewpoints comprise such areas of investigation, as do similar analyses of the functioning of legal-judicial systems, local government, political parties, and so on. Based on the assumption that there is a direct correlation between the breadth and depth of stakeholder partici- pation in political decision making and its quality, a group of scholars have developed the concept of "public brainpower" as key to under- standing relative state performance in managing natural resources.[11] Recent studies of authoritarian government have sought to identify the causes not only of persistence, but of quality of decision making, especially as revealed by management of the economy.[12]

This third component of state effectiveness is, then, the most complex, normatively laden one, requiring investigation of political process as well as an effort to evaluate outcomes. These subjects we shall take up in the following chapter, where commonalities and differences in MENA political systems and their modes of operation will be analyzed. Various indicators of state capacities will be intro- duced by which to compare performance on the four dimensions of generating resources, penetrating society, operating a competent civil service, and compelling the latter to pursue policy mandates coherently while being overseen and held accountable. Before that, however, in the remainder of this chapter, the historical origins and evolutions of MENA states and their capacities will be traced. Linking present levels of state capacities to their historical development should provide a better understanding of the political views and acts of MENA decision makers, shaped as they are by history and the capacities with which they are endowed by their states to provide the public goods of order, development and inclusion.

MENA Path Dependence—History Matters

MENA countries have followed different historical paths while building their states, but most have arrived at reasonably similar destinations. That the MENA states share distinctive characteristics is suggested by the labels typically applied to them, as well as the labels not used. It is rare, for example, for such general, widely used terms as democratic, social democratic, socialist, communist, capitalist, developmental, transitional, or totalitarian to be employed in characterizing MENA states. The vocabulary applied to MENA states instead tends to be more region specific, such as rentier, exclusionary, sultanistic, clientelistic, patrimonial, or simply deep. No MENA state is referred to in the "BRIC" acronym, nor, other than Turkey and occasionally Saudi Arabia, does any play a significant role in debates about so-called "emerging" states. The leading emerging market index, compiled by MSCI, lumps all the MENA economies it lists (Egypt, Turkey and the UAE), into its "other" category, except for Saudi Arabia, which it broke out as a separate listing in 2019.[13]

The lexicon for MENA states, and to some extent the global financial treatment of them, suggests distinctiveness, if not uniqueness, and a certain marginality from the global economic mainstream. Although alleged Middle East "exceptionalism" is frequently decried as reflecting the prejudice of those who refer to or even imply it, such labelling should not deter investigations of the particular configurations of MENA states. Nor should undue emphasis be placed *a priori* on any single variable or historical era, including colonialism, in seeking to account for the present conditions and behavior of MENA states. Like all other states they are the products of multiple causes at sub-national, national, regional and global levels over extended periods of time. This is not to gainsay the profound importance for the MENA of colonialism, but to suggest that its impacts have varied within the region, in significant measure because colonialism was not imposed uniformly nor on *tabula rasas*. It did, however, contribute in the MENA, as elsewhere, to the creation of "incomplete, distorted, and malformed versions of European modern states" which were "then shaped and reshaped by indigenous elites as they sought to control and transform the societies they came to govern."[14]

Colonialism was not uniformly experienced in the MENA or anywhere else in the world; it did not obliterate any and all pre-existing political orders; the independent states established by anti-colonialists varied greatly in their compositions and capacities; and the ability of those post-colonial states to cope with the challenges of globalization that intensified when the Cold War ended suggest that the historical path dependence of the MENA is longer and more complex than a single-minded emphasis on the impacts of colonialism would imply. As for the length and periodization of that history, in some MENA countries it stretches back to what archeologists have termed the pre-historical era of more than 6,000 years ago in, say, Egypt, while for all it includes four reasonably distinct eras: pre-colonial, colonial, post-colonial and post-post-colonial, the last being the era that commenced with the acceleration of globalization some 30 years ago.

Pre-colonial Origins of Stateness

Although the argument that contemporary state capacities are in part the legacy of political authority extant several thousand years ago may at first glance seem fanciful, historical institutionalists have marshalled both theoretical and empirical evidence in support of it.[15] Because China has had the longest imperial regime in the world, with a centralized administrative system for millennia, it has been a natural focus of efforts to identify such historical events, linkages and impacts.[16] Among the findings of these investigations are positive correlations between administrative presence and improved state fiscal performance in ancient China; between that presence and population density and human capital in the Qing Dynasty and in late imperial China—which stretched into the early twentieth century—between capable bureaucracy and the containment of inflation and spread of branch banking.[17] State capacity, in other words, has a venerable history of broad reach and deep penetration, although variable, in more or less the same territory now governed by the People's Republic of China. Esteem for the mandarin tradition of bureaucrat scholars contributes to the legitimation of that government while helping to provide a model for it and its ruling Chinese Communist Party (CCP), one that has enjoyed enormous success, especially compared to territories lacking such venerable traditions of effective statehood.

No MENA country can claim a state patrimony equivalent to China's record of unbroken sovereignty for millennia, with the comparatively brief exception of colonial influence over the Qing Dynasty that commenced in the early nineteenth century. Egypt, Iran, Morocco, Tunisia and Turkey are the only MENA states which have pre-colonial antecedents, but none had traditions of "stateness" of such length, autonomy and capacity as China.[18] Egypt's is the most impressive in terms of the continuity of its territory under central governmental control, which dates back more than 5,000 years to the founding Pharaonic dynasties, but the autonomy and penetration of its central governments was substantially less than its

Chinese equivalent. State autonomy was lost to a series of invaders, stretching from the Persians in the sixth century BC, through the Romans, Arabs, Mamluks, Ottomans and ultimately Western imperialists, commencing with Napoleon's invasion in 1798 and not truly ending until the British evacuation of the Suez Canal Zone in 1954. Successive dynasties exerted varying degrees of control over their nominal territory, with many of them in the Pharaonic and Greco/Roman eras having greater spread and penetration than subsequent ones, whether Arab, Mamluk or Ottoman. Much of Upper Egypt, for example, was ruled by local potentates for centuries. Unlike China, Egypt does not have an unbroken, venerated mandarin tradition of highly trained, disciplined administrators.

Yet by comparison to other MENA countries, Egypt's "stateness" stands out. Within the Arab world only Morocco and Tunisia had pre-colonial states, the former's stretching back to the early Islamic period and coming under the present ruling dynasty in 1667. Tunisia's pre-colonial "stateness" is considerably more discontinuous, having been ruled by various dynasties until it fell under Ottoman rule in 1574, rendering it a relative backwater of that empire. But even in Morocco the sultan directly and continuously ruled only the *blad al mahkzen* (territory of the royal household), asserting his authority just intermittently over the *blad as siba* (territory of dissidence). His administration consisted of "a few ministers and their retainers accompanying the sultan on his armed expeditions to collect the taxes from dissident tribes."[19] As with Tunisia, many tribes enjoyed near complete autonomy from the sultan's government, as did some of its nominal provincial representatives who succeeded in establishing their own semi-sovereign entities. As in Egypt, neither in Morocco nor Tunisia did a mandarin caste emerge to sustain an unbroken administrative tradition.

Turkey and Iran also can be traced back to pre-colonial states, although as empires the states of both those countries, and especially the former, ruled over more extensive territory than those sovereign states do today. Of the two, the Ottoman Empire disposed of substantially more state capacity, at least in its heartland which is more or less contiguous with today's Turkey. Central to that capacity were a reasonably competent civil service and an effective legal-judicial system, while Ottoman society was comparatively easy to govern because in the heartland it rested upon settled peasant agriculture. The Iranian state, by contrast, had to contend with a more tribalized, mobile population and do so with a comparatively smaller, less professionalized bureaucracy.

Of the 21 states the World Bank includes in its definition of the MENA, there are thus only five which have pedigrees as pre-colonial sovereign entities. It is these five, however, that are today the region's most impressive nation states, as attested to by various measures, including population size (with the exception of Tunisia), economic diversification, military strength and political stability, this last indicator reflected by the fact that the three Arab states of Morocco, Tunisia and Egypt did not collapse in the face of the 2011 Arab Spring, even though the latter two underwent regime changes. These states also possess the region's most long-established, effective legislatures, despite their shortcomings. None, however, disposes of state capacity in the magnitude of China, reflecting that country's considerably more substantial historical legacy of stateness.

Saudi Arabia

The MENA countries lacking pre-colonial historical roots of state capacity fall into two categories—those entirely configured by nineteenth- and twentieth-century imperial powers, and those partially based on existing "national" entities but ones lacking clearly defined borders or all but the most rudimentary state capacities. Only three countries—Saudi Arabia, Yemen and Oman—fall into this second category. Contemporary Saudi Arabia traces its antecedents to the mid-eighteenth century, when Muhammad bin Saud, the tribal sheikh founder of the present Saudi dynasty, together with Muhammad ibn Abd al Wahhab, proselytizer of an austere version of Sunni Islam, founded a rudimentary state around Riyadh that steadily expanded over the next 60 years. The Ottomans, acting through Egypt's Muhammad Ali dynasty, pushed that statelet back to its core area around Riyadh, where it largely remained for the next century, contesting with other tribal forces, chief of which were the al Rashid. In the wake of WWI, the new Saudi leader, Abd al Aziz ibn Saud, brilliantly executed a series of military campaigns against the al Rashid and the Hashemites that culminated in the declaration of a Saudi state in 1930, some territory of which was contested with neighboring Yemen and what became the United Arab Emirates, but which largely became the present country of Saudi Arabia. It was not until the 1950s, however, that the kernel of today's state apparatus began to emerge there, and another almost two decades before a vast increase in oil revenues enabled the dramatic expansion of that state core. For all intents and purposes, therefore, the Saudi state is less than half a century old, a fact which accounts in part for various of its frailties. With regard to the legitimacy of its ruling dynasty, however, the fact that the al Saud carved their country out against local, regional and even global challengers—the British in this case—provided substantially more of it than dynasts placed on their thrones by imperial powers, which included those in Libya, Egypt, Iraq, Jordan and the other GCC states, of which those in Libya, Egypt and Iraq were all overthrown in coups d'état. That legitimacy, combined with patronage generated by oil rents, has so far been sufficient to perpetuate Saudi rule despite lingering deficiencies of state capacity, although state weakness limits policy choices and undermines their implementation.

Yemen

The history of the Yemeni state is similar, although its pre-colonial rulers did not survive the nationalist era associated with colonial and post-colonial rule. Given its strategic location and relatively favorable natural endowments, which among other things enabled the country to be the world's only producer of coffee until the eighteenth century, Yemen was a strategic prize which attracted the attentions of external powers. From the early sixteenth century onwards, these included the Portuguese, the Egyptian Mamluks and, following the latter's defeat by the Ottomans, the Ottoman governors of Egypt and subsequently, when they failed to subdue the country, the Ottomans themselves. As a Cairo-based Ottoman commander commented after losing more than 70,000 of the 80,000 troops sent to Yemen from 1539, "We have seen no foundry like Yemen for our soldiers. Each time we have sent an expeditionary force there, it has melted away like salt dissolved in water."[20] Similar sentiments have likely been shared by his twentieth- and twenty-first-century counterparts who also dispatched hapless troops to Yemen, including the Egyptians, Saudis, Emiratis, Russians, British and Americans. Zaydi tribesman in the mountainous north of the country provided then as now the backbone of Yemeni resistance to invading forces. A branch of Shi'a Islam, the Zaydis carved out a separate Imamate in the north, which fought the Ottomans intermittently for some 300 years. In 1839 the British entered the fray, establishing a coaling station in the south in Aden, which in turn caused the Ottomans to try once again to conquer much of the south after an absence of two centuries. With the collapse of the Ottoman Empire at the end of WWI, the Sana'a-based Imam Yahya sought to regain control of the south, launching attacks against the British and their local allies. He failed in this effort and ultimately lost considerable territory to the Saudis, who had allied with his Yemeni opponents on the coastal plain, but he did consolidate his control of the north and in 1926 was recognized as King of Yemen. He was assassinated in 1948 by opposition forces based in the Sunni Muslim community, organized in part by the Muslim Brotherhood. But his son Ahmad mobilized Zaydi tribesman and re-established the Imamate based in Sana'a until his death in 1962, an event which occasioned a coup d'état supported by Egypt, which ultimately dispatched tens of thousands of troops in a vain effort to help consolidate the newly declared Republic. The different historical trajectories of the south and north resulted in a separate, avowedly Marxist-Leninist southern state being created upon the withdrawal of the British in 1967. The near collapse of that state in the wake of the demise of the Soviet Union caused it to merge with the north in 1993, which within a year led to a civil war in which the forces of the north soundly defeated rebelling southerners.

Yemen's history is thus one of extreme turbulence and violence, similar to that of Afghanistan's, with which it shares other common features, including pronounced tribalism, division between Sunnis and Shi'i, poverty and a tradition of weak central government with little administrative reach or societal penetration. The Yemeni government depended on tribal levies to fight the Ottomans in the sixteenth century, as it has in the twenty-first century to fight various internal and external forces. The Imamate that enjoyed some legitimacy because of its role in fighting against the Ottomans, British and Saudis, ended in 1962, with successive rulers in the north being former military officers and those in the south Marxist-Leninist activists. Yemen, in other words, has no tradition of either state capacity or extended dynastic rule, and has only limited oil revenues with which to bind the population to its rulers through the distribution of patronage.

Oman

Omani history is similar to that of Yemen's, a country it borders, so need not be traced here in detail. Whereas about one third of Yemen's population is Zaydi, the majority of Omanis are Ibadis, a sect which split off from Sunni Islam in the seventh century before the Shi'i also did so. As with the Zaydi Yemenis, the Omani Ibadis founded an

Imamate in the rugged interior, which existed for some 1,200 years from 751 and for all intents and purposes became a dynasty ultimately led by the al Bu Said clan which rules Oman today. And as with the Yemeni Zaydis, the Omani Ibadis fought to defend their territory against invaders, also including the Ottomans and Portuguese, while struggling to contain internal challenges arising from schisms within the al Bu Said, from various tribes, from the sharp division along religious and other lines between coastal and interior dwellers, and from conflicts within the mini-empire Oman had created, largely to exploit the slave trade, including the island of Zanzibar and enclaves in East Africa and what is now Pakistan. Restrictions on the slave trade ultimately caused the collapse of that mini-empire, with the British assuming control of its territory and ultimately of Oman itself, the latter by backing one Turki ibn Said al Bu Said, a descendant of whom is the current Sultan of Oman.

In sum, while Oman had a strong mercantile tradition, as was the case with several other territories on the Arabian Peninsula, it was too externally focused on trade and too internally fractious because of religious and tribal divisions ever to establish a state which could extract sufficient resources to ensure that its administrative capacities extended throughout the country. Its current ruling family can trace its lineage back for centuries, but it owes its crown to the British, not to a nationalist uprising against them. It rules over a state that was created under British tutelage and protection, the legitimacy of which is due to the distinctive Omani identity and to very conscious efforts by Sultan Qaboos, who replaced his father Said bin Taimur in 1970, to cultivate an identity that merges his clan with the nation, again as is the case in other GCC countries.[21]

In conclusion, both Yemen and Oman are countries with long histories and episodic experiences with uncontested sovereignty, but which prior to the colonial era did not have sustained traditions of states with adequate capacity to control territory, extract resources and deliver public services. Saudi Arabia's history of statehood is similar, but the country owes its very existence to the al Saud, not to a colonial power, and their writ has run throughout their territory for decades longer than is the case with either Yemen or Oman.

Colonial Creations

The remaining MENA countries of Algeria, Libya, Lebanon, Syria, Iraq, Israel, Jordan, Sudan, Palestine and the four monarchial GCC states other than Saudi Arabia and Oman, are products of colonialism with at best brief, discontinuous prior histories of statehood in the territory they presently occupy. This is not to say, however, that these countries lack history, as they are situated on lands which were once the seats of great empires. Rather, it is that unlike China or, in the MENA, Egypt, Morocco, Tunisia, Turkey or Iran, the history of statehood in this group of countries is intermittent and frequently not contiguous with present territories. So, for example, Libya's Carthage was the home of the Punic civilization, of whom Hannibal is the most well-known historical figure, primarily because of his conquest of substantial parts of Roman-ruled Italy. Northern Sudan was the site of the Pharaonic-era Kingdom of Kush and of several Nubian kingdoms in the period prior to Arabization and Islamization in the seventh century. Lebanon was the home of the Phoenician civilization that colonized much of the Mediterranean world. Syria's Damascus was the seat of the Umayyad Dynasty that prevailed for a century over the then Muslim world that extended from Spain to Central Asia. Iraq's capital Baghdad was the home of the almost equally extensive Abbasid Empire from 750 to 1258. Jordan's Petra was the trading hub of the Nabatean Empire. What is now Israel and the Palestinian Territories includes land that formed part of the Jewish Kingdom as far back as 1000 BC, then a province within the Roman Empire, and subsequently its principal city of Jerusalem served as capital of the Crusader Kingdom.

In all these and related cases, however, the remnants of these once mighty empires are to be found in archeological sites, not in the concepts and practices of contemporary statehood, even though today's nationalisms in these states frequently draw upon these legitimating historical periods and their associated symbols. Algeria was carved out of what was essentially a stateless region of North Africa by the French in the early nineteenth century; Libya was created in much the same fashion by the Italian invasion just before WWI, followed in 1947 by the UN, which filled the vacuum left by Italian defeat and withdrawal in WWII; Syria and Lebanon were formed out of former Ottoman provinces by the French after WWI, as was Iraq by the British. Israel, Jordan and Palestine are the product of British control of that part of the Levant in the wake of WWI, followed by the 1993 Oslo Accords which created the Palestinian Authority. As for the four GCC states referred to above, none since antiquity was the seat of even a mini-empire. All were the products of the convergence of British imperial interests with those of locally dominant tribes. None achieved statehood until 1961 in the case of Kuwait, and a decade later in the cases of Bahrain, Qatar and the UAE.

These then are the many MENA countries which at best experienced varying degrees of central authority intermittently but are not the descendants of historical empires or nation states. They possessed fewer state capacities than Egypt, Morocco, Tunisia, Iran or Turkey, so the task of state building in them under colonial tutelage faced greater obstacles. Not surprisingly, their present conditions bespeak of their relatively impoverished inheritance of stateness. Libya, Yemen and Syria are experiencing intense, protracted domestic conflict that raises questions about their continued national existence, with Iraq not far behind. Algeria underwent a semi-civil war in the early 1990s and is being held together precariously by an oppressive military dictatorship against which, and its handpicked President, hundreds of thousands of Algerians demonstrated in the spring of 2019. Lebanon has never adequately reconstructed its polity, to say nothing of its economy, in the wake of its 15-year-long civil war.

Only in the statelets of Kuwait, Qatar and the UAE is the absence of historical stateness not reflected in contemporary turmoil, thanks largely to their small size, oil wealth, continued support by Western powers and, most importantly, to the fact that their states were essentially imported from Britain, personnel and all. These states served as the administrative arms of the monarchial rulers with which Britain forged alliances dating back to the nineteenth century. They have yet to undergo colonial dialectics of the sort that pitted nationalists against their rulers and foreign backers elsewhere in the MENA. Bahrain, their fellow GCC state that has been wracked intermittently with Sunni–Shi'a tension since the uprising of 2011, has more or less the same degree of stateness, but confronts a much more divided society.

State effectiveness, in sum, varies substantially in the MENA, with the best predictor of it being the degree to which stateness preceded colonial rule in any given country. The precise mechanisms through which path dependency of this nature operates are ambiguous. Presumably they include a mix of expectations and behavioral norms created by institutions over time, the structural legacies of those institutions, and the impacts on populations of shared, known histories. But whatever the actual mix is, the consequence is that it is hard for states to escape their national histories, or lack thereof.

3

COLONIALISM, POST-COLONIALISM, GLOBALIZATION AND THE STATE

The colonial and post-colonial eras are considered jointly here because of their inherent interaction. The former, combined with pre-existing conditions, produced varying anti-colonial reactions ultimately embodied in post-colonial states, as was the case throughout the "third world." Colonialism in the MENA, however, is distinctive by virtue of being but one episode of continuous foreign intervention into the region that persists until today, to say nothing of its remarkably variable length and penetration in MENA countries. Algeria, for example, was invaded by the French in 1832, who dispatched hundreds of thousands of citizens to colonize the conquered territory, the coastal portion of which was officially integrated into France and remained so until the war of independence launched in 1954 finally forced the French to depart in 1962, leaving in their wake a society, economy and polity pulverized by France's long, intrusive presence. British rule in Egypt, by contrast, was officially only from WWI to 1922, even though considerably longer in practice. It never included land seizures or colonial settlement, but was reinforced by a substantial military presence that subdued a countrywide uprising in 1919, though it never faced a protracted national war of liberation by the Egyptians. The sheikhdoms of the Gulf were similarly brought under British control in the nineteenth century, but in them the British presence was still lighter, as reflected in the lack of settlement, a predominantly over the horizon rather than immediate naval presence, and a British "resident" who served as representative of his government simultaneously in several of the sheikhdoms. Such substantial variations in the length and penetration of colonialism in the MENA, to say nothing of participation in it by three European powers (France, Britain and Italy), contrast sharply with, say, Spanish

45

and Portuguese colonialism in Latin America, which commenced in the sixteenth century, included massive migration from the colonial powers and of slaves from Africa, resulted in governments established and operated by those powers, and in much of the region perpetrated genocides of native peoples. The Algerian casualty figure of the war of independence was approximately 1 million, the highest such toll absolutely or relative to population in the MENA, followed by the Palestinians, of whom some 2,000 died fighting Jewish forces in the 1947–48 war, with another 11,000 civilian casualties and some 700,000 residents ethnically cleansed from their homes. Spanish–Portuguese competition, to the extent it existed, did not result in the liberation of Latin American states, whereas Franco–British and British–Italian competitions were responsible for the termination of colonialism in Libya, Lebanon and Syria.

Another distinctive feature of MENA colonialism is that it was embedded in the millennia-long history of external intervention and domination of the region by Western powers, such that many nationalists in the MENA consider colonial rule as simply one phase in that long history and one followed by subsequent interventions, some subtle, others brutal and violent, such as the US-led invasion of Iraq in 2013. The history of Western intervention began with the Romans, who integrated much of the MENA into their empire. No other region of the world has had such extensive and intensive interaction with the West over such a long period, locked as the two have been in what seems a fatal historical embrace. The region served as a primary battleground between external powers in WWI, WWII and the Cold War. The first Arab–Israeli war of 1947–48 was followed by others in 1956, 1967, 1970 and 1973, to say nothing of the Israeli invasions of Lebanon in 1978, 1982 and 2006 or air attacks on Iraq in 1981 or Syria intermittently since 2012. As the creation of British imperial and American neo-imperial power, Israel is viewed by many Arabs as a coercive projection of Western power into their heartland, analogous to the Roman Empire or the Crusades. The MENA has been the epicenter of the global struggle for control of "black gold" since the early twentieth century, with the bulk of oil production directly controlled and owned by British and American companies until the 1970s. Substantial influence over production by foreign companies continues today. Reactions against perceived hostile interventions into the MENA have included violent extremism, especially that perpetrated by Islamists, the most notorious of such attacks being that on New York's World Trade Center in 2001.

Colonial Dialectics

While relations between external powers and MENA nationalists clearly have important perceptual, subjective dimensions, they have also had direct, objective consequences for MENA states, most of which have militated against the development of those states' infrastructural power. Imperialist interest in extracting raw materials from colonies while discouraging opposition resulted in misshapen states, with overdeveloped "output" sides devoted to administration, including suppression of dissent, and underdeveloped "input" sides that lacked robust representative bodies at local and national levels, political parties, formalized interest groups and other means of articulating and aggregating interests. Colonial political economies, in short, cultivated what Michael Mann labeled despotic power while discouraging infrastructural power, because the latter would necessarily include a strengthening of state–society relations, considered inimical to the interests of colonial rulers. Unbalanced states were fostered to preside over and maintain unbalanced economies—ones that relied heavily or even exclusively on the export of raw materials rather than on increasing domestic value added through processing and industrial utilization. Colonial states were thus inherently weak, lacking effective penetration of and engagement with civil society, and hence the ability to mobilize societal capacities in support of national objectives. How these misshapen colonial states impacted post-colonial successor states is partially explained by the differing roles militaries ultimately assumed in the latter, an outcome resulting in part from the relative importance of officers versus civilians in decolonization struggles.

The relative state capacities and development trajectories of Israel, Turkey and Tunisia, in all of which militaries have been subject to greater and relatively more institutionalized civilian control than in other MENA states, illustrate the complex relationships between history, militaries, civil societies and infrastructural power. Israel and Turkey emerged as states thanks to military action, against Palestinians and Arab armies in the case of the former, and against Greeks and European armed forces in the case of the latter. In both countries, however, successful militaries were counterbalanced by effective, civilian-based political parties. Those in Israel had their roots in Europe and early Zionist settlement and were stronger than those in Turkey, which did not emerge until the early 1950s, despite having precursors in the nineteenth-century Ottoman Empire.

While militaries continued to be vitally important state actors in both—with the Turkish military staging four successful coups and one unsuccessful attempt between 1960 and 2016 and the Israeli Defense Forces serving as a major channel of national political recruitment until today, and with both militaries heavily involved in their respective national economies—in neither case were the armed forces as politically hegemonic as in the militarized Arab republics. Civilian institutions enjoyed substantial autonomy from militaries and provided linkages to civil society upon which infrastructural power was built.

The only analogous case to Israel and Turkey in the Arab world is Tunisia, in which the nationalist struggle against France was orchestrated primarily by the Neo-Destour political party, which from the outset subordinated the military to its control. The fact that Tunisia is the only MENA state to have emerged from the 2011 uprisings substantially more democratic than previously attests to the impact of its heritage, in which effective civilian, anti-colonial political mobilization provided the impetus for national liberation and the post-colonial state that followed. By contrast, in Morocco the civilian nationalist movement was immediately subordinated to the monarch on his return from exile in 1955 and successful negotiation of independence from France the following year. Monarchs placed on their thrones by colonial powers in Libya and Iraq, or retained on the throne as a counterbalance to nationalist civilian forces in Egypt, lacked the legitimacy of Morocco's sultan and were ultimately displaced by militaries. Algeria's military, its power greatly expanded by the 1954–62 war of liberation, supplanted the civilian leadership of the FLN in 1965. Syria's fragmented, notable-dominated political parties were spared the task of mobilizing against the French colonizer, so did not deepen political roots in either urban or rural areas. They were relatively easily replaced by the military a few short years after Allied forces drove the French out. In Lebanon similar political parties have held onto power, augmented by the arrival of Iranian-backed Hizbullah that has effectively mobilized Shi'i, in large part because the military was kept small and divided between the various religious "confessions." In Iraq the unpopular, "foreign" Hashemite monarch was easily dispatched by a coup in 1958, with the military and the conspiratorial Ba'th Party sharing power until the fall of Saddam.

In sum, colonial dialectics resulting from intensifying conflicts between colonizers and colonized played out differently across the region, advantaging Morocco's monarch, militaries in Algeria,

48

Libya, Egypt, Syria and Iraq, a mobilized political party in Tunisia and weak, fragmented ones in Lebanon. British-backed monarchs in Jordan and the GCC countries did not face such intense opposition, so retained power. Divided between opposing Russian and British occupying powers, Iran generated a nationalist movement that was pushed aside by a military takeover in 1921 which ultimately gave rise to the British and American supported Pahlavi Dynasty, finally overthrown by the mullah-led uprising of 1979.

Consequences of Decolonization

Clearly colonialism and reactions to it had impacts on stateness in the MENA. In the five countries that enjoyed substantial pre-colonial sovereignty—Egypt, Tunisia, Morocco, Iran and Turkey—stateness is relatively more impressive today than in MENA countries without the benefit of pre-colonial state origins, with Israel's "imported" state, in the sense that it was the product of European political movements, an exception. Yet, among these five, it is only Tunisia and Turkey that have made substantial progress in correcting the imbalance between the output and input sides of their political systems by empowering civilian political actors to contest for power over the state, including most importantly its coercive agencies. In Tunisia this was due to the protracted colonial dialectic driving the creation of an effective, civilian-dominated nationalist movement, while in Turkey it resulted from the military granting sufficient political space after 1950 to civilian political actors for them to organize and ultimately to gain control of the state and subordinate the military under the Islamist AKP which took power in 2002. In contrast, Egypt, Iran and Morocco still have the benefit of coherent states that pre-dated colonialism, but they are misshapen as a result of the imbalance between their preponderant states and disempowered societies, a result of their paths to independence. In none was society success-fully mobilized against colonial rule autonomously from either the monarch or the military, with the partial exception of Iran, in which the monarch was replaced in 1979 by a movement led by the most traditional element of society, the clerics, who were theologically and practically opposed to societal and political pluralism or autonomous societal mobilization. The infrastructural power of these three states, therefore, is less than in Tunisia and Turkey, but greater than in the substantially more fragile Arab republics which did not have the benefit of pre-colonial stateness. Moreover, decolonization within Algeria, Libya, Syria, Iraq, Sudan and Yemen led ultimately to military rule, and in Lebanon to the persistence of a system of confessional balance based on patrimonial clientelism that perpetuated the political influence and economic pre-eminence of traditional elites or warlords empowered by conflict. These then are all unbalanced states, having subordinate societies unable to choose their governments, hold them accountable, or contribute to resource mobilization and deployment.

The GCC monarchies, as well as Jordan and Morocco, have greater infrastructural power than the Arab republics other than Tunisia or Lebanon, because of a mix of three factors. First, state–society linkages, although based heavily on informal, clientelistic relations, tend to be reasonably durable and deep. Those personalistic networks supplement more formal connections between states and citizens, creating more robust parallel channels than are found in the republics. Related to this are two other factors that reinforce these informal ties. One is the relative wealth of the GCC monarchies, hence their ability to service clientelistic networks; while the other, with the exception of Saudi Arabia, is their small populations, thereby making face to face interactions more common while also increasing rents, hence patronage, per capita. Finally, the GCC states themselves were erected in the shadow of Western influence and, in many instances, were manned by Western technocrats. Western powers and GCC monarchs had mutual interests in creating reasonably well performing states that could manage the exploitation of hydrocarbon resources, at least partially diversify economies, and develop human resources. It was not, therefore, a colonial dialectic that drove state building, but a synthesis of colonial and local interests. Jordan and Morocco share some of these characteristics, although they are not as wealthy as the GCC countries. Morocco especially has tended to be more independent of Western powers.

State Consolidation Thwarted

A final feature of the post-colonial era which accounts for the relative underperformance of at least some MENA states is that they are not allowed to fail. The Schumpeter "creative destruction" dictum for capitalist economic growth—that it is propelled by the bankruptcy of non-competitive firms, and hence their replacement by more successful ones—seemed also to apply to European nation building.[1] Smaller and weaker European countries were, primarily in the nineteenth century, gobbled up by larger, stronger ones. Prussia, for example, drove the unification of Germany by extirpating pre-existing, petty principalities. The creation of Italy resulted from a similar process, although with a coalition of its stronger regions rather than one being the principal driving force behind unification.

In the MENA, by contrast, failed states are kept alive by a global consensus against redrawing post-colonial boundaries, mainly out of the fear that once such a process commenced, it might spread out of control in regions where borders are "artificial," dividing potentially national communities while uniting peoples with little shared history, culture, religion, ethnicity or even language. Yemen and Libya are contemporary cases in point. The former is the product of the union of north and south in the early 1990s, regions that have their own distinctive histories, religions and socio-political organizations. The latter is the product of merging three separate regions, Tripolitania, Fezzan and Cyrenaica, again each with its own identity. One solution to their present travails would be to divide them back into their constituent parts, as was proposed by US Vice-President Biden for Iraq during a particularly violent phase of conflict there following the US invasion of 2003, a proposal that gained no traction anywhere. Prussian-style unification, with a strong state annexing surrounding weaker ones, has similarly been opposed, as was the case with Egyptians' efforts to incorporate Sudan after WWII or Syria in the late 1950s, or Syria's efforts to effectively terminate Lebanon's independence from 1976. MENA countries, in short, are either too small to fail or too big to succeed, so there are no state "bankruptcies" to drive state building equivalent to Schumpeter's "gale," his driving force of capitalism. MENA states are condemned to stagger on alone, despite manifestly failed state performance and bleak prospects for improving it in several of them. Had this not been the case, the contemporary MENA would presumably consist of fewer, larger states, possibly with substantially greater capacities.

The dialectic between colonialism and nationalist reactions to it thus did not propel most MENA states to build effective state–society relations, nor even to substantially capitalize on pre-existing traditions of statehood in those countries where they existed. Instead, decolonization typically empowered either coercive forces, or incumbent, traditional ruling elites. Only in Tunisia did it result in civilians taking the lead to establish an independent state not under military or monarchial control. But even that exception ultimately succumbed in 1987 to a military coup, which took almost 24 years and a countrywide uprising to partially reverse with the re-establishment of a civilian government with less than full, institutionalized control of the military and security services. The other success stories of the decolonization era, Israel and Turkey, also failed to establish and consolidate inclusive, institutionalized civilian governance. After 2002 Turkey slid steadily toward Islamist authoritarianism, with Israeli democracy more or less simultaneously declining under Prime Minister Binyamin Netanyahu into Jewish chauvinist authoritarianism. In both cases incumbent, hyper-patriotic, intolerant ruling elites converted their states into vehicles of their own factional interests, thereby violating one of the basic principles of effective state performance. The other MENA countries became either rentier monarchies dependent upon clientelism underpinned by hydrocarbon or, in the case of Morocco, phosphate rents, or, in the case of Jordan, foreign assistance; or military dictatorships, or, in the case of Iran, a theocratic one.

The net result for all the Arab countries was that when legitimating nationalist struggles inevitably faded from popular memory with the passage of time, these authoritarian states faced crises induced by their failures to grant societies adequate access to their political economies. These crises struck those countries simultaneously, attesting to the interconnectedness of the Arab world. They also occurred in the wake of the great wave of globalization that began to sweep through the world in the wake of the collapse of the Soviet Union, thereby also attesting to the inability of most Arab and MENA countries effectively to meet the challenges posed by that globalization.

Globalization and the MENA

Despite its signal contribution to economic growth and equalization of national income between countries of the North and South, globalization's great wave at the end of the Cold War stimulated a matching wave of skepticism in the developed and developing worlds. In both, globalization was rightly seen as contributing to growing inequality within countries of both the North and South. In much of the developing world it was interpreted as yet another manifestation of neo-imperialism. In the MENA this view was particularly widespread, reflecting colonial legacies as much or even more than contemporary relative economic consequences.

In fact, globalization was driving more rapid economic growth in the MENA than in the old colonial powers, growth that compared favorably to that in other emerging regions, with the notable exception of very high performing East Asia. Nevertheless, neo-liberalism and the Washington Consensus became in the MENA derogatory terms, conflated with globalization and employed to discredit it. The Arab uprisings in 2011 were commonly attributed to the effects of globalization, even though they came more than two years after it had gone into dramatic reverse, with world trade falling almost 13% in 2009, having negative consequences for national economic growth almost everywhere. The case could be made, therefore, that it was not rapid globalization, but its sudden, dramatic slowing that has been the cause of Arab, and indeed MENA, discontent. That interpretation is lent further weight by the fact that MENA GDP growth since the global recovery that began to pick up in 2016 has lagged behind almost all other regions, being 1.8% in 2017, leading only Latin America and the Caribbean at 1.7%. The MENA, it seems, suffers from structural liabilities—key of which is its heavy dependence on hydrocarbon exports—that impede its economic growth unless that growth is propelled by very rapid expansion of global trade, hence rising oil and gas prices. The MENA, therefore, is disproportionately dependent upon globalization for its present economic well-being, to say nothing of its future prospects for economic diversification, a virtual precondition for the success of which is expanding globalization.

It is paradoxical, therefore, that globalization in the MENA tends to be commonly viewed more as curse than blessing. Conflated with neo-imperialism and neo-liberalism, both of which it overlaps but with neither of which is it synonymous, globalization has been blamed for undermining social contracts which have sustained authoritarian rule throughout the post-colonial era. Those social contracts were in reality vitiated by the inability of regimes to generate sufficient resources to sustain them, largely because of failures to liberalize state-controlled economies.

Recent research on the negative consequences of cronyism for MENA economic growth, for example, abundantly illustrates the shortcomings of political economies that divide economic actors into insiders and outsiders, privileging the former, punishing the latter.[2] As mentioned above, the 2011 Arab Spring erupted following more than two years of economic stagnation resulting from slowing globalization and accompanying reversals of liberal reforms. Youth protests resulted from the lethal combination of the rapid expansion of university education from the late 1980s with declining employment opportunities as states could no longer afford to further inflate their

civil services and had failed to enable the private sector to create sufficient job opportunities. In Egypt, for example, the overall workforce
expanded by 7.7 million persons from 2005 until 2019, whereas the
civil service grew by only 190,000 during that time. Similarly, in
Saudi Arabia, where 45% of citizens still work for the state, 31%
are over 45 years of age, but only 7% under 30, also reflecting the
slowing rate of civil service recruitment.[3] Rapid population growth,
which contributed to the Arab Spring and state breakdowns, was also
the result in part of ill-conceived, crumbling social contracts, not of
liberalizing reforms, if only because female labor force participation
rates, already low, sank further in tandem with declining opportunities for government employment. In sum, attributing the cause of
political and economic crises from 2011 to globalization and whatever
economic liberalization that accompanied it amounts to blaming the
victim. Moreover, this false indictment has provided justification for
incumbent regimes to reassert authoritarian control over both polities
and economies, spouting nationalist rhetoric as they do so.

Globalization drives limited liberalizations

Globalization's take-off from the mid-1980s, combined with the end
of the Cold War and a reduction in the geo-strategic rents it had
generated for the MENA, induced the region's states to undertake
political and economic reforms required to ride the globalization
wave and extract benefits from it, including capturing more foreign
direct investment (FDI), which in the 1990s became the dominant
source of external financing. Virtually all MENA states adopted
at least some of the "ten commandments" of the Washington
Consensus of measures of economic liberalization, typically coupling
them with cautious political openings.[4] The two decades of rapid
globalization did not produce a new liberal age in the MENA. These
years did, however, witness noticeable shifts from the prevailing, if
already diluted statist economic development model to something
more akin to capitalism; and from unadulterated to what came to
be termed "hybrid" authoritarianism, a system in which elections,
freedom of expression and human rights began to have some, if
limited meaning. Militaries appeared to recede further from seats of
presidential power, while many of the monarchies witnessed expan-
sions of parliamentary activity.

Reform of MENA political economies came to an abrupt halt with
the Arab uprisings of 2011, which themselves followed the global

economic crisis of 2008–9 that presaged several years of stagnating globalization and slower economic growth. As globalization slowed to a crawl, MENA states scrambled to meet intensifying domestic and regional economic and political challenges. Just as they had turned in unison in a liberal direction in the late 1980s as globalization intensified, so they now turned en bloc in a conservative one, shoring up state authority over the polity in their search for ways and means to confront intensifying economic problems.

The MENA's dependence on globalization

As an economic phenomenon globalization is particularly important to the MENA. About three quarters of the region's merchandise exports are hydrocarbons, prices for which are substantially demand driven. As the strongest positive force for world economic growth, globalization thus propels oil and gas prices higher. Even relatively small variations in the rate of globalization, as measured by global trade, can thus be significant for MENA economies, hence for their polities as well. Recent fluctuations in globalization and growth are thus central to understanding the contemporary MENA political economy.

The great wave of globalization that welled up as the Cold War was ending, and which peaked with the 2008–9 financial crisis, ebbed away until 2017, at which time global trade commenced a modest recovery. Between 1985 and 2011 global trade grew at an annual average of almost 6%, with global GDP growth following not far behind. From 2011 until 2016 rates of global trade expansion and GDP growth were low and roughly equal at an annual average of slightly more than 2%. It was during this period of relative stagnation, in 2014, that oil and gas prices plummeted. The WTO anticipated merchandise trade volume growth of 4.4% in 2018, just slightly less than the 4.7% increase recorded for 2017. Growth was projected to be 4% in 2019. For the period 2016 to 2020, therefore, global trade is forecast to expand more slowly than the average rate of 4.8% since 1990, although somewhat faster than the post-crisis 2009–16 average of 3%. Global GDP growth is projected to closely parallel rates of trade growth, at 3.9% in 2018 and 2019 before sliding to 3.7% in 2022. Globalization and growth thus picked up following some eight lackluster years, but they are not forecast to return to the high rates achieved prior to 2008.[5]

The fact that oil prices made a substantial recovery in 2018, by the autumn of which they had doubled in price per barrel in the wake of the 2014 collapse, testifies to the triangular relationship between globalization, growth and hydrocarbon prices. Prognostications for moderate rates of globalization and economic growth thus suggest that those prices may also increase over the next few years, albeit at moderate rates. It should immediately be pointed out, however, that the potential for a renewed, possibly sudden deterioration of global trade and GDP growth is widely feared as a result of the breakdown, in December 2015, of the Doha round of WTO negotiations, followed by an incipient global trade war driven by the Trump administration's "America First" policies. The global financial infrastructure erected in the wake of WWII is facing increased pressure from US disinterest, emerging countries' dissatisfactions with it, and competition from new rivals, such as the Asian Infrastructure Investment Bank initiated by China. Revanchist, anti-globalization political forces are gathering strength, even in much of the OECD. Recalling that a previous wave of globalization that commenced with the rise of steam navigation in the 1870s dramatically ended with the outbreak of WWI, and was not followed by another wave until the 1980s, suggests that globalization cycles have previously been and are likely to continue to be intermittent, unpredictable, subject to political conditions, and punctuated with extended periods of stagnating world trade and economic growth.

Slowing, increasingly uncertain globalization is being succeeded by a gathering storm of difficulties for MENA political economies. The very cause of the region's economic underperformance, which has been the insider/outsider divides inherent in rent seeking associated with authoritarianism, has been reinvigorated by states increasingly fearful of their populations in the wake of the Arab Spring. This revanchism, combined with weakened globalization, virtually guarantees the continuation of stagnating GDPs per capita throughout the MENA, a problem reinforced by rapid population growth combined with the region's continuing economic dependence on oil and gas revenues. What remains of social contracts is insufficient to ensure compliance, so regimes revert to outright repression in grim efforts to hang on to power. The agents of that repression, both militaries and security services, compound the economic problems by themselves appropriating ever larger shares of national budgets and economic activity. Securitization of regimes, driven in the first instance primarily by their inability to foster more rapid economic growth, is economically costly but politically self-sustaining as it engenders the very political opposition it seeks to repress.

Storm in the wake of globalization

The storm gathering over the MENA political economy includes several additional elements. First, Islamism has been a major beneficiary of the dialectical response to globalization, as populations turn to nativist, even chauvinist responses to threats perceived to stem from both economic and cultural globalization. Islamism's comparative popularity divides and weakens political oppositions, while undermining rational policy responses to the threats and challenges posed by globalization. That Egypt's Muslim Brotherhood chose to ally with the military in opposition to liberal reformers in 2011–12 is indicative of this predisposition. Additionally, the excesses of radical Islamism have exacerbated anti-Muslim sentiments and behaviors in the West, which have in turn further stoked anti-Western, anti-liberal and anti-globalization attitudes in the Muslim world. In the face of such polarized antagonisms, it is difficult to the point of impossible for reformers to make a persuasive case for liberalizing political economies and linking them more closely with the West. It is not surprising, therefore, that numerous MENA countries are in the process of reinforcing and broadening their political and economic ties to the leading authoritarian states—China and Russia—a strategy supported both by authoritarian incumbent elites in the MENA as well as by substantial portions of their oppositions.

A second component of what increasingly seems a perfect storm bearing down on MENA political economies is what Giacomo Luciani has called the region-wide civil war, pitting Sunnis against Shi'i backed by Iran; Sunni governments against one another and against or for various types of Islamists; and violent Islamists against more moderate ones.[6] This civil war has already fragmented the GCC and relations between its key member states, thereby undermining the collective political, economic and military capacities of the most dynamic sub-region of the MENA. It has resulted in civil wars and partial or total disintegration in Libya, Syria and Yemen, while preventing the effective political and economic rebuilding of Lebanon and Iraq. It has provided justification for intensifying authoritarian rule in Algeria, Bahrain, Egypt, Kuwait, Morocco, Saudi Arabia, Sudan and the United Arab Emirates. Its economic cost is in the trillions of dollars, while its political cost is to render effective collective, institutionally based behavior, whether across the region or in any of its nation states, impossible or irrelevant. The MENA civil war makes the region too risky a partner for most types of sustained economic relationships, other than extraction of hydrocarbons and selling of arms, so FDI in most sectors has been in more or less continuous decline since the 2008 economic crisis. About half of FDI in the region originates from GCC states and is focused on real estate and tourism, while FDI originating outside the MENA concentrates on hydrocarbon extraction and processing.[7] The region's share of manufactured exports in world trade, which is around 2%, is less than it was in the 1960s.[8]

A third element of the gathering storm consists of global changes and innovations. The key changes have been alluded to above in discussion of the growing constraints on globalization. Whether they are increased tariff protections, competitive currency devaluations, or unravelling of trade blocs, they are driven by a mix of national economic interests and renewed searches for political identity, both of which are by-products of a rapid globalization that was not structured to prevent growing inequality. Threats to globalization are thus arising in various political quarters and seem bound to retard its pace for the foreseeable future, thereby slowing global economic growth just when the MENA needs as much revenue as possible to support much discussed, if scarcely realized, diversification.

A related constraint on globalization is the increased competition between the major players, including the US, EU, Japan, China and Russia. The resurgence of authoritarianism as embodied in Russian and Chinese domestic and foreign policies signals the end not only of the era of US-led, liberal globalization, but of serious challenges to the continuation of even a more gradual form of it. In addition, the securitization of global power relations that increasingly pit the US against both Russia and China renders economic cooperation of any sort more difficult and unlikely, while restricting the freedom of action of third parties, whether the EU, South Korea, Japan or others.

Technological innovations particularly relevant to MENA economies are those related to hydrocarbon extraction and the utilization of unskilled or partially skilled labor in production processes. Extraction of oil and gas by fracking, particularly in the US, has driven dramatic production increases. In 2017, for example, US oil production of some 9.3 million barrels per day was almost double the figure of a decade earlier. The 5% increase projected for 2018 would break the US annual production record of 9.7 million barrels per day set in 1970.[9] Saudi Arabia and the US now share the role of swing producer driving global oil prices, substantially reducing the former's leverage, as well as global oil prices. Australia has become the world's second largest exporter of LNG after Qatar, reflecting the

MENA's smaller, declining share of gas as compared to oil exports. The golden era of hydrocarbon wealth in the MENA is over, thanks in large measure to relevant technological innovations, including LNG transport vessels.

Artificial intelligence, robotization, 3D printing and other increasingly sophisticated technologies integrated into production processes are rendering obsolete the time-tested strategy of initially relying upon the comparative advantage of cheap labor to propel the ascent up production ladders. Bangladesh, the beneficiary of major Chinese investment and technological assistance, has become a world leader in the export of ready-made garments principally because it has integrated new technologies into their production, unlike competitors in the MENA. MENA manpower, relatively expensive in comparison to that in other developing regions, is poorly educated and trained, while MENA investments in research and development are well below levels predicted by GDP per capita. The Arab world produces 5.9% of global GDP, but its governments account for less than 1% of global spending on R and D. The GCC states' average spending is some 0.2%, compared to India's 0.8%. Private firms in the Arab world contribute less than 5% of national R and D spending, compared to Israel where they are responsible for three-quarters of it or the US where the private sector spends two and a half times what the government does.[10] The region's relatively youthful but poorly educated population thus constitutes more of an economic obstacle than a benefit, since it cannot easily be gainfully employed or integrated into technologically advanced production processes.

In conclusion, globalization is widely accused in the MENA of being a false flag for neo-colonialism. Paradoxically, however, it is the slowing of globalization that poses the greater threat to the MENA's political economies because it puts downward pressure on oil and gas prices, renders more difficult the challenge of diversifying economies away from hydrocarbons, and causes increasingly nervous regimes to double down on authoritarianism. Several factors associated with slowing globalization put additional pressures on the MENA, including political polarization between Islamists, secularists and incumbent regimes; a region-wide civil war that has direct economic costs in the trillions of dollars while undermining nation-state coherence and militating against regional integration that could benefit the overall MENA economy and those of its member states; and polarizing relations between global powers that thwart economic cooperation. Simultaneous with slowing globalization, although not necessarily connected to it, have been technological advances in hydrocarbon extraction and production processes that render the region's hopes for capital accumulation and economic diversification yet more difficult to realize.

The MENA, in sum, missed a golden opportunity to benefit from the post-Cold War globalization wave by failing adequately to liberalize its economies and polities while moving up production ladders. No successive wave is currently in sight, probably much to the relief of many in the region, despite the fact that surfing a globalization wave is the most viable solution to the region's current economic and political problems. But riding such a wave requires capacities that most MENA states lack for the historical reasons reviewed in this and the preceding chapter and for resultant structural reasons to be assessed in the next one.

4

LIMITED ACCESS ORDERS AND THE RISE OF DEEP STATES

A state's infrastructural power—its capacity to interact effectively with civil society in the formation and implementation of policies—is typically assessed in relation to provision of order, formation of a coherent national outlook or ideology, and management of the economy.[1] Evidence of the shortcomings of MENA states in maintaining order and propagating shared beliefs (ideology) is plentiful. By various measures, including battlefield deaths, incidents of terrorism, displaced persons, political prisoners, infliction of capital punishment and so on, it is the most disorderly and dangerous of the world's regions. Moreover, even in MENA states and sub-national regions where disorder and violence are relatively uncommon, the sense of personal and economic security is eroded by inadequate rule of law. Institutionalized, effective protection of personal and property rights by legal codes, police and courts is deficient, forcing reliance on personalized means of protection.

As for ideology, it is remarkably fragmented throughout the MENA, divided between state nationalisms, various manifestations of Arabism and Islamism, and loyalties to a host of sub or supranational ethnic, religious, tribal, local and other identities. The authoritarian Arab republics tried but failed in the post-colonial era to homogenize the political belief systems of their populations. Their harsh methods drove antagonistic ideologies underground, from whence they emerged once the heady, unifying days of anti-colonialism had passed.

The capacity of MENA states to manage their economies is similarly deficient, as indicated in general terms by measures reflecting relative lack of diversification, near absence of locally produced sophisticated products, little participation in global production chains, high unemployment—especially among youth—and the "missing middle," referring to the comparative dearth of middle-sized firms amidst a veritable sea of micro, informal enterprises and a small number of large, modern ones typically enjoying favored connections to political elites. A vital question therefore is why MENA state abilities to provide order, ideological consensus and economic growth remain poorly developed.

Limited Access Orders: Definition

The answer to this query is that the region's political economies tend to be dominated by what institutional economists, led by Douglass North, have called limited access orders.[2] These are systems in which order is based on political elites appropriating for themselves "privileged control over parts of the economy, each getting some share of the rents." Rents are returns produced by market restrictions resulting from political interventions, such as "government contracts, land rights, monopolies on business activities, and entry to restricted job markets ... Stability of the rents and thus of the social order requires limiting access and competition." By contrast, open access orders produce order not by limiting competition and extracting rents shared by elites, but by providing open access and stimulating both economic and political competition by guaranteeing that "all citizens have the right to form contractual organizations." According to North, such organizations include political, social and economic ones, such as parties and unions, religious congregations, universities, business firms and other institutionalized collectivities united by a common purpose. Preventing access to and activities by such organizations generates rents for those who are allowed access, while ensuring that incumbent elites are not challenged by organizations capable of mobilizing and structuring oppositional political participation. It is sometimes the case that rents, carefully managed, facilitate economic growth, as they may have done in the case of East Asian developmental states such as Taiwan and South Korea, where they were structured to induce firms in specific sectors to export. More typically, however, and in the MENA certainly, rents are exploitative and "lead to a deadweight loss to the economy."[3]

Transition from closed to open access orders depends upon various preconditions being met, including removal of restrictions on the formation and activities of organizations, imposition of institutionalized civilian control over coercive agencies, and subordination of political and economic interactions to the rule of law. No MENA country, with the partial exception of Israel, has met these "doorstep conditions" for transitions from closed to open access orders. This transition is inherently difficult because limited access orders entail a "double balance in which limited access to politics and limited access to the economy are mutually reinforcing."[4]

The impacts of limited access orders on political economies have received increasing scholarly attention. A study of their negative impacts on FDI, for example, indicates that the influx of foreign capital increases rents to elites because they resist competition so that any "challenger outside of elite businesses will not have the backing of functioning market institutions such as secure property rights or effective regulation."[5] Since 2011 the World Bank's World Development Report and other of its publications have drawn on the concept of limited access orders to guide empirical investigations. The MENA has been a focus of much of that work, which rests on the distinction between "insiders" and "outsiders," referring to those within or connected to ruling elites in limited access orders, as opposed to those lacking such access or connections. Empirical evidence reveals that MENA insiders have benefitted from a host of rents, including preferential access to credit and subsidized inputs, protection of monopolies and oligopolies by selective tariff and non-tariff barriers to trade, awards to insiders of lucrative gatekeeping over entry into labor markets, governmental allocations to businesses in proportion to their levels of electoral support, reduction or removal of bribes required to be paid to obtain government services, preferential granting of security clearances to insiders, and so on.[6] The primary consequence of such discriminatory treatment of economic actors is to increase returns to connected firms at the expense of all others. This in turn negatively impacts economic growth. Connected firms owe their profitability to rents, not performance, so have little incentive to improve productivity. Outsiders, by contrast, know the cards are stacked against them so are disincentivized to invest, innovate and expand their businesses. These conditions are, moreover, frequently not the result just of macro market distortions induced by limited access orders, but of active efforts by firms to recruit political insiders to distort markets to their advantage. A recent study of the Italian political economy, which bears considerable resemblance to MENA limited access orders, found dense networks between politicians and firms, especially larger ones. Industries with a higher share of politically connected firms were much less likely to innovate, but those firms had higher survival rates and employment and revenue growth, although not productivity increases.[7]

Limited Access Orders Preference
Clientelism Over Citizenship

Limited access orders not only militate against economic growth; by encouraging clientelism and discouraging citizenship they also reinforce authoritarian government and material inequality. A World Bank sponsored research project on service delivery in the MENA notes that "ruling elites in the MENA have historically exchanged access to services (e.g., free education, healthcare) and employment in return for popular support." It traced this tradition back to the Ottoman era, after which it was reinforced by colonial powers before becoming incorporated into post-colonial states which "stabilized their rule by doling out access to public goods and services in return for political support, rather than doing so on a meritocratic basis."[8]

Among the many negative consequences of using patronage to engender political support has been the marginalization of the role of representative bodies, the potentially most important of which are national legislatures. This happens "because people recognize that clear bureaucratic procedures do not drive access to state resources and public services." The primary task of elected officials, whose powers are closely circumscribed by executive branches, is to provide personal services. In Jordan, for example, only 15% of respondents to a survey believed that parliamentarians should even try to legislate. Instead it is preferred that they limit their focus to service provision because an MP who "criticizes the system quickly finds that he or she is unable to open doors to jobs or access state coffers."[9]

Similarly, accessing the labor market or obtaining bureaucratic services, such as the issuing of licenses or permits, is believed by large majorities in Egypt, Jordan and Tunisia to require personal intermediation—*wasta*—or bribes, or both. Befitting a limited access order such as Egypt's, only 11% of Egyptian respondents believed they had the *wasta* or financial resources necessary to obtain services, with youth being "the most likely to believe that personal connections are more important in obtaining a government job than merit."[10] A finding of research on the relationship between government and political clientelism is that the quality of public administration is inversely related to the amount of clientelism, i.e., the better the bureaucracy, the less the clientelism.[11] Considerable research also demonstrates a negative relationship between clientelism in the civil service and business dynamism. A survey of Jordanian businessmen, for example, revealed that the need to cultivate clientelistic relations with bureaucrats was emphasized by nearly all respondents, as was the deleterious consequences for their business of that need.[12]

Political clientelism under the limited access orders that prevail in non-oil-rich MENA states has traced a bell-shaped curve elongated on the right side. It expanded rapidly as these post-colonial states consolidated their control, typically through the institutional vehicles of the military, security services, single party and the bureaucracy. In this expansionary phase clientelism extended down into urban and rural peripheries and served to mobilize populations previously excluded both economically and politically. It then began a long period of contraction in which it first ebbed away from the socio-economic peripheries and then from the peripheries of the state itself, including the once vital civil service, leaving little more of the state than its "deep" components enmeshed in tight patronage networks. Not surprising then were the 2011 and subsequent Arab upheavals, products primarily of the decay resulting from ever shrinking resources to sustain clientelism. In those oil-rich MENA states where resources have remained sufficient to service the sprawling clientage networks which grew in tandem with the expansion of oil production, there have been no upheavals other than in Libya. The "Arab Spring 2.0" that erupted in Sudan and Algeria in the spring of 2019 can be linked directly to dramatic falls in government revenues resulting from declining oil earnings. In the former they fell from 16% of GDP in 2007 to less than 1% in 2017, forcing the government to more than halve its expenditures over that period. Oil revenues were halved in Algeria between 2007 and 2017, and while the government sought to sustain spending by drawing down reserves, it was nevertheless forced to reduce subsidies and recruitment into the civil service.[13]

On the periphery of some MENA political economies and in those in which order has collapsed, the patronage machines that thrive are those which are autonomous from or only slightly dependent upon government, and for which the necessary material resources are predominantly private, such as those generated from warfare, smuggling or access to land. This form of clientelism, common throughout the MENA prior to the consolidation of control by colonial and post-colonial states, has recently re-emerged. Anne Marie Baylouny, for example, argues that state retrenchment in the Levant has resulted in a resurgence of political clientelism within pre-existing social formations, most notably those based in extended kinship.[14] Diane Singerman has chronicled the activities of clientelistic networks that emerged in the informal communities of Cairo in the wake of the erosion of the social contract which formerly underpinned the governmental provision of goods and services.[15] In these and other accounts of clientelism on the ever-expanding peripheries of shrinking statist political economies in the MENA, notable in its absence is evidence of political entrepreneurship, other than that by Islamist organizations. As the state recedes there is little evidence that independent patrons, either as individual politicians or political parties, have sought to move into the breach, mobilizing citizens through clientelism. This attests to the absence of democratic space as well as to insufficient autonomous resources in limited access orders with which to construct potential oppositional clientelistic networks. Such orders discourage both economic and political productivity.

The region's limited access orders are inherently clientelism-friendly. They are comparatively authoritarian, with large and inefficient governments. On what is possibly the most standard measure of authoritarianism, which is the World Bank's "Voice and Accountability" indicator, the MENA's annual scores since 1996, the first year the Bank published its governance indicators, have placed it at or next to the bottom of the world's regions, contesting only with Sub-Saharan Africa and Central Asia for the annual booby prize. Government revenues as a percentage of GDP and public employment as a percentage of total employment, the standard indicators of size of government, place MENA governments at the top of the pile. These three characteristics of government—authoritarian, large and inefficient—are noted in comparative research as being the most congenial to political clientelism.

They are not, however, the only causes of clientelism in limited access orders, including in the MENA. Government centralization and restricted access to information are two other factors conducive to the prevalence of political clientelism concentrated in the executive. Few governments in the world are more centralized than Arab ones, which have for years resisted internal and external efforts to decentralize.[16] The region is "info-shy," especially as regards government finances, for which accurate data is notoriously difficult to obtain.[17] It is common practice for ministries and state-owned enterprises to be used as conduits for patronage, most particularly during elections, a practice made possible by centralization and lack of public access to accurate government accounts.

With few exceptions, contemporary research on the relationship between clientelism and citizenship emphasizes the former's negative consequences for the latter. Clientelism reverses the accountability relationship fundamental to democracy in that voters have to surrender their rights, including that of holding government accountable, in order to participate. Clientelism also undermines citizenship because it impedes the development of social trust and other attitudes and values associated with the exercise of citizen rights. To be effective, citizenship must operate through civil society organizations, including political parties, which are themselves not clientelistic, a precondition not met in limited access orders.[18] Gabriela Ippolito-O'Donnell carries the argument for the fundamental incompatibility of clientelism and citizenship yet further. She notes that clientelism absolutely precludes two fundamental rights of citizenship—equality of voting and autonomy of association—so it "undermines the realization of the underlying pillar of democracy, human agency."[19]

The observation that clientelism is antithetical to citizenship is reinforced by the finding that transition to the latter from systems based on the former is inherently a lengthy process. In Jonathan Fox's words, "it takes time and effort to transform clients into citizens."[20] Based on African experience, van de Walle notes that "civic organizations, the press, and the expectations of the citizenry will not immediately adjust to the new dispensation (*i.e., democratic citizenship rights*), but need to be nurtured and encouraged."[21] Democracy is not conceivable without political parties, but building democratic ones requires skill and time, to say nothing of conducive material conditions including economic growth and reduction of poverty. Robert Gay argues that citizenship requires "distribution of state resources not by favor but by rights."[22]

Clientelism, in other words, impedes the development of citizenship, which even under favorable conditions is likely to be a lengthy, complex process, with various intermediate steps along the way. For the MENA, where clientelism is deeply embedded as a by-product of the region's limited access orders, and where other conditions for the transition to citizenship are unfavorable, the implications are ominous. Yet, other regions have confronted the challenge of transforming clients into citizens, so the task is not impossibly difficult. But it does require both broad, systemic change of the political economy as well as more specific developments in governance and politics. The almost unique preponderance of government in the economies of the MENA would have to be reduced by the growth of private capital, which in turn could provide resources upon which independent "voice and accountability" could be built. So long as access to material resources lies overwhelmingly in the hands of those within limited access orders, clientelism will continue to obstruct the emergence of citizenship and the accountability dependent upon it. As for the practice of governance and politics, development of the full panoply of rights, institutions and behavior associated with democracy is ultimately necessary for citizenship to triumph over clientelism. Key in this regard is the emergence of the rule of law and associated institutions and practices capable of combatting corruption. This development in turn requires a rebalancing of the executive–legislative relationship in favor of the latter. Associated with that rebalancing is the creation of electoral systems that are free and fair, and which militate against clientelism and in favor of programmatic political parties. Such structural changes constitute the necessary if not sufficient conditions for the transition from clientelism to full citizenship.

In sum, limited access orders militate against both economic and political development. They deter the formation of independent economic and political organizations. They tilt economic playing fields in favor of insiders and undermine political citizenship by encouraging clientelism. Servicing clientelistic networks in turn necessitates extensive government control of the economy to generate the necessary primary (material) or secondary (network) patronage resources. Fearful of autonomous economic and political behavior, elites in limited access orders centralize power within both the executive and the nation, rendering other branches and agencies of government subordinate while ensuring that all key decisions are made, and all resources held, in the capital. Elites in limited access orders are necessarily distrustful of all opposition, real or imagined. They preside over harsh but brittle states, to use Nazih Ayubi's terms, ones in which there can be no true accountability, so no definitive information on politics or economics, both of which are surrounded with ambiguity and secrecy.[23] These secretive, brittle states must rely upon muscular gatekeepers to prevent outsiders from seeking to join or displace privileged insiders of limited access orders. Those gatekeepers take the form of what has come to be called "deep states," a term originally coined in the MENA, at the core of which are coercive agencies, in turn supported by courts and other bodies involved in the application and adjudication of law. It is to these deep states that we now turn our attention.

Coined in the MENA

The term "deep state" originated in Turkey, where the *derin devlet* (deep state) was a "network of individuals in different branches of government, with links to retired generals and organized crime, that existed without the knowledge of high-ranking military officers and politicians."[24] In Turkey, therefore, the surreptitious deep state was not thought of as being a direct instrument of rule at the disposal of the incumbent regime, but as a freelance network that arrogated to itself the right and power to set the parameters within which the government operated.[25] By contrast, the deep state in Egypt has been depicted as an extension of the regime, the inter-institutional, largely formalized network upon which it relies consciously and actively not only to perpetuate its incumbency, but to implement its rule.[26] Paradoxically although Turkey was the progenitor of the concept, in its subsequent generalization in the Middle East the deep state came to be viewed more as the Egyptian than the Turkish variant. It has not been thought of in most countries in the MENA as just a "hidden hand" keeping the ship of state on course, without the regime having its direct hand on the rudder. Instead the Egyptian model of the regime and deep state being flip sides of the same coin has been deemed to be that more characteristic of MENA polities.

Conceptualization of the deep state as the "real" state in the sense that it constitutes either or both the institutions and networks through which the regime rules is not restricted to the Arab states of the MENA. Indeed, in recent years even Turkey's deep state has been redefined by some observers as now constituting the means through which President Recep Tayyip Erdogan and his AK (Justice and Development) Party govern the country after having dispatched first the military-Kemalist deep state, then the Gulenist one, in some fifteen years of subterranean political war between these competing deep states. Observers of Iran also generally concur that the country is run by a deep state, but disagree over its composition, with some arguing it is comprised solely of the Islamic Revolutionary Guard Corps (IRGC) acting in concert with Supreme Leader Ayatollah Ali Khamenei, and others that it is the broader "intricate security, intelligence, and economic superstructure" cobbled together by him.[27]

Historical Origins of Deep States

The important role of history in shaping contemporary political institutions in the MENA was emphasized in previous chapters. Among those "institutions" are deep states, which are just as beholden to national legacies as are the more visible superstructural state institutions, such as parliaments and legal/judicial systems, copied as they were from those of the colonial powers. Which historical era should be emphasized as having initiated path dependency that led ultimately to the proliferation of contemporary MENA deep states is, however, a matter of contention. The three eras in question are the pre-colonial, colonial and post-colonial ones, assuming we are now in the post-post-colonial era.

In his *From Deep State to Islamic State*, Jean-Pierre Filiu refers to those in control of deep states as "modern Mamluks."[28] He suggests the Mamluks—the medieval "slave" rulers of Egypt and the Levant, who were only finally dispatched to the dustbins of history in the wake of Napoleon's invasion of Egypt in 1798—were the first to establish the system of government that has served as a prototype for contemporary deep states. Foreign to the countries they ruled, Mamluks constituted a military elite, "a counter-society ... alienated from local Arab societies." They widened, according to Filiu, "the classical Islamic divide between the ruling elite or *khassa* (the "special" ones) and the masses of the `amma (the "ordinary" ones)," while militarizing government, subjecting the vizier, the nominal civilian ruler, to their control.[29] Filiu analogizes rulers of most post-colonial Arab republics to these Mamluks, who, "like their medieval predecessors, lacked the legitimacy of century-long dynasties ... [coming] from lower social strata, where the army was the only route to social promotion." These modern Mamluks, among whom he names Presidents Nasser, Boumediene and Asad, "loathed the traditional elite ... and constituted a *khassa* world apart from the rest of the `amma population."[30]

By contrast, Charles Tripp traces contemporary deep states back to the colonial period. According to him, the British, opposed to the creation of a modern, democratic nation state in Iraq, created instead "a dual state—one official and the other a shadow state—consist[ing] of official Iraqi institutions and hidden networks of power and patronage based on allegiance and respect." These institutions and networks were, according to Tripp, "run by British officers, who had little stake or faith in democracy."[31] The culture of "patronage and provincial alliances" they established was inherited by the Sunni Arabs of northwestern Iraq, who left the Kurds and the Shi'i "outside the benefits of the formation of a new state," so much so that "Iraqis were well aware that power did not lie with the official state," but with a deep state which became the "vehicle for the accumulation of wealth, power, and prestige."[32] Tripp concludes by noting that the lineage of the shadow state extends until the present. "Despite being 20th century history, all of this has a very contemporary ring," as

70

reflected in the shadow state established by Nouri Kamal al Maliki and his Dawa Party associates and Iranian backers in the wake of the overthrow of Saddam, copying as they did what the British had done in 1920 and the Americans in 2003.[33]

Joseph Sassoon draws primarily upon memoirs in his attempt to explain dynamics of contemporary authoritarian rule in eight Arab republics, which he describes as being constituted of networks linking political parties, intelligence services, the military, presidencies and economic actors, both public and private. He paints a personalized picture of human and institutional interactions in these deep states, although he does not use the term.[34] In explaining their origins he references the long, in his view unbroken history of authoritarian government dating back to the Ottoman Empire before taking on contemporary forms, such as under President Abd al Fattah al Sisi in Egypt or Bashar al Asad in Syria.

Whatever allegedly formative historical period they have empha-sized, analysts have concurred that the MENA's path dependency is one of authoritarianism, political power having long been concen-trated in the hands of those with coercive power and those recruited by them to assist in their rule—what is in effect a deep state, whether termed such or not. The specific causal factors embedded in these accounts of the rise of authoritarianism and the deep states at the heart of that rule differ, but one theme predominates. It is that the resources necessary to build and sustain these states were primarily exogenous rather than generated and extracted from within national political economies. These resources were acquired by plunder and conquest, in the case of the Mamluks; from imperial powers, in the case of the colonial states; and from rents derived from fossil fuel exports, geo-political leverage, public foreign assistance, or workers' remittances, in the case of post-colonial and now post-post-colonial states. Regardless of the source, the ready availability of exogenous resources militated against MENA states developing infrastructural capacities to foster both the development of national economies and the extraction of resources from them for public purposes.[35]

The purposes MENA deep states were designed to serve were thus not those of performing the three critical governing tasks of providing security to the population, developing the national economy, and building inclusive societies, economies and polities on the foundations of universal, equal citizenship rights. Instead, MENA deep states were intended to impose control over potentially fractious, disobedient populations; to gatekeep the limited access order established by ruling elites to ensure their disproportionate shares of power and material resources; and to prevent or mitigate conflict arising within that elite. The logic of deep states was inimical to good governance. National populations could not be made secure, say through effective and impartial policing, lest that security embolden them to place collective political and economic demands on those within limited access orders. So deep states were intended to heighten insecurity, to intimidate and to divide populations. The development of robust national economies also posed potential threats to deep states, as the endogenous resources such development would generate might accrue to and strengthen potential oppositional forces. Finally, deep states could not grant universal citizenship rights without threatening the very bases of the limited access order of which they were the gatekeepers.

Deep states, in sum, were incentivized to provide bad governance and to do so as secretly as possible. Rendering their self-serving objectives and powers manifest would have been counter-productive. So deep states were hidden behind superstructural state institutions and their official, if largely meaningless rhetoric and stated purposes. Among the consequences were the reduction of visible, public politics to the status of what Mohammed Hachemaoui has labelled with reference to Algeria as "pseudopolitics," by which he means "such politics that works in order to render real politics invisible."[36] According to him the Algerian deep state sponsors elections, legislative assemblies, constitutional conventions and other nominal democratic practices "because they do not affect policymaking or the composition of the ruling elite." They are tools of control and camouflage for real decision-making organizations. They are intended "not to govern or to represent but to implement state policy."[37]

The pseudopolitics of Algeria are indicative of how deep states rob politics of their meaning, rendering them even farcical. Algerian governments have lasted on average just over one year. Abd al Aziz Bouteflika, born in 1937—having served four terms as President, confined by one or more strokes to a wheelchair, having been rarely seen in public for years and under treatment in a hospital in Switzerland—was in March 2019 nominated for a fifth term by his deep-state backers, including his brother, Said.[38] This was too much even for the Algerian public that had been quiescent since the end of the civil war two decades previously. It rose up in its hundreds of thousands in protest against this affront, forcing Bouteflika initially to suspend his candidacy, then when demonstrations intensified and the head of the military withdrew his support, to step down as President. Whether this presaged more direct military control, as it had in Egypt when Mubarak was overthrown, or a transition to an at least semi-civilian government, as it had when Ben Ali was forced to flee Tunisia, remains to be seen. But whatever its final outcome, the dramatic turn of events exemplified the consequence of deep states for civilian politics, which is to render them either farcical or, if meaningful, mass protests lacking effective organizational infrastructure.

5

DEEP STATES: TYPES, RESOURCES AND IMPACTS

Deep states differ along three dimensions. The first, as mentioned with reference to Turkey and Egypt, is their relationship with other actors in the national political economy. Deep states range from being virtually indistinguishable from the formal, ruling elite, as in the cases of Egypt and Saddam's Iraq, to being independent of that elite but supportive of it, as in the case of Turkey prior to the AK Party's rise to power from the 2002 election, to being in opposition to the formal government or at least some components of it, as for example is the case in contemporary Lebanon, where Hizbullah constitutes a deep state, one steadily encroaching upon the government itself.

The second dimension along which deep states can be compared is their composition, the most important sub-dimensions of which are the degree to which they are based on formal institutions as opposed to informal networks, and the degree to which those informal networks are embedded in larger social formations, such as tribes, religious, ethnic, regional or other groupings. Egypt's deep state, for example is at the formal end of the spectrum, comprised as it is primarily of the military, intelligence services and the presidency, between which and from which extend both formal relationships and informal networks. These networks are utilitarian rather than affective in nature, formed as they are out of self-interest, sometimes reinforced by kinship or friendships, but not emerging from deeper social formations.

In Saddam's Iraq and the Asads' Syria, by contrast, the institutional bases of deep states—primarily the Office of the President, the intelligence services, selected units of the military, and leaders of the Ba'th Party—were recruited primarily from Sunni Arabs or Alawis, respectively. The networks within those social forces were of greater

74

importance than formal institutional hierarchies, comprising what might be thought of as a second subterranean layer under the formal state, or in other words, deep, deep states. In Saddam's Iraq, for example, the "shadow state" to use Tripp's term, was reflected in the appointment of "non-Arab Sunnis in many symbolically prominent positions," whereas the inner circle was restricted to "Sunni Arab members of the Ba'th descending mainly from the North-West of Baghdad, where his tribe was dominant." As for the public administration, it was "a hollow shell," reflecting the fact that the shadow state was "a network of power functioning under the shadow (as its name indicates) of the actual state."[1] Yemen's deep state under Ali Abdullah Salih and Libya's under Mu`amar Qadhafi were also of this type, with the former's Sanhan and the latter's Qadhadhfa tribe comprising the deep, deep state under the formal institutions of the deep state itself, such as the presidency, security services and selected military units.

The type and magnitude of resources upon which the power of deep states rest is the third dimension of their variation. These resources consist of material, informational, ideational and relational ones. Material resources are the most important and the best indicator of the breadth and depth of the deep state. They are comprised of those provided directly by the state and those garnered and controlled independently by the deep state itself. In the former category are both human and physical resources, such as military and security personnel and equipment, as well as public economic enterprises, including their personnel, capital equipment and outputs, over which deep states have formal, official control, such as in military-owned and operated enterprises found in many MENA states.

Deep State Resources

Resources generated and controlled by deep states independently of the government consist of those created or captured through both legal and illegal activities. In the former category are resources parasitic on the state, such as the employment of retired military and security officers in the civil administration or state-owned enterprises, as well as those spawned through the deep state's sponsored undertakings made possible by the networks both within it and extending from it, such as companies formed of ex-officers which derive rents from state contracting or restrictions on competition.

Resources generated by the illegal activities of deep states range from the relatively benign if substantial, such as bribes and kickbacks in contracting, to the truly malignant, such as drug, arms and oil smuggling, human trafficking and shakedown rackets. Along the resource sub-dimensions one can thus plot relatively wealthy, integrated, centralized and legalized deep states, such as Egypt's, to those more closely resembling mafia organizations, such as that of Qadhafi's Libya.

Informational resources are those from which infrastructural power is derived. Deep states vary in the amount and type of information they can draw upon in pursuing their interests. Broad, institutionalized deep states, again such as that of Egypt's, possess a wide array of information both through the state itself and from their own sources. This information ranges from that pertaining to the economy, to political activities, to foreign intelligence. Less institutionalized deep states more anchored in a single, dominating social force, such as those in Iraq and Syria, have fewer capacities to gather general governmental information and more restricted needs for it. Their overriding interest, since they are essentially at war or potential war with the societies they rule, is political control. They concentrate therefore on information relevant to that task, as Saddam's security services' records of individuals, their families and tribal connections attest.[2] Since their material resources are generated more through outright theft and other criminal activities, their need for accurate, up to date information on the national economy is limited.

Ideational resources are those both internal to the deep state and those projected by it. Internal ideational resources are comprised of the messages and means of delivering them through which the deep state maintains its own ideological coherence. The Turkish deep state, for example, depended heavily on the Kemalist message propagated in military academies, a message that underscored not just the ideology of the state's founding father, Mustafa Kemal (Ataturk), but the responsibility and indeed right of the deep state to defend it, including from Turks themselves who might not subscribe to Kemalist secularism.

Iran's IRGC, which comprises either a part or virtually the entirety of that country's deep state, is yet more ideologically coherent. It assumes responsibilities and rights to defend the "Islamic Revolution," of which the Iranian state and even nation are defined as the products. The standard message of deep states to their members, conveyed through a variety of educational, training and other methods of indoctrination, is that sovereignty is vested in them, not the population as a whole, which is too naive, untrustworthy, and maybe even disloyal to have the nation's fate in its hands. Brigadier

76

General Yadollah Javani, for example, one of the leading theoreticians in the IRGC, argues that the Iranian identity is composed of "Islam, revolution and historical depth," all of which render it subject to permanent, unceasing attack by "America and the Zionist regime," from which it can only be successfully defended by the IRGC.[3]

Relational resources consist of formal and informal linkages that connect the deep state internally to formal state institutions, and outward to civil and political societies, including the economy. Some deep states, like that of Egypt, possess truly sprawling networks that connect their constituent institutions and their whole to the executive, legislative and judicial branches of government, to civil society organizations and political parties, as well as to public and private sectors of the economy. Ben Ali's deep state in Tunisia was not as interlinked, in part because it depended more on his family ties and in part because—based on the intelligence services rather than the military—it was smaller and lacked its own institutionally generated material resources. Consequently, Tunisian political and civil society institutions, enjoying more freedom from the deep state than Egypt's, were able to play more effective roles than were their Egyptian counterparts once their respective regimes collapsed.

Because deep states are purposely opaque, it is only when regimes collapse above them that their nature and strength is truly revealed. Tunisia's was not strong enough nor sufficiently independent of Ben Ali to reconstitute itself, although its coercive residues still lurk under the present, democratically elected government.[4] The legal framework created by Ben Ali to develop and protect the financial interests of his cronies within the deep state also remains unchanged.[5] Egypt's deep state, by contrast, more independent of Mubarak and more firmly based in the military, quickly reasserted its power after the 2011 uprising.

The manner in which deep states are reconstituted reflects the distribution of power within them. In the Soviet Union, for example—a classic police rather than military state—the intelligence services provided the institutional base and linkages with which Vladimir Putin built his successor Russian regime. Through first the KGB, then its successor organization, the FSB, Putin spread his personal network into the military, political organizations and, most importantly, into the freshly privatized economy, the reins of power of which he plucked from the hands of Yeltsin-era oligarchs and placed in the hands of his own cronies.

The struggle by remnants of Ali Abdullah Salih's Yemeni deep state to reconstitute their power after losing it in 2012 reflects its more informal, personalized nature and its tribal base. The coercive power of that deep state was vested primarily in military units commanded by Salih's son and other relatives, which deserted the elected successor government headed by President Abd Rabbuh Mansur Hadi. Lacking the capacity to unseat that government by itself, these military units under Salih family leadership forged a tactical alliance with the Iranian backed Houthi insurgency against which the Salih regime had paradoxically previously conducted a decade-long counterinsurgency campaign. The outcome of the present struggle, which has sucked in Saudi Arabia, the United Arab Emirates, Sudan, and even naval units from Egypt, to say nothing of US participation in aerial bombardment, is yet to be determined. It is clear from events thus far, however, that the once Salih-controlled deep state provided a firm foundation upon which the power of that family and its allies could be reasserted, albeit in alliance with the Houthis and, at a distance, Iran. Similarly, in Libya, residues of Qadhafi's deep state, in the form of military units gathered under the leadership of former Qadhafi general turned CIA agent, Khalifa Haftar, are operating with the external support of Egypt, Saudi Arabia, the UAE, France and Russia to bring down the Tripoli-based competitive successor government to Qadhafi.

Given variations in the composition, internal and external relationships, and resources of deep states, it is hardly surprising that they take different forms. But such variation is also true of, say, parliamentary democracies, which are commonly deemed to constitute a distinctive type of political system. Deep states, however, are more complex and difficult to understand, not only because of their novelty in social science analysis, but precisely because they are purposely hidden from view by those within or allied to them.

"Bottom up" Deep States

Deep states vary along three dimensions—their relationship with the ruling elite; their composition; and their resources. The first two dimensions array types of deep states, while the third measures their strength. In MENA republics, the classic, top down model of relations between rulers and deep states was that the former created and then based their rule on a deep state. Or, in the case of Turkey, elements in the military surreptitiously nurtured at arms' length a deep state to limit the sovereign powers of the democratically elected superstructural state, at least when the military itself was not directly ruling. Subordination of deep states to the rulers of these republics was not, however, constitutionally mandated nor politically preordained, but was fluid and subject to contestation. Egypt's deep state, for example, removed President Husni Mubarak in 2011 when it became evident that continued support for him would threaten the deep state itself.

Because several of these "top down" deep states have passed into history, the question of what has succeeded them arises. The answer is a new type of deep state, one formed from the bottom up, typically "with a little help from their friends." Lebanon's was the pioneering bottom up deep state, followed by Iraq and Turkey. Libya, Syria and Yemen are now witnessing efforts to cobble together what may ultimately become similar bottom up deep states. What is meant by bottom up is that these deep states result from mobilized social forces penetrating state superstructures, then steadily encroaching on the powers of existing regimes.

Lebanon

In the case of Lebanon, the social force in question is that of Arab Shi'i Muslims, organized since the early 1980s by Hizbullah under the tutelage and with the support of its Iranian backer.[6] Hizbullah has during that period come to penetrate and exert predominant influence over most state institutions, including the military. By 2017 it had accumulated sufficient power to impose the Maronite Christian, Michel Aoun, its choice for President, on the country, and consolidated control of parliament in the 2018 elections thanks in part to a favorable new electoral law it pushed through parliament. More crucial to Hizbullah's erecting a deep state with which to penetrate and control the nominal state was its accumulation of coercive power, initially by building its own militia with Iranian backing, which ultimately has come to outgun the weaker Lebanese army, and then by becoming the dominant force within the army itself. Accompanying this process was an ever-expanding propaganda effort to identify Hizbullah's interest with the national interest and to present itself as the primary defender of the sovereignty and welfare of Lebanon. The apotheosis of this public relations campaign was reached during Hizbullah's successful summer 2017 offensive against the jihadi organization, Tahrir al Sham, in Arsal, which borders Syria. Secretary General Hassan Nasrallah claimed in a televised speech on 26 July that Hizbullah's victory was for "all Lebanese and peoples in the region, Christians and Muslims, who have suffered from takfiri terrorism."[7] The speech was preceded by footage showing Hizbullah troops replacing Tahrir al Sham's flags with newly created ones divided between the Lebanese flag on the top and Hizbullah's on the bottom, as well as those troops holding placards with pictures and names of Lebanese soldiers killed in the brief operation, "further promoting unity and shared sympathy between the Shia organization and state forces."[8] Coming to depend ever more heavily on the stronger Hizbullah not only for combat capacities but for intelligence, the Lebanese Armed Forces (LAF) were by this stage "held hostage" by that organization.[9]

Resources for Hizbullah's deep-state-building project come from three sources. The initial provider was Iran, which continues to provide some $200 million annually for "political and social services," as well as military aid, a figure that substantially exceeds the military assistance provided to the LAF by various Western countries.[10] The next resource to be tapped as Hizbullah's strength increased was that from a range of illegal activities, key of which was drug smuggling. This expanded from its original focus on hashish produced in Lebanon's Biq'a Valley, one of the two heartlands of Hizbullah, into a wide array of illegal substances, including the Arabian peninsula's "most popular illegal drug," Captagon—by 2015 Hizbullah had become "the only faction systematically involved in producing the drug."[11] Finally, as Hizbullah's penetration of the Lebanese state increased, so did it increasingly drain resources away from it. Hizbullah did so through both legal and illegal, direct and indirect means, ranging from allocations for reconstruction conducted by companies controlled by it, to complicity by Hizbullah-penetrated security services in drug trafficking.

Iraq

The Lebanese prototype of the construction of a deep state from the bottom up is currently being replicated in Iraq, with similar, if less successful, efforts also underway in Syria, Yemen and Libya. In Iraq, Syria and Yemen, Hizbullah itself, under Iran's guidance, is playing a direct role in training and equipping militias overwhelmingly composed of local Shi'i.[12] As in Lebanon, these militias, usually with their attendant party organizations, appear to be implementing a three-phased program. The initial phase is building a political-military capacity with external support, in these three cases directly or indirectly provided by Iran. Following on from that, as in Lebanon, is the penetration of the state's administrative, political and judicial institutions. The next step, if possible, is assertion of direct control over the state, as has been achieved in Lebanon, where Hizbullah is steadily eliding the distinction between itself and the nation's interests and indeed sovereignty.

Iraq has travelled furthest down this path of the existing state being hollowed out and maybe ultimately effectively displaced by a deep state built upon a social force, again that being Arab Shi'i Muslims. Unlike in Lebanon, however, the organizational vehicle through which Iran has sought to hollow out and control the Iraqi state erected in the wake of the American invasion in 2003 has been composed of multiple overlapping and intertwined political and military organizations. This web has camouflaged Iran's involvement and enabled it better to manipulate potentially rebellious Iraqi allies and outright clients. The Badr Organization has since 2014 become "Iran's most important instrument in Iraq," so tracing its rise is equivalent to mapping the expansion of the emerging deep state more generally.[13]

As in Lebanon with Hizbullah, the initial phase in the development of the Badr Organization was focused on its coercive capacities. It was founded as the Badr Corps in 1983, probably not by coincidence the same year in which Hizbullah was created. Initially the armed wing of the Supreme Council for the Islamic Revolution in Iraq (SCIRI), composed overwhelmingly of Shi'i who fled Saddam's Iraq to Iran, the Badr Corps was under direct operational control of Iran's then newly created Quds (Jerusalem) Force within the IRGC and linked through it to Hizbullah. It was renamed the Badr Organization in 2003 when it entered Iraq in the wake of the US invasion, with which it temporarily cooperated. It operated under the cloak of SCIRI, which in 2007 was renamed the Islamic Supreme Council of Iraq and formed a key base of support for the government of Prime Minister Nouri al Maliki formed in 2006.

As the main coercive arm of Iran's subterranean intervention in Iraq—one increasingly involved in combat against American troops—the Badr Organization necessarily played a more covert political role, this division of labor between coercion and politics widening as violence and the need for armed forces intensified. In 2007, Badr's former official leader and probably still its de facto one, Abu Mahdi al Muhandis, founded the Kata'ib (Battalions) Hizbullah, also under the IRGC and used by it as the key force to combat American forces, then conducting a "surge" against Iraqi resistance to the occupation.

Under the triumvirate of Badr, the Supreme Council and Kata'ib Hizbullah, several smaller militias cum political organizations were created. This complicated network of personal and organizational ties took on an ever more coherent, deep state form, which reached new heights during the fight against ISIS from 2014 to 2017. In that initial year the Badr Organization and Kata'ib Hizbullah assumed command of the so-called Popular Mobilization Forces (al Hashd al Sha'bi), the creation of which marked the transition of this collection of Shi'a militias into *a* if not *the* principal coercive force of the Iraqi state. That transition was facilitated by the capture of state resources resulting from these interlinked Shi'a military and political organizations penetrating the superstructural state.

Hadi al Amiri, for example, Secretary General of the Badr Organization, was recruited by fellow-traveler and Dawa Party leader, Prime Minister Nouri al Maliki, into his initial cabinet formed in 2006. Al Amiri served as Minister of Transport until 2014, siphoning funds away from that ministry into his Badr Organization.[14] In June of that year he left the government to resume direct command of the Badr forces and, along with both Abu Mahdi al Muhandis and the Iranian head of the Quds Force, Qassim Sulimani, of the newly formed Popular Mobilization Forces. Three months later in one of his final acts as Prime Minister, al Maliki appointed al Amiri as governor of Diyala Province, thus giving him control of the army and security forces in that vital, religiously and ethnically mixed region to the northeast of Baghdad. The Badr Organization's power base in the central government was secured by the appointment as Interior Minister of Muhammad al Ghabban, a client of al Amiri whose appointment to that post the Americans had blocked. According to reliable accounts, al Amiri exercised real control through al Ghabban over that vital ministry and its security and intelligence forces. When al Ghabban was forced to resign after his ministry failed to deter a July 2016 ISIS-backed attack in Baghdad, he was replaced by another Badr subordinate to al Amiri, one Qassim al Araji. Drawing upon these governmental resources provided through the ministries of transport and interior, and from control over Diyala and other governorates, by 2017 the Badr Organization had built up its forces to some 50,000 men under arms, supported by heavy artillery, armored troop carriers and tanks.[15] The budget provided by the government of Iraq to the Popular Mobilization Forces, of which the Badr Organization is the strongest component, amounted to $1.5 billion in 2016, half a billion dollars more than in the previous year despite a dramatic downturn in governmental revenues. According to one analyst, "the Badr Organization is well on its way to establishing a state within a state that is dependent on Iran."[16]

Turkey

Turkey is another MENA republic within which bottom up deep-state-building projects have occurred. In its case three have been pursued sequentially. The first was the Kemalist deep state erected on the main foundation of the military but extending through informal networks into even the Turkish criminal underworld. For half a century, it acted as the guardian of "democracy," which it interpreted as elected governments that posed no threat to the material or ideational interests of the deep state and the military at its core. With four coups in its republican history—to say nothing of dirty wars against Kurds and systematic violations of the human and civil rights of those in the leftist and Islamist political oppositions—the deep state gradually became the primary target of opposition forces, much the most important of which were Islamists.

Their operating assumption, based on two generations' political experience with the Kemalist deep state, was that they could not assume sovereign power through strictly democratic means, but would have to construct their own, parallel deep state to neutralize the Kemalist one. They began the project under Turgut Ozal, who, as the civilian Prime Minister following the military government that ruled from 1980 to 1983, opened both political and economic space for Islamists. Ozal likely did this partly out of sympathy and partly out of the calculation of his need for a political support base to reduce the deep state's leverage over him. This opening ultimately gave rise to competitive Islamist deep states. The first to emerge was that associated with Fethullah Gulen, originally a village Imam whose moderate Islamist message, combined with his organizational skills, enabled him to construct a sprawling network that included as many as 3 million members in Turkey. Gulen also oversaw the establishment of hundreds of schools in Turkey and worldwide, the prominent newspaper *Zaman* and the Samanyolu television network, Bank Asya, and from the mid-1990s on, increasing penetration of non-state and state institutions. These ranged from the Turkish Confederation of Businessmen and Industrialists (TUSKON) and parliament, where it had some 60 members—or 10% of the total—to institutions more central to power, such as the police force and judiciary: the bedrocks of the Gulenist deep state.[17] By 2013 it had also made inroads into the military.

The exact nature of the relationship between the sprawling Gulenist network and the political party face of Turkish Islamism remains unclear. It could have been a conscious division of labor, or simply two like-minded actors coordinating efforts. In any event, initially the Welfare Party in the mid-1990s provided the political face for Islamism, while the Gulenists provided the organizational and institutional muscle to support it. After that party was dismissed from government and declared illegal in 1998, its role was inherited by the AK Party, which assumed control of government due to its success in the 2002 parliamentary election. At some stage, most probably once Recep Tayyip Erdogan became Prime Minister, the political face of the Islamist movement embodied in the AK Party began to construct its own deep state lest it be dependent upon and possibly even replaced by the Gulenists. But between 2002 and 2013, cooperation between the two enabled them to root out the Kemalist deep state, a task which they managed primarily through their control of the judiciary and police forces. Having finally uprooted the Kemalist deep state by 2013, the Gulenist–AK Party alliance collapsed as both sides sought to inherit its powers. Over the following three years a subterranean war—conducted initially within the court system and among the police forces, then ultimately in the military—was played out. Erdogan and his deep state ultimately defeated the Gulenists, who were purged in their tens of thousands from state institutions and private organizations, including business and the media, in the wake of the failed July 2016 coup, which Erdogan accused them of organizing. The high command of the military along with mid-ranking officer corps were decimated by these purges. Within a year of the failed coup Erdogan had discharged 169 generals and admirals, fully half of the high command. This move suggested that in one fell swoop Erdogan—now President serving under the new, undemocratic constitution drafted under his supervision and approved in April 2017—had mopped up the remnants of both the Kemalist and Gulenist deep states.[18]

The Turkish case thus exemplifies the "pseudopolitics" associated with deep states, in the sense that the determinative struggles for power were within and between deep states rather than within the formal political superstructure. It is true that the formal political superstructure played a more important role in Turkey than in Algeria. Actors in the Turkish deep state had to take account of elections and parliaments over which they could not exert absolute control. Yet ultimately the decisive struggle for power took place between the competitive deep states.[19] In Algeria, by contrast, with the exception of the period 1989–91, when the deep state was divided and thus opened the door to a free and fair election, that deep state ensured that all politics were of the pseudo variety, meaning they had no real impact on political outcomes, which are determined by the deep state itself. This left no political channel open other than mass protests, which duly erupted in the spring of 2019.

Resource Capture by Deep States— Top Down versus Bottom Up

The types and magnitudes of resources deep states capture are largely shaped by two factors: whether the deep state is top down or bottom up; and the primary sources of governmental revenues. Those built from the top down, especially those resting not on a particular social force but on more inclusive institutions, command more informational, ideational and relational resources than those built from the bottom up, all of which are comprised primarily of a single social force. This is because the infrastructural power produced as a result of these three types of resources depends on the deep state's willingness and ability to penetrate broadly and deeply into the political economy and community and reshape both. Deep, deep states, being those based in a single social force, face inherent obstacles in those quests. Because they are perceived to reflect that narrow interest, they necessarily have to rely more upon despotic than infrastructural power in dealings with members of excluded social forces. It is also inherently difficult for them to create narratives that conflate the deep, deep state's interests with the nation's as a whole, or even to formally inculcate a loyalty narrative within the deep, deep state, precisely because real loyalty is based on kinship and shared religious, tribal and ethnic, rather than broader national, identities. Top down deep states comprised more of networks within and between formal institutions, such as those in Egypt, Algeria, Iran, Tunisia and Palestine, have not faced similar constraints, so their infrastructural power, based on informational, ideational and relational resources, has been greater.

The types and quantities of material resources under the control of deep states reflect not only their nature, but also the sources and magnitudes of the nation's wealth. Deep, deep states rely on plunder and criminal earnings, with the balance between those two determined primarily by the amount of resources under the nation state's control. In wealthy oil exporting Libya and Iraq, Qadhafi's and Saddam's deep states simply plundered oil revenues, having little need for additional earnings from crime. Syria and Yemen, with substantially smaller hydrocarbon-generated revenues, gave rise to deep, deep states that plundered those revenues, but also siphoned off additional ones. They did so largely by creating monopolies for those within the limited access order, and by engaging in criminal activities, typically smuggling.[20] After the 2011 uprising in Syria, violence and criminality became yet more central to its deep state's revenue raising. "Fuel supplies to regime territory and energy dealings with areas under the control of the so-called Islamic State became big business." Former pillars of the business community were forcibly displaced by militia leaders and "new trading and smuggling rings displaced the old landowning nobility at the top of the social pyramid."[21] One such militia figure based in Latakia is Ahmad al Foz, whose profits from extortion, theft and smuggling—condoned, even assisted by the elite around Bashar al Asad—enabled him to purchase the very symbol of the old Damascene elite, the Orient Club.

Iran

Iran's deep state apparently comprised of the Office of the Supreme Leader, generals from the IRGC, and "the wider security-intelligence apparatus," has generated rents from plunder of the country's hydrocarbon resources as well as by creating monopolies, preferential access and other legal and semi-legal means that favor elements within the limited access order that the deep state gatekeeps.[22] The very language of those within the Office of the Supreme Leader and the IRGC reflects their concern with guarding that limited access order, as they verbally divide the population into "one of us" (*khodi*) and "not one of us" (*naa-khodi*).[23]

The Bonyad-e Mostazafan, ostensibly a religious foundation whose purpose is to provide charity for the poor, is the tip of the iceberg of the Iranian deep state's economic empire. In reality, this Bonyad, or foundation, like others, is a multibillion-dollar "slush fund for regime insiders and particularly the generals from the Revolutionary Guards."[24] The IRGC controls 40% of the country's nominally private banks, as well as the country's largest engineering firm, Khatam al Anbiya Construction Headquarters, which employs more than 160,000.[25] The "semi-state sector," which includes "religious, revolutionary, military foundations and cooperatives, as well as social security and pension funds," is larger than the private or public sector. At its heart is the "network of companies around the IRGC," which expanded enormously during the 2005–13 presidency of Mahmoud Ahmadinejad.[26] At that time the head of the Khatam al Anbiya, Rostam Qassemi, was made Minister of Petroleum, thereby opening that sector up yet further to the IRGC. In early 2019 the head of Khatam al Anbiya announced that his firm was ready to replace the French oil major Total in the development of the South Pars gas field, Iran's key fossil fuel project.[27] Not surprising is that "Iran's deep state, the security and intelligence forces and their hardline supporters that hide behind Supreme Leader Ayatollah Ali Khamenei, does not want (President) Rouhani to accomplish his goal of normalization of relations with the West," as it would "lead to a loosening of the deep state's grip ... and loss of economic might and privileges."[28] The main area of conflict between President Rouhani and the IRGC is, accordingly, not the 2015 nuclear deal (the Joint Comprehensive Plan of Action) and Iran's missile programs, but "the IRGC's dominance of Iran's political and economic spheres." Shortly after his re-election Rouhani accused the IRGC of "plundering the country's wealth through its control over economic institutions in the name of privatization."[29] It should be noted, however, that Rouhani himself served in the IRGC, heading its Air Defense Division, before becoming a director of Khatam al Anbiya, suggesting that his criticism was more tactical than strategic as he jockeyed for power within the elite.

Egypt and Tunisia

Egypt's deep state similarly depended initially on assets seized from the colonial power and the *comprador bourgeoisie* which prospered in its shadow, then from oil and gas export revenues and internal allocations of those fuels to energy intensive processing industries owned by cronies. Revenues derived from hydrocarbons have never been sufficient, however, so they have been augmented through a legalized system of crony capitalism that created rents in various sectors of the domestic economy, probably the largest being the allocation of state land for private purposes.

Tunisia's endowment of natural resources is even less than Egypt's, so its deep state has had to rely yet more heavily on cronyism, aptly described in a 2014 World Bank sponsored report.[30] Tax data analyzed after the fall of the Ben Ali regime revealed that 220 companies owned by his relatives "earned 21 per cent of all the country's private sector profits between 1996 and 2010, in large part benefitting from rules in their favor." Those companies controlled on average "6.3 per cent more market share than ordinary businesses," entirely because they benefitted from regulations, many of which were specifically granted for such purposes. A 2007 rule that required the government's permission to produce cement, for example, was drafted to provide a virtual monopoly to Ben Ali's brother-in-law's newly created Carthage Cement Company.[31] As a World Bank co-author of the report noted, "there is nothing illegal happening here, it is just that these laws do not necessarily benefit the public."[32]

Turkey

Turkey's sequential deep states have amassed resources differently. The Kemalist deep state, more authorized than created by a ruling military—hence based more in informal networks than established relationships between formal state institutions—garnered resources through both plunder and theft. The military economy provided it with access to state funding, while the government's extensive intervention into the economy enabled it to favor the business interests of the Kemalist economic elite which in turn provided resources to sustain the networked deep state. As for theft, connections into Turkey's criminal underworld, heavily involved in drug smuggling among other nefarious activities, provided the networked Kemalist deep state with illegal gains. What ultimately led to the dismantling of that deep state was its relative tolerance of oppositional political and economic activities, the latter of which generated increasingly substantial resources. This is especially evident in the case of the so-called "Anatolian Tigers"—small and medium-sized entrepreneurs with Islamist leanings who took advantage of duty-free entry into the EU after 1995 to export both manufactures and agricultural commodities. Resentful of the state's privileging of Istanbul-based Kemalist economic elites, this newly energized Islamist bourgeoisie contributed resources to Islamist political activists, of whom the most successful were Gulen and Erdogan. Now that the latter has gained control of the Turkish state and built under it his own deep state, he is in a position to generate resources from that control. The massive increase since 2002 in state-funded construction, carried out largely by firms connected to the AK Party, is indicative of Erdogan's strategy of plunder.

External resources

Virtually all MENA deep states also obtain resources from foreign backers. The Palestinian Authority and the deep state controlled by Fatah that underpins it are the most dependent of the MENA states and deep states upon such external resources, which consist primarily of subsidies provided by the EU. Next in order of dependence upon external subventions are the bottom up deep states cobbled together in resource poor countries. Lebanon is the prime example of this, dependent on Iran as its deep state fabricated by Hizbullah has been. Similarly, Bashar al Asad's deep state would have collapsed in the absence of Iranian support. Libya's competing deep states are both sustained primarily by domestically produced oil revenues, although both also receive external support, those in the west from Qatar primarily, and those in the east from the UAE and Saudi Arabia. Resources for Iraq's deep states, first Saddam's, now the one emerging primarily under Iranian and secondarily American tutelage, have come principally from the country's oil revenues, augmented by Iranian and US support. In the remaining contemporary Arab republics under consideration—Algeria, Tunisia and Egypt—only in the last have externally provided resources been of great importance to the deep state, whether provided by the USSR to Nasser or by the US to all subsequent presidents. Algeria's hydrocarbon wealth has obviated the need for external resources, whereas Tunisia has been too marginal to the geo-political strategies of potential donors for its deep state under either Bourguiba or Ben Ali, or for the struggling successor one based on the intelligence services, to receive substantial external resources.

In sum, the differential resource bases of these republican deep states, combined with their composition and relationship with regimes, have impacted how they deal with national economies. At one end of the spectrum is Qadhafi's Libya, in which the deep state simply plundered the economy, preventing it from nurturing the growth of fixed capital assets by depriving it of appropriate constitutional, legal and administrative frameworks. At the other is Kemalist Turkey, within which the deep state at least allowed, if it did not actually facilitate, the emergence of an alternative, dynamic economy, which ultimately undermined that deep state, while laying the foundations for new ones. In all cases, those in the limited access orders gate-kept by deep states benefitted disproportionately from national economies, the rents they extracted being dead weights on economic growth.

Do MENA Monarchies Have Deep States?

All MENA deep states considered thus far are in republics, begging the question of whether deep states also exist in MENA monarchies. The simple, straightforward answer is "no," with one possible exception and some qualifications. The monarchies have in general rested on patrimonial rule, rather than deep states. This is not to say, however, that the monarchies are open access orders. They rely more on rents than coercion both to induce compliance and to reduce demands for access to their limited access orders, membership in which is restricted to ruling families and those closely associated with them. The monarchies are, in other words, softer versions of the harsh republican limited access orders that rely more heavily on coercion.

The three factors that determine the nature of all MENA states suggest why the monarchies emerged and have survived as patrimonial systems. The first is the role played by specific actors in state building. The second is the degree of national homogeneity. The third is the availability of economic resources. In the case of monarchies, a fourth factor, the nature of the royal family, is also relevant.

State builders

Post-colonial state builders in the republics were in all cases commoners, typically of relatively humble origins, whose power was initially based on their membership in the military, intelligence services, or a Leninist-style political party, such as the Ba'th, and subsequently on a deep state comprised of those bodies augmented by police forces, the judiciary, and public and private economic actors. By contrast, monarchial states were in six cases built from the top down by the British selecting a ruling family with which first to share, then to devolve sovereign power. The two exceptions are Morocco, where the King sided with the nationalists against the French colonial power; and Saudi Arabia, where Abd al Aziz Ibn Saud orchestrated a successful revolt against British efforts to install the Hashemites as principal rulers of the Arabian Peninsula. Both these ruling families, therefore, were legitimated by their pre-colonial status as well as by their nationalist credentials earned through their opposition to a real or potential colonial power. As for the other six monarchies, only in Jordan was the military a vital actor in the state-building process. The British-commanded Arab Legion augmented Hashemite King Abdullah's tribal levies. After his grandson King Hussein assumed direct command of that force in 1956, as the renamed Royal Jordanian Army, it became the vital prop of monarchial rule. Royal legitimacy was substantially less in Jordan than in Morocco or Saudi Arabia because the Hashemites were not native to its territory, had been imposed by the British, and after 1948 came to rule over Palestinians on the West Bank, a people who aspired to their own nation state. The only other monarchy in which the military played a similar, albeit considerably less important role, is Oman, where a British-officered force underpinned Sultan Qaboos' rise to and then exercise of power, with that Sultan's Armed Forces subsequently being brought under Omani command. But unlike in Jordan, the Omani al bu Said ruling family had historical roots in the country dating back 14 generations, claimed leadership of the dominant Ibadi Muslim sect, and did not rule over subjects who longed to have an independent state ruled by themselves.

Societal cohesion

The degree of societal cohesiveness has been central to the type of deep states erected in the republics. In those republics with heterogeneous societies divided into sharply competitive social forces, such as Iraq, Syria, Yemen, Libya and Lebanon, deep states have perched precariously on a particular social force, whether religious, ethnic (now in the case of Kurdish Iraq) or tribal. In Libya, for example, at the core of the deep state were security brigades "that reported directly to Qadhafi's residences at Bab al-Aziziyya, and were often headed and staffed by Qadhafi's loyalists and confidants," including the 32nd Reinforced Brigade, commanded by Mu`amar's son Khamis Qadhafi. These brigades were "organized along community and tribal lines," whereas the next layer up of the deep state, the broader military, was commanded by officers recruited primarily from the Qaddadfa, Warfalla and Magarha tribes, considered to be those most closely associated with Qadhafi's regime.[33] In Libya and these other countries the task of building inclusive, accountable governments on those fragmented social foundations was beyond the capacities and will of either colonial or post-colonial state makers, as now seems also to be the case with post-post-colonial states.

The only absolutely homogeneous monarchy is the smallest, Qatar. Minority religious or ethnically based social forces are to be found in all the others, but in none, until recently in Bahrain and Saudi Arabia, has the degree of conflict and contestation between them been anything like as pronounced as in Iraq, Syria, Libya or Yemen. The challenge of knitting together a national political community, therefore, was not as daunting as in most republics.

Resources

The relative magnitude of national resources also impacts the need for deep states. The greater the patronage available to MENA rulers, the less they have had to rely upon repression—the bigger the carrot, the smaller the stick.[34] The ratio of hydrocarbon revenues to populations in all GCC monarchies has considerably exceeded the average in MENA republics. But while ample oil revenues have until now been sufficient to sustain those monarchies, they are not a *deus ex machina*. Oil revenues in Libya under Qadhafi matched those on a per capita basis in the GCC. In the two other major oil and gas exporting republics, Algeria and Iran, per capita rents have been similar to those in monarchies, even slightly exceeding those in Bahrain and Oman. In Iran, they were insufficient to sustain the Shah's regime, although he was not a "real" monarch in that he owed his crown not to being the scion of a historic ruling family, but to his military officer father having seized power, and to the Americans and British who first facilitated his succession, then intervened covertly in 1953 to save his throne. As for non-hydrocarbon national wealth, GDP per capita in Morocco and Jordan is similar to that in Tunisia, albeit somewhat higher than in Egypt, thereby suggesting that rents alone do not explain the rise and persistence of monarchial rule. Overall though, the monarchies have enjoyed substantially greater oil rents per capita than republics.

Size of dynasties

As Michael Herb has argued, the monarchies differ in the size of their ruling "families," with all of those in the GCC other than Oman being more accurately described as family dynasties because they are actually extended clans or tribes.[35] There is strength in numbers. The Saudi ruling family, for example, numbers some 20,000 princes, of whom a substantial portion serve in the military and intelligence services, elsewhere in state institutions, and in the public sector of the economy, to say nothing of being key figures in private business. Similar, if less sprawling dynastic family networks rule in Kuwait, Qatar, Bahrain and the UAE. Their primary vulnerability has been intra-family tensions, commonly manifested during successions, which have been chronic in Kuwait, intermittent in Qatar and now greatly intensified in King Salman's Saudi Arabia.

Oman, Morocco and Jordan are ruled by monarchs, not family dynasties. They are therefore inherently less stable since their rule, like that of the presidents of the republics, necessarily depends heavily on non-family members. In the case of Jordan, the monarchy with the shallowest historical roots and fewest family members, this has led successive kings to rely on the military and security agencies to govern the country in a fashion akin to that in the republican top-down deep states. In Morocco and Oman there has been more carrot and less stick than in Jordan, so to the extent deep states are defined as having coercive agencies at their core, they cannot be said to exist in either. In both these cases monarchs have combined a cult of personality with extensive patronage networks as vital underpinnings of their rule.[36] Morocco's famous *makhzan*, a classic limited access order, evolved in the twentieth century from the monarch's household into a sprawling modern financial and business conglomerate spreading downward from the palace through holding companies and controlling a dominant proportion of the country's entire economy.

Sultan Qaboos seems to have copied the Moroccan ruling family's playbook in building a similar network more or less from the ground up, relying heavily on his relatives from the al bu Said family in so doing. His uncle Sayyid Shabib, for example, was put in charge of the Tawoos Group in 1982, since which time it has become the leading business conglomerate in Oman, "involved in various sectors ranging from agriculture, telephones and services to leisure, and concluding contracts with Petroleum Development Oman, the Diwan of the Royal Court and the Minister of Defence and Oil."[37] Another uncle, Shaykh Mustahil al Ma'ashani, served in the cabinet before taking over Muscat Overseas Holding, "the most active business group in Dhofar." One of his sons was given control of leading telecommunications companies before being recruited into the Royal Court, while

93

another son was placed in charge of the leading banking consortium, Bank Muscat. Various other relatives are sprinkled throughout leadership positions in the government, public and private sectors.[38]

But Qaboos' cult of personality and sprawling, familial-led patronage network have not provided the political security of his fellow king in Morocco, a deficiency now highlighted by his lack of heirs and failing health, and further exacerbated by declining oil revenues. Continuing to dole out patronage since opening the taps in 2011 to calm widespread protests, the Sultan ran budget deficits of 15% of GDP in 2015 and 21% in 2016, in which year he "doubled the unaccounted part of the budget, which includes his own allowance, promised state employees another salary rise, and took delivery of a fresh batch of British-made Typhoon warplanes."[39] Also in late 2016 he stepped up repressive measures, jailing editors and reporters as well as cracking down on independent jurists. The 2020 Vision declared in 1995 committed Oman to bolstering its private sector, creating a broad industrial base, and most importantly, weaning the country off oil. In 2016—by which time oil exports were to have provided only 40% of government revues as opposed to 66% in 1995, but had grown to more than 80%—the obviously overly ambitious plan was renamed the 2040 Vision.[40] As in the case of Jordan's kings, Sultan Qaboos has relied heavily on external support for his military and security services and, also as in Jordan in the 1970s, even for direct intervention to combat a domestic insurgency.

Deep states in monarchial futures

To return to the question of whether or not deep states are to be found in monarchies, the equivocal, theoretical answer is "yes." Empirically, however, since there appears to be only one such case, that of Jordan with its unique history as a militarized buffer state, the more accurate answer might be "no," with that single exception. But this begs the question of whether or not deep states might be emerging in these patrimonial monarchies.

Certainly, the conditions that have supported them in the past are changing. The favorable rent to population ratios they enjoyed as a result of oil and gas revenues are in decline. Presumably, therefore, more sticks than carrots will be required to induce compliance. Increased repression in the wake of Arab Springs, such as in Bahrain, Saudi Arabia and even Kuwait, suggests such a trend has commenced. A related factor is the militarization of the monarchies. Morocco,

Jordan and Oman have comparatively large, well-financed armed forces, with spending on them accounting on average for about 20% of all government spending. These three monarchies have 8.3, 20.5 and 17.9 military personnel, respectively, for each 1,000 people, compared to the MENA, NATO and emerging countries' averages of 13.9, 6.0, and 5.1, respectively.[41] But their military spending pales in comparison to that of the GCC monarchies, several of which, led by the UAE, Qatar and Saudi Arabia, are among the world's highest spenders on their militaries, whether by absolute amounts or as proportions of their budgets, populations or GDPs. Qatar introduced conscription in 2013, followed by the UAE a year later, then in 2017 by Kuwait. In 2018 the Saudi Grand Mufti called for it in his country.[42]

Ballooning of the personnel and financial resources of monarchial armed forces has been associated with an increased tendency to deploy them, such as by the Emirates and Saudi Arabia in Yemen or Libya at present, or to implicitly threaten their use, as is the case in the dispute that commenced in 2017 between Qatar and other GCC states. As the monarchies expand their militaries and base ever more of their foreign policy leverage upon them, so will the domestic political clout of those armed forces grow. Much the same can be said of security and intelligence agencies, which are being beefed up to confront real and perceived domestic challenges.

Finally, the Achilles heel of all authoritarian political systems, which is leadership succession, is now afflicting many of the monarchies, just as it has always afflicted the MENA republics. In Jordan, Oman and Morocco the challenge of succession is choosing from a limited number of candidates from within comparatively small royal families. The present case of Oman, where no clear successor has yet emerged, illustrates that problem, as does the last-minute choice in 1999 of Abdullah as successor to his father King Hussein, rather than Crown Prince Hassan, in Jordan.

But in the family dynasties succession poses a much greater challenge. Those dynasties have swollen into sprawling conglomerates, divided vertically between contending lines, horizontally between generations. The struggle over the succession to King Salman in Saudi Arabia illustrates the problem and its consequences for a potential deep state emerging there. In seeking to ensure the succession of his young son Muhammad, the King was forced to sideline his nephew, Crown Prince Muhammad bin Nayif, then serving as Minister of Interior. Among other things this necessitated a reshuffle of power within the sprawling security and intelligence system so as to eliminate the chance that Muhammad bin Nayif's supporters might challenge Muhammad bin Salman's ascendency. So in June 2017, the King issued a decree changing the name of the Investigation and Prosecution Authority to that of Public Prosecution, removing the head of the Authority, who was a supporter of Muhammad bin Nayif, and simultaneously awarding himself the power to fill the newly created post of Public Prosecutor, attached directly to the office of the King. Named as the new Public Prosecutor was Shaikh Saud al Mu`jab, a close confidant of Muhammad bin Salman's. Accompanying this move was the promotion of General Saud bin Abd al Aziz al Hilal to Director of General Security Services, thereby placing the two key institutions with direct, potentially coercive power over other members of the royal family in the hands of the King and his son Muhammad. Six months previously the King had established the National Security Center directly under his control, as a competitor to the Ministry of Interior and intended to neutralize it. Accompanying these changes was a smear campaign against Muhammad bin Nayif, including charges that he was a drug addict and supporter of the Qatari ruling family.[43] In September 2017, as opposition to the apparent succession from King Salman to his son Muhammad was mounting, General Security Services rounded up some 30 prominent Saudis, including Prince Abd al Aziz bin Fahd, son of the former King Fahd and nephew of King Salman, on the grounds that they were "working for the benefit of foreign parties against the security of the kingdom."[44]

While the Saudi dynasty has been riven in the past by succession struggles, most notably that which erupted in the late 1950s and pitted King Saud against the future King Faisal, never before have royal divisions penetrated so far down into the coercive agencies of the state, or sounded so much like intrigues in republican deep states. Intra-family struggles in Saudi Arabia, and, by extension, in many if not all of the other family dynasties, will in future almost necessarily involve at least the veiled threat if not the actual use of force. This condition alone elevates the relative power of coercive agencies, already being beefed up in the face of both domestic and foreign challengers.

Jumlukiyya

In conclusion, the border between deep state republics and patrimonial monarchies is becoming more porous, with a growing possibility that more of the latter will cross over into deep state political territory formerly occupied almost exclusively by republics. Prior to the Arab Spring, the term *Jumlukiyya*, combining the Arabic words for republic (*Jumhuriyya*) and monarchy (*Malakiyya*), was coined by Egyptian sociologist Saad al Din Ibrahim.[45] At that time many Arab "presidents for life," as Roger Owen dubbed them, were scrambling to secure successions for their sons, thereby founding family dynasties.[46] In the wake of the failure of such efforts the tide is flowing the other way. There is, for example, steadily less to distinguish the dependence of Jordan's King Abdullah on his military and security services and network of crony capitalists from the similar dependencies of several presidents. The exercise of power in family dynasties also increasingly resembles that in republics. Contending royals are seeking to establish their own lineage as permanently paramount, entrenching their power in coercive agencies. It is as if they were battening down the hatches in preparation for coming political storms whipped up by intensifying intra-familial conflicts, declining rents, more mobilized populations, and intensifying regional hostilities. This hunkering down will inevitably foster the growth of subterranean coercive politics, converting visible political interactions into pseudopolitics of the republican variety.

6

INCLUSION, HUMAN RESOURCES
AND STATE POWER

The traditional measures of state capacity to effect citizen inclusion
are the institutional performances of bureaucracies and representative
bodies, such as local governments and national legislatures. In recent
years with the growth of e-government, indicators of electronic
connectivity are also relevant to the assessment of inclusion. With
regard to administrations, the typical rule of thumb is that their
inclusion of citizens is inversely related to their degree of centralization. It is assumed that decentralized administrative powers and
functions provide more entry points for citizens. As regards elected
bodies, for them to facilitate inclusion they need to be representative,
influential and engaged in public policy making.

MENA bureaucracies are centralized and stove-piped, thus offering
little access to citizens, to say nothing of providing inadequate
administration. A recent study of localization and decentralization
evaluated countries on those two characteristics along political, fiscal
and administrative sub-dimensions, then combined those indicators
into an overall ranking of countries "on the closeness of their
government to the people."[1] The researchers found a strong, positive
correlation between rank on their scale of closeness and higher levels
of human development and lower levels of corruption. Their measure
of closeness rested heavily on the size of populations and territory
served by local government units, with the smaller of both being
positively related to closeness. Local governments in the MENA
served larger numbers of citizens than those in any region other than
East Asia and the Pacific and presided over areas on average about
four times larger than any other world region, with the exception
of Sub-Saharan Africa. The sub-dimensions on which the overall
Government Closeness Index was based were those of the relative

importance of local government, its security of existence, and the degrees of financial, political and administrative decentralization. Of the 182 ranked countries, only four of the 17 MENA countries included were in the upper half—the UAE, Turkey, Sudan and Lebanon. The large republics ranked between Iran at 100 and Syria at 120. The result was similar for the fiscal decentralization index, in which only four MENA countries appeared in the upper half. For the political decentralization index the result was yet less favorable for the MENA. Other than Israel, only Turkey and Iraq were in the upper half of 182 ranked countries, 17 were in the lower half, and nine were in the lowest quartile. The MENA, in short, is characterized by centralized local government that does little to include citizens in public policy decision making. According to Laurie Brand's review of Janine Clark's study of decentralization in Jordan and Morocco, it reflects regime strategy in both countries, where "it seems that there has been little will to engage in anything other than cosmetic decentralization ... avoiding any meaningful devolution of power."[2]

The World Bank has developed measures of citizen engagement in rule making and regulation, sampling 185 countries for its Global Indicators of Regulatory Governance.[3] The key sub-dimensions on which citizen engagement in regulation are evaluated are engagement of stakeholders in rule-making processes, consulting with them about regulations once applied, and providing access to information about regulations. On the first dimension, the MENA is the lowest scoring region, the Bank observing that "the Middle East and North Africa stands out as the region with the least inclusive rulemaking." As for consultation, the Bank notes that "among all regions, South Asia, Sub-Saharan Africa and the Middle East and North Africa have the least advanced consultative practices." On the sub-dimension of providing access to regulatory information, the MENA has the highest proportion of countries of any region for which there is "no consultation," that being half of them. Regulatory impact assessments are conducted by about a quarter of MENA governments, the only lower proportion being those in Sub-Saharan Africa in which one in five do. On the overall citizen engagement in rule-making score, the MENA slightly outperforms Sub-Saharan Africa, the only region it does. Rankings within the MENA place all the big republics at the bottom of the seven indicators with scores of zero for all of them, with the exception of Egypt which scores 0.6 because it publishes some proposed regulations. Only Morocco and Tunisia are credited with undertaking three of the seven procedures that make up the overall index. Indicators of citizen engagement in rule making are important, according to the authors of the World Bank study, because, "Where citizens know the rules that govern their society and have a role in shaping them, they are more likely to comply with those rules. Corruption is lower and the quality of regulation higher."[4]

Overly centralized, underperforming bureaucracies

Bureaucratic competence is a prerequisite not just for inclusion, but for the exercise of infrastructural power in general. An assessment of the importance of effective decentralization to both inclusion and to the implementation of governmental policy is provided by Hadi Fathallah's consideration of the capacities of the Saudi bureaucracy to implement the ambitious Vision 2030 economic plan put forward by Crown Prince Muhammad bin Salman.[5] Fathallah paints a picture of centralized, stove-piped, dysfunctional administrative institutions unable as he says to provide simple services such as "waste management, food safety, and water," much less the complicated services required under Vision 2030. Confronted for example with repeated floods that caused deaths and property damage, in 2013 the Saudi government bypassed regional and local authorities by empowering Aramco, the state oil company, to "oversee and manage improvements to local infrastructure." In 2018, despite Aramco's involvement, Jeddah continued to flood. The national government blamed the Amir (governor) of the province, who had no authority over Jeddah. He in turn blamed the municipality, which in turn blamed Aramco. According to Fathallah, the range of regional and local institutions involved and intended to implement Vision 2030 is complex, inefficient and dysfunctional. Provincial Amirs are appointed by the King, typically from among princes of the royal family, the purpose being to consolidate royal control. These Amirs, not being from the region they are governing, "lost touch with the needs of the people and with the tribal networks that would facilitate development projects." As a result, their administrations have become "ceremonial governmental entities." A parallel local government system exists under the Ministry of Interior, while yet another consists of hundreds of municipalities. "With such a labyrinth of national and local governmental entities—themselves governed by laws that are issued by different ministries—not only is there much confusion over hierarchy and legal authority, these entities compete for resources, power and visibility." They are, in a word, stove-piped.

Presiding over all of this is a myriad of government institutions with overlapping and intertwined authorities, including "the crown, the diwan, the Council of Economic and Developmental Affairs, assorted ministries, a range of strategy committees and project management offices," and so on. The overall result is to erode "the credibility of both local and central institutions."

In its annual overview of MENA economies in 2018, the World Bank noted that "If Arab countries can improve the capacity of their local governments to plan, finance, and deliver key services, they could make great strides towards building confidence with their citizens, and towards achieving the ambitious Sustainable Development Goals."[6] As a model for MENA countries to copy, the Bank cites South Korea's reforms of its civil service, which prior to 1960 was a body based on a spoils system "where civil service positions were used to reward political allies and supporters."[7] Reforms commencing at that time included requirements for open, competitive exams for recruitment and linking promotions to job performance evaluations. In the MENA, by contrast, the Bank notes the pressure to convert virtually any public administrative body, including those paid for by the Bank's funds, into "a source of patronage jobs."[8] Unless and until they are reformed, most MENA executive branches can neither effectively integrate citizens into their broader communities nor provide public goods and services at adequate levels.

Weak representative bodies

Representative bodies are more directly responsible for inclusion because it is for access to them that citizens compete in elections and these bodies in turn are intended to reflect and act upon citizens' collective policy preferences. MENA parliaments do not perform representation functions adequately. They serve primarily as mediators between citizens and executive branches, thereby extending rather than curtailing executive power. A survey conducted in Jordan, Tunisia and Egypt, for example, found that "voters elect those whom they believe would be willing and able to provide services, as opposed to following their party's program or voting according to national interest."[9] More than 80% of respondents said that service provision, by which is meant access to resources provided by executive branches, was the primary criterion they used to decide their vote. Not surprisingly MENA parliaments are not assessed as being powerful. M. Steven Fish and Matthew Kroenig have evaluated 158 parliaments in creating a "parliamentary powers index." The 18 MENA parliaments listed, other than that of Israel, have an average score of 0.28, which 123 of the 158 parliaments exceed and three equal.[10]

One reason why MENA parliaments are so comparatively powerless is that executive branches frequently ignore the constitutional provisions, amendments, laws and regulations they produce. This is a principal finding of the fifth iteration of the Arab Democracy Index, produced by the Arab Reform Initiative in 2017.[11] Virtually unique among such indices, this one seeks to evaluate separately the "means" and the "practices" of democracy and then compare the results. Means refer to the formal constitutional and legal structure, while practices refer to what individuals and institutions actually do. Those compiling the index note that MENA parliaments frequently produce legislation in response to foreign pressures to democratize, but that such legislation is essentially a dead letter, as reflected by the wide gap between the means index, on which the average Arab country score is 788, compared to the practices index, on which the average is only 504, some 40% lower. This is the widest gap between means and practices in the some 20-year history of conducting the five iterations of the survey on which the index is based. In other words, MENA and especially Arab parliaments are disempowered because those elected to them typically see their role as service providers rather than as policy advocates, and because sensitive policies they might enact can be easily ignored in practice, thereby enervating reform momentum and even public desire to work politically through parliaments. In the MENA, inclusion appears to remain the preserve of clientage networks, hence controlled from the top down, rather than resulting from bottom up access for citizens to policy making or implementation. Inclusion is necessarily then limited in societal scope and depth.

Obstacles to e-government

The most recently developed means of extending inclusion is through electronic connectivity. While e-government is the most sophisticated, formal manifestation of that connectivity, day to day citizen interaction through the social media provides at least some inclusion. While numerous factors impact how and in what degree electronic connectivity facilitates inclusion, the most basic and important one consists of access to the physical requirements for such connectivity. In 2018 the World Bank published a review of digital infrastructure in the MENA, from which it concluded that it "lags that of other emerging regions. Internet speed is slow. Prices, while lower, remain high ... Many internet markets in MENA countries have monopolies or entry barriers."[12] The report continues in this vein, observing that "Mobile broadband use in the MENA region is more limited than in other regions ... Low quality is also an issue." All MENA countries have mobile broadband speeds "below the global average." Most rely on copper wires rather than fiber-optic technology for connections to internet service providers. The fundamental cause of these shortcomings, according to the report, is that "the broadband infrastructure in MENA is still influenced by mostly overstaffed, state-owned incumbent operators with legacy infrastructure ... MENA countries are still paralyzed by state-owned incumbent operators." In a word, according to the Bank, dominant, state-owned telecom companies refuse to forgo their rents, although "these rents create a model that is unsustainable in the long term."[13] The Bank does not mention the security aspects of this arrangement, but they are also important. States seek to maintain control of electronic connectivity of all sorts in order better to monitor personal communications, censor websites, distribute "fake news," and so on. Since the Arab Spring the sophistication of such monitoring and censorship has vastly increased, thereby deterring social media and even informal, day to day communications between citizens. Even cyberspace, therefore, does not provide an arena within which they can feel and indeed be effectively included in the nation's socio-political and economic systems.

State Capacity: Developing Human Resources

Education

Mark Dincecco argues that one of the principal "channels" through which state capacities can be increased is that of mass public education, which "can increase the overall level of educational attainment—and thus human capital ... Greater human capital in turn can improve economic productivity."[14] By virtually all standard measures other than proportion of age cohorts in school, MENA education is underperforming. Equivalent years of schooling based on standardized, globalized tests such as Trends in International

103

Mathematics and Science Study (TIMMS) and the Program for International Student Assessment (PISA), indicate that MENA students are not learning at globally competitive rates. When actual years of schooling are compared to learning adjusted years based on performance on TIMMS, the gap is greater for all MENA countries compared to non-MENA ones. A student in Egypt, for example, who has completed 11 years of schooling, has only finished a bit more than six years if learning adjusted.[15] In primary schools in the world's five developing regions the World Bank in 2018 administered standardized learning assessments of reading and mathematics by senior students, then compared the median percentage of those who scored above a minimum proficiency level. Only Sub-Saharan Africa scored lower on the two skills than the MENA, with less than half of MENA students being in the upper half of performers.[16] As for educational impacts and rewards, they appear to be lower for males in the MENA than in any other region according to the same World Bank study. The median wage increase for each year of school in the MENA is about 5%, the lowest increase for any world region.[17]

Public health

Human capital growth is not just the product of good schooling and appropriate employment. It also depends on the level of public health. The World Bank unveiled its new Human Capital Index (HCI) in the 2019 edition of its *World Development Report*. Its three dimensions are whether children survive from birth to school age; expected years of "quality-adjusted" school; and rates of stunting and adult survival. In the initial iteration of that index based on 2018 data, 157 countries were included, of which 16 are in the MENA. One MENA country ranks among the top 50—the UAE. Ten rank in the bottom half, with only Turkey at 53 and Iran at 71 being among the large MENA countries ranking in the top half. The large Arab countries of Egypt, Iraq, Sudan and Yemen rank in the bottom third.[18] The MENA's relatively poor performance on the Human Capital Index is yet worse if controlled for GDP per capita, which the Bank's report does. All MENA countries fall below levels predicted by their relative wealth, with only Morocco and Iran coming close to the line produced by plotting GDP per capita on the x axis and "productivity relative to frontier" (the estimated productivity of the next generation of workers based on the HCI) on the y axis. The MENA countries falling furthest below that line are all the GCC countries and Iraq.[19]

Even the poorest of MENA countries, however, including Yemen and Sudan, fail to achieve levels on the HCI equivalent to what would be expected by their low GDPs per capita, whereas comparator countries such as Niger, Liberia, the Democratic Republic of the Congo, Burundi, Haiti and other low income countries substantially outperform predicted levels. According to these global comparisons, the MENA is not producing levels of human capital predicted by its GDP per capita and essential if it is to become more competitive in the coming generation. Capacities of MENA states to deliver educational and health services fall below those of both rich and poor comparator countries.

Citizen discontent

Given the objectively poor performance of MENA states in developing human resources it would hardly be surprising if citizens in the region resent what they perceive as poor treatment and are, therefore, discontented. This is in fact the principal finding of a major investigation into the causes of the 2011 Arab Spring. A puzzle driving that enquiry was to determine the major cause of the rebellions, given that none of the countries concerned was experiencing dramatic reductions in personal wealth as measured by household consumption surveys. So if they were not becoming poorer, why were Egyptians, Tunisians, Syrians, Libyans, Yemenis and other Arabs so unhappy as to pour into the streets to demand fundamental change?

The answer is that they were fed up with what they deemed to be inadequate state performance in providing public goods and services as well as suitable employment, all of which they wanted within a framework of effective governance based on citizenship rights rather than through *wasta*, or influence-peddling within patronage systems. As MENA limited access orders gave progressively less importance to outsiders, so was there "a precipitous decline in life satisfaction scores on the eve of the Arab Spring, especially for the middle class." The World Bank report on the survey-based investigation notes that "These declines reflected perceptions of falling standards of living related to the shortage of formal-sector jobs, the dissatisfaction with the quality of public services, and government accountability. Ordinary people were frustrated as they could not share in the prosperity generated by the relatively few, large and successful Arab firms." According to the report, "The middle class wanted more—it wanted voice, real opportunities and accountability."[20] It was particularly unhappy with the poor quality of public goods, "such as health, education, transport, electricity and other types of government services," including public safety, control of corruption and the fairness of the justice system.[21] Small surprise that life satisfaction data revealed that subjective well-being was "low and plummeting." By the eve of the Arab Spring, "life satisfaction in most countries was below the average for countries at similar states in their development."[22] The report concludes that "these grievances were symptoms of the deep structural issues in Arab economies," at the core of which were "weak institutions plagued by corruption, and the high incidence of rent-seeking practices that constrained the growth of the private sector."[23] MENA state capacities, in sum, have not been equal to the task of satisfying their citizens' aspirations, so these citizens are unhappy, discontented and potentially rebellious.

Political and economic costs of inadequate human resource development

MENA states have inadequate power and capacities, so are not effectively including or serving their citizens, who are in turn becoming increasingly disenchanted. Virtually all states have responded not by improving their powers and capacities so as better to serve the needs of citizens, but by increasing repression of them. This downward spiral of state–society relations further undermines what limited infrastructural powers those states have, rendering the challenge of economic growth ever more difficult to meet.

Recent disappointing MENA economic performance reflects these difficulties. Over the past decade six MENA countries remained high-income, five stayed trapped in the middle-income bracket (Algeria, Egypt, Jordan, Morocco and Tunisia), and three fell from high to middle income (Iran, Lebanon and Libya). None escaped the so-called middle-income trap upward.[24] Average per capita GDP growth has been only about 2% annually for the poorest countries. The growth rate steadily decreases as relative income increases, indicating that the comparatively wealthy MENA states are far from being engines of growth for the region as a whole. Mediocre growth in national income results from an almost complete absence of productivity growth throughout the region. Average growth of Total Factor Productivity (TFP), a measure of management effectiveness, has in the MENA been extremely low, between 0 and 1% for the poorer countries, negative for the richer ones.[25] This poor result is due in part to the failure to adequately develop human resources and to the exclusion of citizens from participating effectively in national political economies. But it is also due to the failure to provide sufficient public order and effective management of the economy, issues to which we shall now turn.

Developmental States and Public Order

The interest of political economy in state capacities was stimulated by the post-1960s East Asian "Economic Miracle" of rapid growth driven by manufactured exports. The orthodox explanation of that "miracle" had by the 1980s come to be that the "developmental states" of East Asia had been sufficiently strong and far-sighted to adopt not only facilitative macroeconomic policies, such as balanced budgets and undervalued currencies, but also microeconomic policies that targeted state support on promising sectors, such as electronics, automobile manufacturing and shipbuilding, while encouraging competition between private businesses to export.[26] Indirect assistance to export-oriented manufacturing was provided by physical and especially human infrastructural development, the latter consisting primarily of major investments in public education at all levels. Political economy thus "brought the state back in" to its analysis of economic growth, implying that competitive, efficient markets did not develop and operate autonomously, but depended upon states fostering enabling conditions.

Possibly because the leading East Asian states and the entire region then enjoyed relative peace and security, the importance of domestic and external order to their development was accorded little attention. Similarly, possibly because these were comparatively homogeneous societies, socio-political inclusion was not attributed great importance for economic development. The East Asian post-WWII experience, in other words, played a key role in shaping the political economy of development and its primary focus on the state. That experience and the theorizing it generated, however, does not apply without modification to the more fractious MENA.[27]

The challenges of providing order and including more disparate social forces pose greater obstacles to MENA than they had to East Asian development. Fortunately, scholars working in the disciplines of political economy, institutional economics and historical sociology have long recognized that states face diverse development challenges, which those scholars have sought to identify and measure. Michael

Mann, for example, specified three such challenges—providing order, engendering ideological coherence and developing the "infrastructural power" with which to administer effectively, meaning "the capacity of the state actually to penetrate civil society, and to implement logistically political decisions throughout the realm."[28] Effective administration thus requires states to be embedded in their societies and accountable to them, rather than ruling over them dictatorially. States, in short, have to provide order and foster inclusion if they are to develop effective capacities.

Initially state capacity was measured by revenue extraction, but over time the measure has been broadened to include not only market regulation and enforcement of property rights and contracts more generally, but also provision of public goods, such as education and health services. A related evolution in theorizing about state capacities has been to more clearly separate coercive state powers— the ability to exert military and police power—from extractive, regulatory and public good provision capacities, recognizing that development requires both, i.e., domestic law and order and military defense against external enemies, on the one hand, and secure private property rights, on the other.[29] Among other benefits, this division enabled institutional economists, such as Mancur Olson, to calculate the negative development consequences of coercion and to posit that incentives for power wielders to promote economic activity depend primarily on the anticipated time required for returns on such investments. If they are short, the states under their control behave as "roving bandits," grabbing whatever resources they can without regard to systemic consequences, whereas if they are longer, state power wielders are likely to be "stationary bandits," for whom it is profitable to develop state capacity and a peaceful environment.[30] The broad distinction between state power and state capacities, as well as the narrower focus on the behavior of those exerting state power, are of particular relevance to the MENA, where modes of coercion and their direct and indirect costs are particularly high and militate against effective state capacities.

State Power in the MENA

Although MENA states invest disproportionately in security, they generally fail adequately to deliver it to their populations. The Global Peace Index ranks 163 countries that contain 99.7% of the world's population on 23 indicators that measure peace using three broad themes: the level of safety and security in society, the extent of domestic and international conflict, and the degree of militarization.[31] In 2018, countries in the Middle East and Africa were the world's least peaceful. Of the world's ten most dangerous countries in that year, five were in the MENA. Of the 25 most dangerous, 11 were in the MENA. Sixteen MENA countries ranked among the half of countries most dangerous in 2018, while only five were among the least dangerous half, and those five included three of the smallest GCC states along with Tunisia and Morocco. In other words, about 90% of the MENA population lives in countries more dangerous than the world average, while almost 100 million live in five of the most dangerous. MENA residents, in short, experience comparatively little safety and security, are exposed to high levels of domestic and international conflict, and are compelled to support costly militarization.

An indirect measure of state power is provided by the State Fragility Index, which compares 167 countries on four measures of fragility—security, political, economic and social. According to its compilers, "a country's fragility is closely associated with its state capacity to manage conflict; make and implement public policy; and deliver essential services."[32] The index thus purports to measure both state power and state capacity and ranks all countries included from 0 to 25, the higher the score, the more fragile the country. In 2015, the most recent year for which the index is available, in the three categories of most fragile states—alert, high alert, and very high alert—the scores of which ranked from 12 to 24, seven of the 27 were MENA states with a total population in excess of 200 million, some 40% of the region's entire population. The six least fragile MENA states ranked between 43 and 66 with overall scores of 5, but these included four small GCC states, Lebanon and Tunisia, with a total native population of less than 25 million.

Of the State Fragility Index's 12 dimensions, the security dimension is arguably that most reflective of state power. It is comprised of indicators for internal conflict, small arms proliferation, riots and protests, fatalities from conflict, military coups, rebel activity, militancy, bombings and political prisoners. On this dimension the MENA states with populations in excess of 30 million—Egypt, Iran, Iraq, Turkey, Algeria, Morocco, Sudan, Iraq, Iran and Saudi Arabia, the combined population of which is some 450 million, or about 90% of the region's people—have an average score of just over 8. The only countries with higher scores than this average are several African ones along with Pakistan, Afghanistan, North Korea, Russia and the Philippines. For the vast majority of MENA citizens, state power does not provide as much domestic order or security as most citizens enjoy in Latin America and Asia, to say nothing of Europe and North America.

The threat of external war is also comparatively high in MENA countries, as reflected in data reported by the Center for Systemic Peace.[33] What is most striking in the comparison of global trends in armed conflict is their spike in Muslim-majority countries—all of the 37 of which except for Bangladesh, Indonesia and Malaysia are in or on the periphery of the MENA—that began in the mid-1970s and persisted unbroken for a quarter of a century. From 1974 to 1980, the number of wars in Muslim-majority countries tripled (from 21 in 1974 to 64 in 1980), all but three of which occurred in the MENA. After a two-year interlude, 2001–2, when incidence of armed conflicts in Muslim-majority countries dropped, in 2003 it commenced a sharp increase which has never abated. The societal impact of warfare for these countries is some three times more intense than for countries in all other regions and leads "to both societal and systemic disintegration, making the coordination of policy initiatives, particularly those designed to alter the current momentum, extremely difficult to implement and sustain."[34] According to the Center's report, "The systemic repercussions and human trauma associated with major episodes of political violence, in general, appear to persist for twenty-five to seventy-five years, depending on the scope, magnitude, and duration of the experience."[35] State power in the MENA, insufficient to secure domestic order or prevent cross-border conflict, is thus also inadequate to permit the development of state capacities essential to addressing the consequences of conflict.

Weak state power in the MENA does not result from a comparative lack of resources devoted to its exercise. The region's countries spend more on their militaries as a proportion of GDP and state budgets than any other. Saudi Arabia, for example, has for years been spending about a third of its budget on its military.[36] Nine of the world's 20 countries that spend the most on importing arms are in the MENA.[37] According to the Stockholm International Peace Research Institute's (SIPRI) 2019 annual report, Middle Eastern countries increased their arms imports by 87% between 2009–13 and 2014–18, accounting for 35% of global arms imports in the latter period, during which time relatively impoverished Egypt became the world's third largest importer of arms. Moreover, as Diwan and Akin note, intermittent reductions in defense spending over the past several decades have not resulted in overall reductions in security spending, but have typically been offset by increases in spending on internal security and police. In Mubarak's Egypt, for example, as official spending on defense stagnated in real terms from the 1990s, spending on security services rose dramatically, resulting in an increase in personnel in those services such that by 2011 they outnumbered the 450,000 strong military by a factor of some four times.[38]

As Douglass North and his institutional economist colleagues observed, plentiful resources make possible large ruling coalitions and more stable, less violent political orders, whereas resource constraints narrow ruling coalitions and lead them to be more repressive.[39] The recent history of the MENA attests to this relationship. As rents from oil and gas exports per capita have declined and GDP per capita has stagnated, so has political repression increased, with no end in sight for this vicious cycle as hydrocarbon prices stagnate, populations expand rapidly, and elites grow ever more fearful of being removed by discontented populations.

7

STATE CAPACITIES FOR ECONOMIC MANAGEMENT

The most critical of state capacities is the ability to generate revenue, without which a state cannot function. Both the amount and sources of revenues are of importance. Mark Dincecco's analysis of more than 140 contemporary countries found a strong positive correlation between the tax/GDP ratio, "a raw measure of the extractive capacity of the state," and per capita GDP. Wealthier nations extract higher tax revenue relative to their GDPs than poorer ones. Moreover, wealthier states rely more heavily on income tax than do poorer ones, as revealed by the strong correlation between income tax/total tax and per capita GDP.[1] As Besley and Persson observe, taxation of income requires comparatively high administrative capacities, so the share of income tax of total tax revenue is a key measure of a state's "fiscal prowess."[2] Dincecco's data also reveals a strong positive correlation between contemporary states' contract enforcement and their per capita GDPs, while Acemoglu as well as Besley and Persson observe that tax revenue is higher in states where there are institutional constraints on executive power.[3] In sum, taxes, and especially direct ones in the form of income taxes, are closely correlated with state capacities and national wealth. Dincecco's investigation of the possibility that economic development is the cause, not the consequence, of state capacity improvement causes him to conclude otherwise—namely, that greater state capacity as measured by revenue extraction through taxation, and especially direct taxation, facilitates economic development.[4]

Oil is the primary source of government revenue in the ten leading Arab oil exporting countries. The share of oil revenue in total revenue according to the IMF in 2016 ranged from 47% to 94% and averaged 77% across this group.[5] Oil and gas exports as well as

112

indirect benefits from such exports by neighboring countries, such as through subventions, also provide a substantial share of revenues in other Arab countries. International multilateral and bilateral aid pours into MENA countries in greater amounts absolutely and relatively than into any other region. In total amount of such aid, five of the top 20 recipients globally are MENA countries. On an aid/ per capita basis, the world's three highest recipients are all MENA countries.[6]

Heavily dependent upon direct or indirect revenue from hydro-carbon exports and public foreign assistance, most MENA economies not only have low taxation rates, but also low proportions of direct taxes, especially personal income taxes, to total taxation. They tend to rely instead on indirect taxes, tariffs and fees. In the large oil exporting countries, even indirect taxes have been minimal until recently. Saudi Arabia and the UAE, for example, were finally forced by mounting budget deficits to introduce 5% value added taxes only in January 2018. As one expert on Gulf economies noted, however, in "GCC countries, it will likely take years (if not decades) to fully develop and implement VAT."[7]

Unfortunately, reliable, current data on MENA governmental revenues is not readily available. The World Bank's most recent World Development Indicators, for example, provide data on "taxes on income, profits and capital gains" for only Egypt, Israel, Jordan, Lebanon, Oman, Turkey, the West Bank and Gaza. In those seven countries, which constitute only a third of all MENA countries, direct taxes as a percentage of total revenues averaged 15%. This compares to averages of 32% in East Asia and the Pacific, 30% in Latin America and the Caribbean, 54% in North America, 22% in South Asia, 20% in lower-middle-income countries and 21% in upper-middle-income countries. The MENA, according to this relatively scanty data, thus extracts less revenue from direct taxation than any other global region or comparator lower-middle and middle-income countries.[8]

The Heritage Foundation's "tax burden" index assigns each of 180 countries a score from 0 to 100, the higher the number, the lower the "tax burden." In 2018, the 15 MENA countries listed, omitting Israel, averaged over 90, much the highest number, so lowest level of taxation, of all global regions.[9] The two lowest scoring MENA countries (i.e., those with the highest tax burdens) other than Israel were Tunisia and Morocco, suggesting their comparatively greater extractive capacities. The Heritage Foundation data also reveals that despite having the lowest proportion of taxes to revenues, MENA countries have the highest proportion of government expenditures to GDP and that the region's "fiscal health" is the world's poorest. An effort to calculate total tax revenue as a percentage of GDP for 180 countries that relied upon Heritage Foundation and other data sources found that of the ten countries with the lowest tax as a percentage of GDP, seven were in the MENA. Of the 20 countries with the lowest tax to GDP ratio, fully half were in the MENA. The only MENA countries with relatively high rates of taxation to GDP were Algeria, at 64.07% the world's highest, which is a very misleading artifact of its unique method of recording oil revenue, and Israel, at 36.8%, which placed it about equal to the OECD average of 34.5%. The only other two MENA countries in the top half of countries according to their tax/GDP ratio were Morocco and Jordan, reflecting the relatively well-developed extraction capacities of these two kingdoms, at least by MENA standards. Egypt was the only other MENA country not to fall into the lowest third of countries ranked according to the tax/GDP ratio.

An indirect measure of state capacity to tax is the relative efficiency of tax collection. According to the World Bank, "A good tax system should ensure that taxes are proportionate and certain (not arbitrary) and that the method of paying taxes is convenient to taxpayers. Lastly, taxes should be easy to administer and collect."[10] For the tax component of its Ease of Doing Business Index, the Bank focuses on the rate as a percentage of profits, as well as the relative difficulty and time taken to prepare, file and pay corporate, value added and labor taxes. The average rank out of 190 countries for the five small GCC countries in 2018 was just below 5, reflecting the fact that citizens of those countries basically are not taxed. These rentier states have focused on distribution, not extraction. Morocco ranked 25th. For the remainder of the MENA countries, however, the average ranking is much lower—about 120th. The lowest scorers were the republics with the largest populations— Algeria, Egypt, Iran, Iraq, Sudan and Tunisia, the average for which was just less than 160th. The relative efficiency of MENA taxation for the great majority of its citizens is thus in the bottom third of ranked countries. Taxation in Egypt exemplifies the broader situation. According to the World Bank's 2018 *Doing Business* report, Egyptian businesses must make 29 tax payments annually, which require on average 392 hours to file and pay, and of their profits, fully 45% are taken by taxes.[11] The Bank concludes from its taxation data that "Arab countries are among the least efficient tax collectors in the world."[12]

Finally, the relative proportion of the MENA population that can be subject to direct personal income taxes is small because of the remarkably low labor force participation rates in the MENA. Of the 20 countries globally with the lowest percentage of the population in work or looking for work, 12 are in the MENA. Of the ten countries with the world's lowest labor force participation rate, six—Jordan, Syria, Iraq, Algeria, Iran and Lebanon—are in the MENA.[13]

State Capacity: Fiscal Management

How states manage financial assets is another measure of their capacities. Such management involves not only direct governmental handling of macroeconomic tasks such as balancing budgets and ensuring appropriate interest and currency exchange rates, but also regulatory functions involving interactions with private actors, such as supervising the financial sector, preventing illicit financial flows, deterring corruption, and inducing formalization of business enterprises so as to minimize the size of shadow economies.

Special conditions in the MENA

The MENA confronts at least two unique challenges of fiscal management. One is the intensity and unpredictability of revenue cycles driven by fluctuations in hydrocarbon prices, further magnified by the uniquely large role of governments in economies.[14] Falling oil prices diminish state revenue, typically requiring reductions in public spending, which in turn militate against growth in non-oil sectors, reinforcing the downward economic spiral. Downward momentum is further reinforced by current account deficits necessitating drawdowns of capital reserves and, increasingly since 2014, accumulation of foreign debt. Domestic economic demand is also reduced by increased unemployment and associated reductions in household income. GCC countries, for example, experienced such a cycle driven by declining oil prices in the early 1980s, which lasted almost 20 years until dramatic increases in oil prices in the early twenty-first century restored domestic consumption to early 1980s levels. During this period Saudi Arabia racked up fiscal deficits 18 years in a row, which it covered primarily with domestic borrowing.[15]

A new cycle commenced in 2014 with the downturn in oil prices, which have yet to recover to even half the level reached prior to the decline. During this recent cycle international borrowing by many of the leading oil exporters, most notably Saudi Arabia, has intensified, thereby likely protracting both the length and the depth of the cycle as repayment of interest and capital will further reduce domestic demand. The only long-term remedy to recurrent fiscal cycles is reducing state reliance on hydrocarbon exports through economic diversification, a challenge which has since the 1990s received considerable lip-service among the MENA oil exporters. Only after 2014, however, were some reasonably substantial remedial actions taken, such as reductions of subsidies, introduction of new taxes, measures to encourage employment of nationals and discourage that of expatriates, investment in downstream oil and gas processing and utilization, and some encouragement of business start-ups in non-oil and gas sectors. Such measures may have slightly lessened immediate fiscal burdens on the oil exporting states, but have yet to be of such magnitude as to delink oil prices from fiscal cycles, as reflected in stagnating rates of economic growth and mounting foreign debts. Low rates of economic growth are due in part to cyclicality itself. The standard deviation of GCC growth was 7% from 1976 to 1990, falling to 4% until 2010, as compared to the much less cyclical OECD, where it is 2%. Private business in the GCC thus rides a financial roller coaster that drives big swings in profits, thereby complicating investment decision making, hence discouraging it. This volatility alone was found in 2013 to reduce growth by 0.3% in the GCC.[16]

Fiscal responsibility

Possibly the two most relevant indicators of fiscal responsibility are the budget deficit and public debt as a percentage of GDP. The Central Intelligence Agency's *World Factbook* for 2018 provides up-to-date statistics for both. Of the 19 MENA countries listed, including Israel, only four—the UAE, Turkey, Israel and Iran—had budget deficits that placed them in the lower half of the 222 listed countries, with Iran's being the highest deficit in that group at 2.3%. The other 15 MENA countries ranked among the half of countries with above average deficits, ranging from Morocco at 3.6% to Libya with 25.1%. The average deficit for all MENA countries was 7.9% of GDP, a figure almost four times the maximum deficit permitted in the EU, within which, in the Eurozone, the aggregate budget deficit in 2018 was a paltry 0.69%.[17]

Not surprisingly, with budget deficits of this magnitude MENA governments have accumulated substantial debt. Of the 21 MENA countries listed in the *World Factbook*, out of the total of 210 countries for which data is reported, nine were among the half of more heavily indebted countries, 12 among the half less indebted. The median level of debt was about 50% of GDP. While this breakdown seems to suggest that MENA countries as a whole are not heavily indebted, closer examination reveals that other than Turkey and the West Bank/Gaza, all the MENA countries with debts in the lower half of listed countries are oil exporters, including all the GCC countries, Iran, Algeria and Libya. The only significant oil exporter with public debt in the top half of countries is Iraq. All the rest of the listed MENA countries export minimal quantities of oil or none at all. They include Lebanon, the world's third most indebted country as a percentage of GDP, and relatively populous countries such as Egypt, Sudan, Yemen, Morocco and Syria. The median debt proportion of these countries is 88% of GDP. The working assumption in the IMF is that debt to GDP ratios in excess of 60% in developed and 40% in developing economies threaten fiscal sustainability.[18] Large and growing budget deficits and accumulating debt suggest that MENA state fiscal capacities are weak.

Dutch Disease

Another, related challenge to fiscal management in the MENA is coping with the Dutch Disease of overvalued currencies resulting primarily from oil and gas export revenues and secondarily from import dependence and the consequent desire by governments to reduce import costs in local currency terms. For the major oil exporters, the primary cause is the more important, whereas for MENA states less or not at all directly dependent on oil exports, the secondary cause of reducing import bills is the more vital. GCC currencies have traditionally been pegged to the US dollar, which has gradually undermined the competitiveness of their economies and is reaching the point that the peg will not be sustainable as revenues to support it are increasingly insufficient. Egypt, for example, which depends on imports for more than half the foodstuffs required to feed its population (which exceeded 100 million in 2018), goes through cycles of seeking desperately to peg its local currency to a basket of foreign hard currencies, then suddenly devaluing, dramatically increasing domestic inflation and interest rates and the costs of imports. Over the long haul, though, MENA currencies have been substantially overvalued, bringing short-term benefits principally in the form of enhanced consumption of cheaper imported goods, at the expense of long-term economic growth of the sort East Asia experienced in part because that region purposely undervalued national currencies. Hydrocarbon dependence, in sum, has intensified the challenge of fiscal management for the MENA, a challenge which has grown in magnitude since the 1970s and has yet to be met.

Recurrent vs capital expenditures

Other challenges of fiscal management are not so unique to the MENA as are those related to dependence on hydrocarbon exports, but the region does not deal with them as well as comparator regions do. All states not only determine how to spend their revenues, but also influence credit allocations by financial institutions. In both cases MENA states make poor investment decisions.

As for state expenditures, the share of recurrent ones has been steadily rising as the portion of capital investment has been dropping in most MENA states since about the beginning of the twenty-first century. During the second oil boom that lasted from then until 2014, government spending was increasingly devoted to wages, subsidies, education and health, a tendency that was accelerated in response to the Arab Spring of 2011 that saw most governments seek to mollify their populations by employing more of them, paying higher salaries, and providing handouts of various sorts, including subsidized food, energy and housing. Saudi Arabia alone spent $130 billion in 2012 for such purposes. These recurrent expenditures reduce budget flexibility and in most MENA countries now account for between two thirds and fourth fifths of budgets, thus dramatically shrinking public investment.[19]

Egypt's recent budgetary history exemplifies the larger picture. Public investment decreased from 13.9% of total expenditures in 2003/4 to only 6.5% in 2015/16. By contrast, the ratio of recurrent to capital expenditure in Vietnam has for several years been 70/30, causing the World Bank to caution the country about overly generous salaries to civil servants that were in turn reducing the level of investment.[20] To make matters yet worse for Egypt, it has increased its borrowing to cover recurrent, not capital expenditures, thereby rendering debt servicing all the more difficult. The budget deficit climbed from 9.8% of GDP in 2010 to 11.5% in 2015 and over 12%

thereafter, increasing public debt from 82% to over 100% of GDP by the end of 2017, of which a steadily greater proportion was in foreign currencies, thereby substantially increasing the financial burden if the value of the Egyptian pound falls in relation to them. Heavy borrowing in turn drove interest rates up so that by that by 2018, at more than 20% for local currency debts and an average of almost 8% for dollar and euro denominated bonds, they were absorbing over a third of budgetary expenditures, with subsidies claiming almost another third and civil service wages about the same, leaving a small fraction of the budget for all other expenditures.[21] Egypt, like many other MENA countries, has been living beyond its means for many years, as is reflected in its increasingly parlous fiscal position.

Budgetary process

Fiscal imbalances result from both policy choices and capacity limitations, to say nothing of the challenges faced by MENA countries in dealing with accentuated cyclicality and overvalued currencies. The common policy of MENA elites has been to substitute social contracts for political participation. Those contracts, now fraying due to too much population and too little productivity growth, have required increasing proportions of budgetary expenditures. But even if elites were to recognize the negative economic consequences of their politically driven budgetary choices, difficulties of budgetary formation would remain.

Again, Egypt provides abundant evidence of relevant capacity weaknesses, the key ones being a lack of fiscal rules regarding public expenditure and budget deficits; no legal restraints on borrowing for current spending; and what amounts to a dualistic budgetary system in which the accounts of some 700 governmental units are not included in the national budget, thereby ensuring not only a lack of transparency for a significant proportion of public revenues, but administrative malfunction. All of those some 700 budget authorities prepare their own budgets in collaboration with the Ministry of Finance, leading to "fiscal fragmentation and inefficient use of public resources." Addressing capacity shortcomings of the budgetary process in Egypt would require a host of reforms to "the budget institutions to improve the structures, rules and procedures that govern the formulation, approval, and execution of government budgets."[22] Since opacity of the budgetary process serves the interests of those within and exercising power over the relevant governmental

119

institutions, fundamental reforms of this nature are continually postponed.

That Egypt is not alone among MENA countries in having a less than transparent budgetary process is indicated by the region's standing on the Open Budget Index. This assigns 102 countries a transparency score on a 100-point scale using questions that assess the amount and timeliness of budget information that governments make publicly available. Each country is given a score between 0 and 100 that determines its ranking. In the most recent version, 2017, of MENA countries only Jordan was credited with having "substantial information available."[23] Turkey, Morocco and Egypt had "limited information available," Tunisia had "minimal information available," while Algeria, Iraq, Lebanon, Sudan, Saudi Arabia, Qatar and Yemen "had scant or no information available." Only two of 11 MENA countries scored in the top half of the index, while seven of the 13 lowest performers were MENA countries. The average score of those seven countries was 1.7, whereas the average of the top 13 performers was just over 80. Only Sub-Saharan African countries score as poorly as MENA ones. Given the strong correlation between transparent budget information and GDP per capita, which in the MENA at $7,350 is almost five times that of Sub-Saharan Africa's of $1,550, MENA countries have remarkably opaque budgetary processes given their relative wealth.[24]

Credit allocation

The state's fiscal capacity can also be measured by how it impacts the allocation of credit. Heavily indebted states borrow from their nations' banks, among other lenders, thus crowding out potential private borrowers. In Lebanon, for example, the government sucks up two thirds of all bank credit, primarily in order to sustain the overvalued local currency. Crowding out of private borrowers is aggravated in limited access orders by states steering credit to insiders. Cronies in all MENA countries in which the phenomenon has been studied capture a disproportionate amount of credit, typically leaving small and medium-sized enterprises to rely on profits and personal savings to finance their operations.

Credit is an important stimulant to growth, so long as it is allocated appropriately. There is a strong positive correlation between credit to the private sector as a percentage of GDP, on the one hand, and GDP per capita and GDP growth rates, on the other. In OECD countries, for example, private sectors receive credit equivalent to 145% of GDP. In East Asia the proportion is 143%, whereas in Sub-Saharan Africa it is 32% and in the next lowest region, Latin America and the Caribbean, it is 49%. Those are the only two global regions in which the private sector receives less credit proportionately than in the Arab World, where it is 58%, or in the MENA, where it is 63%.[25] In low and middle-income countries as a whole it is 105%, suggesting how significantly the Arab World and the MENA are underperforming by this measure of fiscal capacity. The private sector's share of credit in Yemen is 5%, in Sudan 7%, in Iraq 9%, in Libya 17%, in Algeria 24% and in Egypt 28%, all below the Sub-Saharan African mean and on average less than one fifth of the level prevailing in low and middle-income countries.

As for crony capture of bank credit, Ishac Diwan and his colleagues have investigated that topic in several Arab countries. In Egypt, for example, he and Marc Schiffbauer found that by the end of the Mubarak era politically connected firms had captured 92% of the loans held by private firms listed in the country's main commercial register.[26] The impact of political connections on credit misallocation is heightened by discrimination against start-ups and other younger firms. The World Bank notes that in Egypt, "capital in the industrial sector is misallocated towards a few large old firms ... reallocating capital from large to smaller industrial establishments would raise aggregate productivity in Egypt."[27] A major World Bank report on inadequate job creation in the MENA identifies various constraints on the growth of micro, small and medium firms, of which inadequate credit for them is one of the most important.[28]

Small and medium-sized firms throughout the MENA find it difficult to obtain finance for several interrelated reasons. Banks are ill equipped to evaluate private credit risks in general, and those pertaining to individuals and small businesses in particular. Among the reasons for that is the comparatively short paper trail left by most citizens, itself an indicator of the low level of state infrastructural power. Less than 10% of employed Egyptians, for example, file income tax returns, so knowledge of a third party's financial situation is necessarily limited not only for the state, but also for private actors seeking to enter contractual relations with one another, including borrowing and lending money. A related cause of the reluctance to extend credit is the difficulty of enforcing contracts in general, those pertaining to loans in particular, and even more so those extended to informal enterprises, which constitute the overwhelming majority of small firms in most MENA countries. Financial institutions typically require comparatively valuable collateral to secure loans, or demand from debtors post-dated checks. These constraints on financial interactions, which reflect the state's inadequate infrastructural power, are compounded for small and medium businesses by the need for connections into the limited access order, which by virtue of their small size they lack virtually by definition. The World Bank's regular Ease of Doing Business surveys report access to credit as a problem facing many MENA businesses, but since those surveys tend to focus on medium and large firms, they do not reveal the magnitude of the challenge facing smaller businesses in obtaining credit.

To address this deficiency two surveys have recently been conducted in various Arab countries of owners of micro, small and medium-sized firms in an attempt to assess their special problems.[29] They found that micro and small enterprises—defined as having less than four or ten employees depending on the country, and which constitute between 89% and 98% of all firms in Jordan, Egypt, Tunisia and Morocco—faced what their owners described as virtually insurmountable challenges in obtaining financing, with only 6% of them in Egypt and 8.5% of them in Jordan able to do so, despite accounting for 76% of credit applications.[30] No other problem plagued their business to such a degree. In Egypt and Tunisia another survey reported that far and away the main source of financing for nascent, micro and small enterprises was self-financing through savings and profits. The survey reported in both countries the counter-intuitive finding that small size is a greater barrier to firms obtaining credit than is their informality.[31] The survey also revealed that obtaining capital from investors through "venture capital or stock issuance," rather than banks, was about as difficult for small and medium businesses; 10% of business respondents in Egypt resorted to either of these two methods, while in Tunisia 7% raised funds in the stock market. In the MENA as a whole, the share of loans extended to small and medium enterprises is between 8% and 10% of total credit, depending on the purpose, while in Brazil it is 14%, Croatia 18%, Bangladesh 20% and Ecuador 24%.[32]

Given the difficulties small and even medium-sized firms in the MENA encounter in raising capital, to say nothing of various other hurdles, it is hardly surprising that the vast majority fail to grow. According to the World Bank, micro firms in the MENA with fewer than ten employees "almost never enter larger size categories." In the period from 2007 to 2011 in Tunisia, for example, of all one-person firms 22% exited, 76% remained one-person firms and only 2% hired at least one more worker. The probability that non-farm firms will grow from less to more than ten employees in five years is a low of 2% in Gaza and the West Bank and a high of 12% in Lebanon.[33]

Aggregate measures of fiscal management

Estimations of states' fiscal management capacities are provided by two aggregated indices. The Natural Resource Governance Institute's Resource Governance Index ranks 81 countries that together produce 82% of the world's oil and 78% of its gas on the quality of their resource governance along the dimensions of revenue management, value realization and enabling environment.[34] In the bottom of five categories—"failing"—are ten states, two of which are in the MENA—Libya and Sudan. In the next to the bottom category of "poor" resource governance are 29 states, nine of which are in the MENA. Only three MENA states are among the 14 that rank within the middle category, "weak," and none do better than that. As for the revenue management index that comprises one third of the overall resource governance index, the MENA country average is 34, the lowest of its scores on the three sub-indices. The Institute also assesses the governance of both state-owned enterprises (SOEs) involved in natural resource production and sovereign wealth funds (SWFs) that receive their revenues from them. Of the 74 ranked SOEs, the 15 in the MENA have a median rank of 52, placing the majority just above the bottom quarter performers. Fully a third of MENA SOEs were assessed as having "failing" governance, while the median governance performance was "poor." As for SWF governance performance, 33 were ranked, including ten from the MENA. The median ranking was 25, placing the majority of MENA SWFs in the bottom third of the rankings. Seven of the ten were ranked as having either "failing" or "poor" governance, including the very largest of them, located in Qatar, the UAE, Saudi Arabia, Algeria and Libya. So, in the MENA's most vital sector, that of oil and gas, financial management capacity is particularly deficient, in significant measure because of its remarkable lack of transparency, as noted by the compilers of the Resource Governance Index.[35]

The other relevant aggregated index that reflects state fiscal capacities is that provided by the Bertelsmann Foundation.[36] Its "Transformation Index" is comprised of political and economic transformation (to democratic market capitalism) indices, which are made up of a total of 12 sub-dimensions, many of which provide indications of state capacities. The index lists 19 MENA countries, of which only five score in the top half of the rankings of 129 countries. The median rank is 90, so the average MENA country is in the bottom third of listed countries. Within the ten bottom scores on the index are Iran, Libya, Sudan, Yemen and Syria. The most recent Bertelsmann Index, for 2016, suggests that the probability of a broad transformation of MENA political economies into democratic capitalism is extremely low. That conclusion is reinforced if the first iteration of the index, conducted in 2006, is compared to that completed a decade later. Over that ten-year period, 11 of the 16 MENA countries ranked in both fell in the rankings, while only four improved, with one, Jordan, remaining unchanged. All of the big MENA republics, with the exceptions of Iraq and Algeria, fell in the rankings, indicating that the majority of citizens of the region experienced deterioration in their prospects for political and economic transitions away from economically underperforming authoritarian states.

State Capacity: Supervising the Financial Sector

Credit to the private sector was assessed in the preceding section because governments in the MENA exert strong direct and indirect pressures over credit allocations, in part because of their total or partial ownership of banks, and in part because of their interest rate policies. In this section state regulatory capacities will be assessed. Together these state functions direct the flow of capital into and from financial sectors, serving as the brains of national economies by determining shares of capital lifeblood. This was a key organizing device of East Asian developmental states, which purposely steered financial credit to chosen sectors and even private actors within those sectors in order to stimulate production and exports.

The three principal sources of business investment capital in most economies are banks, equity markets and corporate bonds. Banks provide the overwhelming share of capital in the MENA, as equity markets are comparatively small and private bond issues uncommon. Although there are several reasons for bank predominance—including the desire of elites to preserve control over credit allocation, which is more difficult with freely traded stocks and bonds, as well as the pronounced role of family-owned businesses which abhor sharing information or control with non-family members—what concerns us here is the impact of the financial regulatory structure. In a word, it has to be of sufficient capacity and objectivity to instill trust in investors. As the Turkish academic Nihal Bayraktar notes, "it is notable that both the significance and the magnitude of the impact of institutional and governance quality indexes on market capitalization are very strong. This outcome indicates that countries with better institutional quality can potentially develop their stock markets with fewer burdens on the economy."[37]

Equity markets

Results in the MENA speak for themselves in that regulatory quality has been insufficient to develop adequate trust in equity markets, so they remain underdeveloped by global standards, thereby depriving MENA businesses of a potentially important source of capital. Moreover, MENA markets are not growing. Market capitalization in the MENA amounted to 53% of the region's GDP in 2009, but only 52% in 2017. The Egyptian market fell in that period from a capitalization to GDP ratio of 48% to 20%, Jordan's from 134% to 60%, and Saudi Arabia's from 74% to 66%. During that same period global stock market capitalization grew from 83% of the world's GDP to 112%, East Asia's from 92% to 111%, while South Asia's remained flat at 83% for those eight years.[38] The gap between the MENA and much of the rest of the world in stock market capitalization is yet greater if one compares not total market capitalization, but stocks traded as a percentage of GDP. This is because the turnover rates in most MENA markets are low. Companies frequently list their shares for reputational, rather than capital purposes, having no intent to sell large numbers or proportions of shares. By the measure of stocks traded as a percentage of GDP, the MENA fell from 34% in 2009 to a paltry 15% in 2017, a period during which global share trading remained constant at 117% of GDP, while that in both low and middle-income countries rose from 77% to 82%.[39] The lack of activity on typical MENA exchanges is reflected in the very low value of stocks traded as a percentage of GDP on, say, the Bahrain exchange at 5%, the Iranian exchange at 3%, or the Lebanese exchange at 2%. Only the exchanges in Saudi Arabia, the UAE, Kuwait and Turkey managed to exceed 20%. In the US, turnover as a percentage of GDP is 176%, while in South Korea it is 110% and in Malaysia 67%.[40]

One of the regulatory deficiencies regarding MENA equity markets is direct governmental intervention into them, typically in the form of driving up total valuation as a surrogate indicator of confidence in the government itself. The Saudi government, for example, which has long been a major purchaser of shares on Tadawul, the national exchange, commenced the practice in 2016 of aggressively countering negative impacts of unfavorable news on stock valuations by secretly purchasing large blocs of shares. It has routed these purchases through third parties, including asset managers at Saudi banks which are not required to reveal the identity of their clients. The news reports to which it has responded with such purchases include those about the economic consequences of the blockade of Qatar, the detention of the Lebanese Prime Minister, and the killing of Saudi journalist Jamal Khashoggi in Istanbul, presumably on the orders of the Crown Prince. As one government spokesperson replied to journalists investigating governmental purchases, "We need to highlight to the world that Saudi investment is good." While China and other countries engage in this practice in part to attract foreign investors, only about 4% of the stocks listed on Tadawul are owned by non-Saudis. But as Antoine van Agtmael, who coined the term "emerging market" almost 40 years ago, observed, government manipulation makes the Saudi stock exchange "more of a fake market, and that kind of undermines the trust of investors in the long run."[41] In the run up to being included among emerging-market indices in 2019, the Saudi government was especially keen to make the market attractive, a motive that accounts in large measure for the Tadawul being up almost 10% over the year ending in December 2018, compared to the MSCI All Country World Index which fell by some 5.5% over that period. Using funds from its Public Investment Fund, the country's sovereign wealth fund, by the end of 2018 the Saudi government had come officially to own some 40% of shares traded on the exchange, but substantially more in reality.[42] In addition to making potential investors wary of a market dominated by a single purchaser driven by political rather than economic imperatives and subject to the whims of a single person, the use of PIF monies to purchase shares deprives it of the capital to invest in the major projects that have been bally-hooed as driving employment and the economy more generally in the years ahead.[43]

As for private bonds, they account for a very small percentage of MENA business capital, as elsewhere in the developing world. In lower middle-income countries their share of GDP is about 5%, while for upper-middle-income countries it is just above 10%.[44] Regulation of markets for both stocks and bonds in the MENA remains too weak to instill sufficient confidence to attract large proportions of the region's investment capital.

Financial inclusion

Banking regulation tends to be of higher quality than that of stock and bond markets in the MENA, but that central core of the financial sector also has some, if varying, difficulty in attracting private capital, as evidenced by the comparatively low ratio of bank account holders among populations as well as low national contract intensive money ratios. According to the World Bank, "For the third consecutive update (2011, 2014, 2017) the Global Findex Survey found that the MENA region has the lowest financial inclusion in the world." In the developing world as a whole, 63% of adults have bank accounts, as compared to only 52% of men and 35% of women in the MENA; 145 million of the region's 250 million adults are thus unbanked. This deficiency cannot be explained by the growth of electronic banking. Mobile money account ownership in the MENA is 7% despite the fact that 80% of the unbanked have cell phones. In 2017 one third of adults in the MENA made or received digital payments, compared to 44% of adults in other developing countries. Cash on delivery accounts for 51% of even e-commerce purchases.[45]

So just as regards stock and bond markets, MENA citizens are comparatively reluctant to trust banks with their money. The manifest lack of trust in financial institutions reflects poorly on MENA states' fiscal management and regulation. Sudden, dramatic currency devaluations, widely fluctuating interest and inflation rates, imposition of new taxes with little debate, and inadequate guarantees for depositors are some of the manifestations of deficient fiscal management and regulation that retard the growth of the financial sector. This in turn reflects the shortcomings of state capacity when it rests more on despotic than infrastructural power, the latter of which is the product of state–society interactions that over time generate trust in institutions, including financial ones.

Relative national rates of so-called contract intensive money (CIM) reflect trust in the banking system so, along with bank account density, provide another indicator of infrastructural power. As Lewis Snider explains, "Where institutions are highly informal, i.e., where contract enforcement and security of property rights are inadequate, and the policy environment is uncertain, transactions will generally be self-enforcing and currency will be the only money that is widely used."[46] The proportion of money that passes through official banking systems in different MENA countries, their so-called "CIM ratios," reflects the degree to which they enforce contracts and secure

127

property, with the lowest ratios in Iraq, Syria, Sudan, Yemen and Algeria, and the highest in the GCC countries, Lebanon and Israel.[47] So in much of the MENA cash is king rather than credit cards or other modes of transaction, further reflecting the region's limited infrastructural power.

Islamic finance

A final concern about MENA state supervision of financial sectors is the emergence of so-called "Islamic finance," the key definitional element of which is interest-free financing, which in turn requires various workarounds to factor in the cost of money over time. From the 1960s three types of Islamic finance have developed. The initial one was at its core intended as Muslim, self-help development financing, designed primarily to assist the rural poor. Some of its ideas and practices were then picked up by two other strains, one of which was intended as the financial adjunct to the Islamist movement, mobilizing capital primarily for Islamist activities and their supporters. The other was what might be thought of as "establishment" Islamic finance, meaning Islamic financial practices adopted by states and private financial institutions. From the 1980s an increasing number of MENA states found Islamic financial instruments, key of which were "sukuk," a form of Islamic bonds, convenient tools with which to raise funds. Private financial institutions similarly discovered that the very label "Islamic" would attract customers keen to have their financial behavior appear to comply with Quranic prescriptions, although, other than the prohibition of interest, there is little about Islamic finance in the Quran. The precepts and practices of Islamic finance were developed from the 1970s onwards based on retrospective interpretations of medieval financial practices in the Middle East. Eventually the development-focused Islamic finance faltered, while that associated with Islamist political movements was extirpated by regimes fearful of it. This left establishment Islamic finance to absorb and use the capital of believers attracted by the idea of applying their beliefs in the real world.

The dramatic growth of this third form has posed major regulatory challenges to all countries in which Islamic finance has flourished, of which those in the MENA and especially the Gulf are most notable. As both states and private institutions began to deal in the billions of dollars with sukuk and other forms of Islamic financing, such as that of mortgages and consumer credit, so did it give rise to problems with both the definition of the term "Islamic" and the appropriate operationalization of it. Possibly of greatest importance was the question of how the burden of financial loss should be borne, since interest in Islamic financing is replaced by risk sharing. This was not an issue so long as those utilizing these instruments did not incur losses, which has been more or less the case with states and the large Islamic banks. But it is less the case with non-financial private parties, including businesses, many of which have issued sukuk. One such firm, for example, Dana Gas, an Abu Dhabi listed gas exploration business, sought in 2017 to default on a $700 million sukuk issue dating to 2013. It argued it had received legal advice that the bonds were no longer deemed compliant with *sharia*. It was seeking to have them declared invalid in a court in the UAE and in the English High Court, and replaced with new sukuk bearing less than half the rate of return of the replaced ones. Following half a year of litigation the English court issued a decision against Dana Gas, ordering it to pay its UK creditors, a ruling that induced Dana Gas to commence negotiations with all sukuk holders on terms more favorable to them.[48] It thus took a court in the UK to adjudicate what in essence was a MENA issue and one that threatened the viability of the sukuk industry, which by that time was worth in excess of $400 billion, with Islamic banking assets accounting for more than 15% of total bank assets in the MENA. The rating firm Moody's noted that the very lodging of the case would "diminish the liquidity and growth of the sukuk market."[49] In sum, MENA states sat by as Islamic finance took off, themselves seeking to take advantage of it rather than to properly regulate it. Ultimately the ambiguities and possibly even contradictions involved in Islamic finance have brought much of the enterprise into question, with potentially serious ramifications for both public and private finance in the region.

State Capacity: Stemming Illicit Financial Flows, Deterring Corruption and Shrinking Shadow Economies

Illicit financial flows

Effective fiscal control necessarily involves preventing illegal cross-border flows of funds, deterring corruption more broadly, and seeking to reduce if not eliminate shadow economies, meaning unregistered, unlicensed activities that thus fall outside the scope of the state's administrative systems, including taxation, regulation, certification, etc. As for illicit financial flows, Global Financial Integrity tracked them for developing and emerging economies from 2005 to 2014, discovering that during that period roughly $1 trillion annually flowed out of those economies "due to crime, corruption, and tax evasion—more than these countries receive in foreign direct investment and foreign aid combined."[50] The 14 MENA countries assessed averaged annual illicit flows of some $2.25 billion, a relatively small portion of the total but reasonably significant for most of the national MENA economies concerned. Iran and Iraq, for example, during that period averaged outflows of about $8.5 billion each, and Egypt about half that amount, in its case almost double the $2.5 billion of public foreign assistance it received in 2015.[51] Given that these and many other of the listed MENA countries have extensive currency and banking controls, their inability to stem the outward flow of capital suggests complicity, which would be consistent with the interests of those in limited access orders.

Corruption

Transparency International introduces its most recent Corruption Perception Index report on the Arab world as follows: "In a region stricken by violent conflicts and dictatorships, corruption remains endemic in the Arab states while assaults on freedom of expression, press freedoms and civil society continue to escalate. In this environment, it is no surprise that 19 of 21 Arab states score below 50 in the Corruption Perceptions Index 2017, which captures levels of corruption in the public sector."[52] The three non-Arab MENA states—Israel, Turkey and Iran—also did not score well as a group, their scores being 62, 40 and 30, respectively, for ranks of 32nd, 81st and 130th, respectively. Four GCC countries as well as Jordan and Tunisia ranked within the upper half of the index, with all the other MENA states other than Israel in the bottom half. Among the 11 countries perceived to be the world's most corrupt, five are in the MENA—Iraq, Libya, Sudan, Yemen and Syria. The World Bank's "Control of Corruption" governance indicator reports similar findings. The MENA's rank has steadily deteriorated over the past decade, from 47, to 45, to 43 from 2007 through 2012 to 2017.[53] Only two of the world's regions, South Asia and Sub-Saharan Africa, scored lower over those years.

Informality

The term "shadow economies" is used interchangeably with "informal economies." Both refer to activities, key of which are housing and work, that fall outside of formal regulation and recording by the state. The proportion of the total of such activities that are "extra-state" provides a good indication of not only a state's overall capacity, but especially of its infrastructural power because that proportion is determined by interactions between citizens and their government. Residents may choose to live in informal housing, meaning that built on land to which they do not have formal title, or work in an informal business, meaning one not officially registered nor paying social security or taxes, because it is cheaper, avoids cumbersome regulations, or because they have no alternatives. For its part the state may seek to compel formalization in order to regulate and extract more taxes, or it may turn a blind eye to informality, knowing that it lacks the capacity to force formalization or indeed even the desire since it is unable to provide sufficient housing or employment and therefore leaves such tasks to be performed on a self-help basis by citizens. So the placement of states on the formal–informal continuum reveals the intensity and breadth of interactions with their citizens—their infrastructural power.

There is a strong, positive correlation between level of economic development, as measured, say, by GDP per capita, and formality. The economies of poorer countries are characterized by much higher proportions of informalism and the poor within them are more likely to live and work in informal contexts than the wealthy. Although economists dispute the costs and benefits of shadow economies, with many arguing that in their absence poor countries would have less housing and employment because their states lack the capacities to meet those needs, virtually all the relevant data indicate that informalism comes with substantial costs to quality, security, productivity, investment, innovation and so on. Hernando de Soto, a Peruvian economist, has argued that formalization alone would free up substantial capital for the poor because the assets they control could then be used as collateral.[54] Efforts to formalize MENA economies based on the Peruvian model de Soto pioneered have not, however, enjoyed much success, suggesting that a minimum of state capacity may be necessary for formalization to proceed. In major urban centers in Egypt, for example, as much as three quarters of new housing is estimated to be informal, suggesting that the government

131

turns a blind eye to land encroachments for that purpose. Otherwise the housing crisis would be much worse.

The World Bank and the IMF have devoted substantial resources to both studying shadow economies and seeking to bring them into the sunlight of officialdom.[55] Results in the MENA have been discouraging, as suggested by the World Bank's 2014 conclusion that "informality in the MENA has been rising in recent years."[56] According to the Schneider Index, which measures informality on the basis of the share of production not declared to the tax or regulatory authorities, the annual growth rate of informality in the MENA is surpassed only in two regions, Latin America/Caribbean and Europe/Central Asia. But on the basis of firms commencing business informally, the MENA has the world's highest share, more than double that in either of those two regions.[57] Moreover, informal firms remain as such for longer than in any other region, including those two. Finally, mobility from informal to formal jobs is "extremely limited," with an informal worker in Egypt, for example, having a 4% chance of so doing.[58] Informality in the MENA overall, "involves the vast majority of workers outside of the public sector." It is only because MENA public sectors absorb the world's leading proportions of labor forces that gross comparative rates of informal employment between that region and the rest of the world place the MENA at about the mid-level of informalism in the developing world. The IMF's estimate of the comparative prevalence of shadow economies, which it defines as "all economic activities which are hidden from official authorities for monetary, regulatory, and institutional reasons,"[59] places the MENA's total shadow economy, which is about one quarter of the entire economy, as less pervasive than in South Asia, Sub-Saharan Africa or Latin America/Caribbean. It is about double the proportion of the shadow economy in OECD countries.[60] But the relatively small proportion of GCC economies that are informal distorts the broader MENA picture. Non-GCC MENA economies ranked by the IMF, including Egypt, Algeria, Lebanon, Libya, Morocco, Tunisia and Turkey, have on average economies characterized by being one third informal, slightly above the average of some 31% for 158 countries ranked.[61]

The World Bank's explanation of high and rising proportions of informal employment in the MENA is that it "displays lower employment and higher unemployment rates than any other region in the world." This results from high population growth rates and job creation being limited mainly to "low value-added service sectors, most of which are associated with high rates of informal employment." As a result, a "typical country in the MENA produces about one-third of its GDP and employs about 65% of its labor force informally."[62] The consequence is that two-thirds of those in the MENA private labor force do not have pensions and about one third of total economic output is undeclared, hence untaxed.

Another manifestation of informality that bears on national accounts is the relatively low level of written business contracts. The survey mentioned above of Tunisian and Egyptian small and medium enterprises found that only 20% of businesspersons in the former and 14% in the latter always used formal contracts when engaging in business transactions. The primary reason given by two thirds of respondents for avoiding written contracts was that they believed they would not be able to enforce them, with younger businesspersons being more doubtful than older ones of effective rule of law governing contract enforcement. Those conducting the survey concluded that "entrepreneurs may actually want to use formal contracts, but they cannot afford the risk and cost of weak rule of law," an observation reinforced by the finding that respondents who operated formal businesses reported being "more exposed to corruption and extortion than those operating in the informal sector."[63]

MENA state capacity is insufficient to shrink shadow economies or even to prevent their growth. Unable to provide the housing, jobs and contractual enforcement their citizens need, MENA states seem to be purposely permitting informal arrangements to fill those gaps. But the more they step back from these economic activities, the less they interact with citizens in mutually beneficial ways, thus undermining their already tenuous infrastructural power. Its decline is manifested in reduced extraction and regulation, inadequate business and human resource development, and inefficient business and commercial transactions due to deficiencies of contract enforcement against the backdrop of weak rule of law.

8

THE MENA: REGIONALIZED
BUT NOT INTEGRATED

The MENA's paradox is that it leads the world in regionalization but trails it in regionalism. Its peoples, in other words, interact across national borders socially and politically more than those of other developing regions. According to Giacomo Luciani, "major political developments take place at the regional rather than at the single-state level."[1] But as is the case with its states, the MENA's regional institutions are remarkably weak. Its modern history is littered with failed state-led attempts to create political unions, regional economic integration associations and socio-political organizations such as professional and business associations. Its economic elites have similarly failed to create integrated regional businesses on anything like the scale of those in East Asia, the broader Pacific Region, Europe, or North America.

By contrast, from the bottom up Middle Easterners have forged transnational movements based in pan-Arabism and pan-Islamism, while their nation states have meddled incessantly in the affairs of neighboring countries. "The basic puzzle of the region," according to Matteo Legrenzi and Cilja Harders, is why, given the "geographic proximity, the relatively high degree of social, cultural and religious homogeneity as well as political, economic and military interaction," there is such a "low degree of institutional regional cooperation, let alone integration."[2] Leon Carl Brown's classic study of the international relations of the MENA suggests that answers to this puzzle are to be found in its external and internal relations as well as in its special characteristics. He noted that the Middle East is "a penetrated system, one subject to an exceptional level of external intervention and yet, by virtue of its cultural distinctiveness, is stubbornly resistant to subordination."[3] This subsystem of international relations is "characterized by frequent shifts in alliances, heavy penetration of the system by outside powers, a zero-sum logic and an overall trend towards 'homeostasis,' featuring the inability of any regional player to substantially modify the existing balance of power."[4]

Since the Ottoman Empire's ultimately fatal weakening commenced at the end of the eighteenth century, the MENA has been swept by successive waves of unification attempts, instigated by regional states seeking unsuccessfully to emulate Prussia by imposing union, by movements swelling up from popular bases, and by various combinations of the two. All have failed, in large measure due to opposition from external powers driven by fears either of setting precedents for redrawing colonial-era boundaries or of strong MENA states becoming yet stronger by devouring weaker ones, as they did in Europe. Egypt's Muhammad Ali's efforts in the 1820s and 1830s to bring key Arab areas of the weakening Ottoman Empire under Cairo's control might have succeeded had European powers, led by the British, not decided to prop up the "sick man of Europe" lest Egypt become the core of a larger, powerful Arab successor state. The "Arab Revolt" that broke out during WWI, in which "Lawrence of Arabia" is reputed to have played a key role, sought to create a unified Arab kingdom driven by emerging Arab identity coupled with the territorial ambitions of Sharif Husayn of Mecca and his sons. When Turkey's Ataturk dissolved the Islamic Caliphate in 1924, Egypt's King Fuad toyed with the idea of resuscitating it under his tutelage, primarily as an effort to extend Cairo's influence throughout the MENA. Egypt's Nasser competed with Ba'th Party leaders in Syria and Iraq in the heyday of Pan-Arabism in the 1950s and 1960s to lead that movement and bring it under the control of their respective capitals. Since the formation of the Gulf Cooperation Council (GCC) in 1981 by the six Arab states of the Gulf, that once most effective and enduring of structural efforts to unite Arab countries has not only itself fragmented, but its internal divisions have driven fault lines through the broader Arab world.

The pendular swings between Islamism and Arabism as primary identities and motivational forces for unification have vacillated for more than a century. Islamic reformism beginning in the late nineteenth century as championed by such figures as Gamal al Din al Afghani, Muhammad Abduh and Rashid Rida, was then eclipsed by the competing appeal of Arabism, largely because it was the ideology of choice of partially secularized army officers who seized power in several newly independent states. Their efforts to enhance personal and national appeals by linking them to Arabism were paralleled by

135

the mutation of Islamic reformism into political Islam in the form of the Muslim Brotherhood, which from its base in Egypt began to construct a region-wide movement to Islamicize societies, economies and polities under its guidance. As the twentieth century progressed, the bipolar ideological cum identity struggle between Arabism and Islamism became a three-way contest as nation-state loyalties gained more traction. The twenty-first century has witnessed the partial eclipse of Arab identity in favor of state-based nationalism and Islamism, the latter of which has embarked on renewed unification efforts, the most ambitious of which has been that by the so-called Islamic State, known in Arabic as Da'ish, which in 2014 declared the recreation of a Caliphate based in Iraq and Syria. As this cursory overview of failed unification efforts over more than two centuries suggests, this is an urge that mutates but does not disappear, despite seeming destined never to be fulfilled.

The persistence of shared, region-wide identities among Arabs and their present configurations are reflected in answers in response to a question in the 2016 fourth "wave" of the Arab Barometer Survey, which asked respondents to indicate that with which they most identified: country of birth, religion, Arabism, region, local community, tribe/extended family or other. More than half chose as their primary identity one other than state nationalism, the largest share at 28% identifying with the Muslim or Christian religions. Four percent identified as Arabs and 13% with their local community, tribe or extended family.[5] Other survey data as reviewed in the 2016 Arab Human Development Report do not report such low levels of Arab identification, but do confirm that over the last generation state-based nationalisms and religious identities have grown.[6] Data from numerous WVS and Pew Global Attitude surveys have consistently reported that the MENA's people are the world's most religious.[7] The Arab Opinion Index issued by the Arab Center for Research and Policy Studies reports that 79% of respondents to its 2015 survey in 12 Arab countries "expressed views supportive of the unity of the Arab nation," with 37% supporting the statement that "the Arab peoples are one nation, divided by artificial boundaries" while a further 42% supported the statement that the Arab peoples form "one nation, but each of the peoples within that nation has its own distinct characteristics." Seventy-five percent of respondents expressed the belief that the Palestinian cause is not solely a Palestinian issue, but also an Arab one.[8]

In sum, the region's states face the continuing challenge of inducing their citizens to answer the "who am I" question by saying they are

Algerian, Tunisian, Egyptian and so on, rather than by indicating their primary identification is at the supra- or sub-state level. The contemporary MENA thus remains afflicted by the paradox of regionalization without regionalism as the former has never provided sufficient or appropriate impetus for the latter. Today's regionalization is driven by economic factors and technology that directly impact the region's citizens, rendering them aware of one another and their shared values, interests and problems. By contrast, regionalism is undermined by intensifying competition between MENA states and sub-state actors, heightened by deepening identity divides, principally along religious and ethno-sectarian lines. The ideological, practical and intermittently powerful forces of regionalization swelling up from below are too weak and divided to provide bases for institutionalized regional integration, while MENA states are being sucked into an intensifying civil war that is destroying hopes for effective regionwide political and economic institutions. Regionalization without regionalism, now more than two centuries old, looks set to continue.

Regionalization: Too Little and Too Much

While regionalization is strong enough to provide competition for national identities, to fuel trans-regional political movements and to justify interference by the region's states in neighboring countries, it is neither so strong nor gathering such momentum that it is about to overwhelm existing states. As IS forces were sweeping through Syria and Iraq in 2015, for example, the Arab Opinion Survey reported that 89% of its respondents in 12 Arab countries had a negative view of the organization.[9]

The "al Jazeera effect"—which refers to the impact that the pan-Arab, Qatari-based satellite television broadcasting station had on the Arab world when from 1996 it pioneered region-wide news coverage that previously had been dominated by national broadcasters—is losing its strength for four inter-related reasons. First, emulators have arisen with support from various governments, most notably those in Saudi Arabia and the United Arab Emirates, that blunt the quasi-Islamist, pan-Arab message of al Jazeera. Al Arabiya, for example, associated with Saudi Arabia, was the primary source of news for some 8% of respondents to the 2015 Arab Opinion Survey, compared to 12% who preferred al Jazeera.[10]

Second, the proliferation of both satellite and terrestrial broadcasters aimed directly at national audiences, many of them now privately owned and with more interesting and competitive programming than was the case back in 1996, have captured a growing share of the market. Indeed, state-owned TV stations in that 2015 survey were the most important sources of news for more respondents than any other category of broadcasters.[11]

Third, social media have assumed ever greater importance as sources of news and opinion and they are overwhelmingly national in source and focus. The Arab Opinion Survey reported that internet usage increased from 42% of respondents in 2012 to 50% in 2014 to 61% in 2015, with 80% of those using the internet connected to social media.[12] The 2016 Arab Human Development Report notes that the rise from 5 million Arab internet subscribers in 2000 to 141 million in 2015 has catapulted the Arab world into being the most internet-connected region of the developing world.[13] An Arab Youth Survey conducted in 2013 cited in that Report confirmed the centrality of social media to Arab youths, finding that more than half were active on Twitter, that almost one fifth have their own blogs, and that 59% obtain their news from online sources, compared to 24% who do so from newspapers.[14]

Finally, the Arabic language, which in its "modern standard" version provided the linguistic basis for pan-Arabism, including in its al Jazeera manifestation, is being eroded by the use of national dialects in the social media, in other broadcasting, in movies and literature, and increasingly, even by politicians. Arabic, in other words, having been transnationalized since the 1950s, is being re-nationalized.

Declining inter-Arab migration

What appears to be stagnation of trans-regional broadcasting and the wider cultural integration to which it contributed is paralleled by a tailing off of intra-regional human movement. As a proportion of the region's population, both tourists and migrants from within it are declining. The waves of tourists from the Gulf that swept into Egypt, Lebanon, Tunisia, Turkey and Morocco in the 1990s and early 2000s have receded for security and financial reasons. Dubai's rapid growth as a touristic destination for Middle Easterners reflects the trend away from intra-regional tourism, as that city is for all intents and purposes culturally and economically globalized out of the MENA. In 2015 the Middle East became the world's fastest growing "outbound" travel market as ever more residents of the region left it altogether when they departed temporarily from their own country.[15]

But it is the relative and absolute decline of intra-Arab migration that is having the more profound impact on regionalization and regionalism. The downward trend of migration has been underway for more than a generation, having commenced in earnest in the wake of Iraq's 1990 invasion of Kuwait and perceived support for it by Yemen, Jordan and the Palestinians. Some 1.5 million Yemenis, Jordanians, Palestinians and other Arabs were expelled from Kuwait and Saudi Arabia alone, resulting for example in a reduction of the Palestinian population of Kuwait from 400,000 to 80,000.[16] In 1975 Arabs comprised almost three quarters of the foreign population of GCC states.[17] Between 1990 and 2010, the number of migrant workers in the GCC countries more than doubled, but the share of Arabs among them fell from one half to one third.[18] Those countries host an estimated 27 million immigrants, which is some 80% of all immigrants in the region, of whom Indians comprise the largest single national group.[19] The International Organization for Migration reported that in the wake of the 2007–8 global financial crisis, the number of Arab migrants in the MENA dropped below 6 million, which constituted just under half of total Arab migrants worldwide.[20] Subsequent economic recovery drove the number of Arabs resident in GCC states back up, such that by 2015 it had reached some 7 million.[21] In 2018 the population of the Arab world was almost 400 million, suggesting that less than 2% of Arabs are presently living as immigrants in an Arab country. Only 29% of remittances that flow out of Arab countries go to other ones, even though such remittances constitute a large portion of total remittances in those receiving Arab countries.

The great surge of intra-Arab human movement that commenced in the wake of the first oil boom of 1973–4 has been ebbing away proportionately, even absolutely as far as migration is concerned, for almost 30 years, and with regard to tourism for almost a decade. Two measures, one economic, the other political, of the impacts of that human movement suggest how important it has been and how its decline militates against regionalization and regionalism. The economic measure is remittances from the rich oil producing Arab states to poorer countries, the biggest recipients of which are Egypt, Lebanon and Jordan. Remittances to them from the GCC countries, Iraq and Libya are in decline in relative terms. Egypt's total remittances, for example, peaked in 2012 at $19.2 billion, falling in current dollars to $18.1 billion in 2018, the GCC's share of which has steadily declined as the United States' and Europe's shares have increased.[22] In 2018 remittances to the MENA fell 6% from the preceding year, whereas those to South Asia doubled, taking them to some two and a half times those of the MENA. In that year, of the six global regions receiving substantial remittances, the MENA ranked ahead of only Sub-Saharan Africa and Europe/Central Asia.[23]

Declining inter-Arab capital flows

At the broader level, the flow of capital in the form of inter-Arab FDI, which grew rapidly from 2000 and reached a peak of just over $35 billion in 2005, plunged in the wake of the 2007–8 global financial crisis. Its hesitant recovery was then cut short by the 2011 Arab Spring. But even at its peak, inter-Arab capital flows did little to bring the people of the region together. The bulk of it has been "highly concentrated on a few large-scale projects, frequently initiated by state-owned entities ... It remains an unstable and occasional source of funding ... and the employment effects on the receiving countries ... are likely to be minor."[24]

Consequences of declining interactions

A political indicator of declining regionalization resulting from reduced personal interactions is fluctuation in the fortunes of the Muslim Brotherhood and its "franchises." Arab migrants, especially from Egypt, began spreading in earnest the message of Islamism in general and that of the Brotherhood in particular into GCC countries and Libya from the early 1970s. As teachers and other professionals, they played key roles in inculcating Islamist beliefs in young Arabs. Originally, they were supported at least tacitly in so doing by many host governments, key of which was Saudi Arabia. But as the strength of Islamism grew, it came to be perceived as a threat by host governments, one of the principal reasons they began to impose tighter limits on the numbers of Arab migrants allowed into their countries. By the time of the 2011 Arab Spring, other than Qatar, all GCC countries and Libya were taking measures against migrant and domestic Islamists.

In sum, the seemingly bright prospects of the 1970s and 1980s for political and economic integration being driven by temporary and long-term residence of Arabs in other Arab countries, and by the capital flows that accompanied it, have failed to materialize. Reaction by host countries against perceived political threats combined with the region's generalized political and economic insecurity have substantially reduced the presence and impacts of Arab migrants, in both hosting and sending countries. Increasingly stringent visa requirements and other restrictions on travel and residence, including outright bans, have been imposed on various non-national Arabs by not just the major oil exporters, but by many other Arab countries as well.[25] According to the World Bank, movement of labor in the MENA region is increasingly constrained by labor market laws that specify "burdensome and costly procedures for obtaining work permits, limitations on the length of stay, quantitative limits and sectoral bans on work permits, job nationalization, workers' educational status, restrictions on foreign investment, and restrictions on the mobility of family members."[26] The Arab world has steadily become less receptive to fellow Arabs as the need for effective region-wide economic and political institutions has increased.

The MENA Civil War

Just as there are insufficient and declining shared communications and experiences of living together among Arabs to strongly propel the growth of regional institutions, so too is that growth hindered by the intensification of regional conflicts and violence that pit states against states, states against their own peoples, and transnational Islamist movements against the very idea of statehood as well as its specific manifestations. The MENA is sliding into a Hobbesian world where life for many is nasty, brutish and short. The direct and indirect costs of warfare have ballooned. The Arab world has 5% of the world's population, but by 2018 over 57% of global refugees, 47% of internally displaced persons and 40% of the world's forcibly displaced population, rates that increased five times from 2000.[27] It has almost 70% of the world's battle deaths and almost half of global terrorist attacks.[28] International Institute for Security Studies' (IISS) reports on military spending give a figure of $181 billion for Arab spending in 2014, but that excludes Libya, Syria, the UAE, Yemen and Sudan, for which there was no reporting or reliable data. For those countries on which there is reporting, the average level of Arab state spending on military forces consumed over 6% of GDPs, but exceeded 10% in Iraq, almost 13% in Saudi Arabia and 15% in Oman. These figures, according to Anthony Cordesman, "ignore major internal security

141

spending, counterterrorism activity, and the cost of military industries and arms purchases." The Arab world, then, even on the basis of
statistics that substantially understate expenditures and exclude those
for security/intelligence agencies, spends far more proportionately on
militaries than any other region of the world. It spends some three
times the global average of just over 2% of GDP on militaries and
more than double that of the developing world's next highest spender,
which is South Asia, at 2.5%.[29]

A major driver of such high expenditures is the never-ending Arab
Cold War, originally dubbed such by Malcolm Kerr to characterize
inter-Arab relations in the 1950s and 1960s. It has become an ever
hotter war since Iraq's invasion of Kuwait in 1990, followed by the
US-led invasion of Iraq in 2003 and then by the 2011 Arab Spring,
since which time it has morphed into a region-wide civil war in which
the non-Arab Muslim states of Turkey and Iran are increasingly
implicated.[30] The main combatants as described by Giacomo Luciani
are the incumbent Sunni Muslim "sultans" governing MENA states;
Shi'i Muslims led by Iran; moderate Islamist forces embodied in the
Muslim Brotherhood; and takfiri jihadis of whom the most numerous
and successful were those organized within the so-called Islamic State,
driven out of Iraq and Syria by 2019. These fault lines in the region's
politics are accompanied with further divisions within the combatting
camps. The Sunni "sultans," for example, are divided by their stances
toward moderate Islamists and Iran. Qatar, Turkey and Sudan have
been favorably disposed toward both, whereas Saudi Arabia, the
UAE, Bahrain and Egypt have been antagonistic, with other countries
perched uncomfortably between the two hostile camps.

The Lebanese "model" proliferates

Political vacuums in ungoverned spaces created by the MENA's failed
and faltering states suck in these competing forces, with devastating
consequences. Lebanon, with its historically weak state, was the
precursor battleground for MENA competitors. In the 1950s they
consisted primarily of Arab nationalists, of which the strongest
variant was Egypt's Nasserism, versus traditional Lebanese political
actors rooted in religion and region, in turn backed by the Saudis,
the US and other external powers. Civil war was narrowly averted
in 1958, but a decade later in the wake of the 1967 Arab–Israeli
war and the second major influx of Palestinian refugees, the stage
was set for renewed hostilities. Those erupted in 1975 and pitted a

now broader array of actors that included the Palestinians and newly mobilized Shi'i Muslims, each backed by one or more regional or extra-regional state. It was 15 years before the fighting was ended by the Ta`if Accords, which essentially handed the country over to Syria, the most tenacious of the interventionists, while promising political reforms, the most important of which were to be down the road. Agreement on those reforms has yet to be reached, as attested to by ongoing political struggles and sectarian animosities that intermittently bubble up violently.

The Lebanese prototype of a state unable to defend its sovereignty has subsequently been duplicated elsewhere, first in Iraq in the wake of the 2003 US-led invasion, then as a result of the 2011 Arab Spring, which weakened the Syrian state and altogether destroyed those in Libya and Yemen. Their territories became venues in which the region's hardening fault lines were replicated. In Iraq, Iranian backed Shi'i militias came to control the state, overwhelming potential Sunni "sultans" backed primarily by Saudi Arabia. Transnational jihadis then flowed into the vacated Sunni political space, soon to be widened by the collapse of the Syrian government's authority over bordering territory. For almost four years from 2014 Iraq was effectively partitioned between the so-called Islamic State (IS) based in the northwest; the Kurdish Regional Government striving for complete autonomy if not actual sovereignty, adjoining it to the east and supported in varying degrees by the US and Israel; and the rest of Iraq under the sway of the Baghdad-based Shi'i government, itself divided between pro- and anti-Iranian elements. The defeat of IS in late 2017 and the simultaneous weakening of the Kurdish Regional Government, due primarily to Kurdish political infighting, paved the way for considerable reconsolidation of Baghdad's authority throughout the country. That authority, however, remains tenuous, both because of unresolved hostilities between the many competing actors and their external supporters, and the huge financial and other challenges involved in physical reconstruction of much of the country laid to waste by incessant fighting. As of early 2018, for example, Iraqi officials reported that the country had received less than 1% of the funding required to rebuild the country.[31]

Bad as the situation has been in Iraq since 2003, it is even worse in Libya, Yemen and Syria, where the fragmentation of local antagonistic forces is yet greater. At the national level Libya is divided between governments based primarily in Tripoli in the west and Benghazi in the east, the former dominated by Islamists and members of western tribes, in turn backed by Qatar and Turkey; the latter by the so-called Libyan National Army, cobbled together by former Qadhafi general turned CIA agent, Khalifa Haftar, now working in league with various domestic forces, including local tribal allies and eastern Islamists, and backed by regional actors Egypt and the UAE, with Russia providing further military support. The US backs a third, still weaker government formed under UN auspices, while European countries are divided between support for that UN governmental effort, as in the case of the UK, or for the "Libyan National Army," as in the case of France. The Special UN Envoy, Ghassan Salame, a former Lebanese cabinet member forced into exile in the wake of the assassination of Prime Minister Rafiq al Hariri in 2005 and Hizbullah's consolidation of power, has had little success in reconciling the factions. To further complicate matters, much of the south of the country is under the effective control of different tribal and ethnic groupings, some of which are involved in transnational smuggling and political organizations, so disinterested in having a reconsolidation of Libyan national authority in Tripoli, Benghazi, or anywhere else.

While differing in detail, the story is pretty much the same in Yemen and Syria, where various local forces are supported by a similar array of regional and global actors. The Islamist-leaning governments of Qatar and Turkey back like-minded elements in those countries, while the "Sunni sultans" of the UAE, Saudi Arabia and, to a lesser extent, Egypt, generally back opponents of the Qataris and Turks, although these are shifting alliances, especially in Syria. Russia is supporting the Syrian government while the US is opposing it. In Yemen, by contrast, Russia provides at least diplomatic support to the Houthi rebels, currently holding power in the capital Sana`a and dependent upon Iran for military backing. The US has been acting through the UAE and Saudi Arabia in support of the "legitimate" government that for two years was based in Aden before fragmenting in early 2018 between factions supported by the UAE and forces that remained loyal to the nominal Yemeni President, Abed Rabbo Mansur Hadi, who had been backed by Saudi Arabia.

As is apparent from these cases, ungoverned spaces in the MENA invite Hobbesian struggles that pit arrays of local, regional and global actors in shifting coalitions. The task of nation building—or more accurately, nation-state reconstruction—in such circumstances is complicated and difficult, as the failure of the Lebanese state to be effectively rebuilt since the civil war ended in 1990 attests. Moreover, it is not just totally ungoverned spaces in collapsed states that are parlous. As the MENA civil war intensifies, its states are becoming more aggressive as they face externally supported insurgencies, while global actors, especially Americans, Russians and Europeans, are backing various of the competing states and transnational and sub-national forces.

Irredentism even in Egypt

Egypt's northern Sinai Peninsula illustrates how a MENA state threatened with losing its grip on some of its own territory typically responds to an irredentist threat. Long-simmering discontent among the tribalized northern Sinai population, resentful of the government's appropriation of their land and apparent lack of interest in their general welfare, finally boiled over in the wake of the Arab Spring. Within weeks of its outbreak in Egypt, Sinai activists commenced attacks on governmental installations, key of which was the pipeline through which gas flowed to Israel. Logistical support and training were provided by Palestinian Islamists in neighboring Gaza to these increasingly well-organized and radicalized forces, the most prominent element within which was the so-called Ansar Bayt al Maqdis (Partisans of Jerusalem). In November 2014 members of that organization swore allegiance to the then named Islamic State of Iraq and the Levant (ISIL, subsequently IS), adopted the name ISIL-Sinai Province, and stepped up their campaign of violence against the government and its supporters. For the first time in its modern history Egypt witnessed citizens collaborating with external forces, in this case violent Islamists based in Gaza, Syria and Iraq, possibly supported by Turkey and Qatar—as the Egyptian government claims—to undermine the national government. Its reaction has been a clumsy counter-terrorism campaign supported by the US, various European states and, increasingly, by Russia.

GCC fragments

Another example of political disruption and economic loss resulting from the regional civil war is the fracturing of the only even semi-effective regional integration association—the Gulf Cooperation Council (GCC). Formed in 1981, its ambitious aims once included a customs union, passport-free travel, a common currency à la the Euro, as well as the integration of national military forces. By 2018 those hopes had been dashed by intensification of the conflict between Qatar, on the one hand, and the UAE, Saudi Arabia and Bahrain, backed at distance by Kuwait, on the other, with Oman, the sixth GCC country, trying to remain neutral. The key divisive issues were Qatar's alleged support for Islamists and its reluctance to join the anti-Iranian front pushed by the UAE, Saudi Arabia and Bahrain. For its part Turkey has supported Qatar, toward which the US has cautiously leaned, as paradoxically so have Iran and Russia. So the last surviving, functioning institutional manifestation of Arab unity has effectively collapsed, bringing to an end, at least for the time being, the long and unhappy history of such integration efforts. One immediate, negative impact of that collapse was capital flight from several GCC countries, with Qatar alone losing some $20 billion in a single month at the outset of the crisis.[32]

The economic costs of the splintering of the GCC were not only incurred by its member states. They compounded throughout the Arab world as those GCC states sought through financial means to win or maintain allies and to punish backsliders or outright opponents. Jordan provides an example of the consequences of this manipulation. Facing mass protests in response to the declaration of austerity measures in May 2018, the Jordanian government rescinded proposed tax hikes and subsidy cuts mandated by the IMF, thereby intensifying the economic crisis that had seen public debt rise to almost 100% of GDP and unemployment to some 20%. This left Jordan dependent upon GCC states, whose five-year Gulf Aid Package had expired the previous year. Saudi Arabia refused to renew it on the grounds that Jordan had not bowed to Saudi pressure to drop its support for a Palestinian state, to ban the Muslim Brotherhood, to mute its opposition to the US decision to move its embassy from Tel Aviv to Jerusalem and, most importantly, to sever ties with Qatar. Having tried to straddle the widening gap between Saudi Arabia and its allies, on the one hand, and Qatar and its allies on the other, driven by financial necessity Jordan had little choice but to tilt further in the Saudi's direction. In June 2018 it secured from Riyadh a new five-year $2.5 billion aid package, some 3.5 times larger than the IMF loan. In addition to political strings attached, economic conditions were imposed to ensure Jordanian compliance, including the provision that aid in the form of deposits in the central bank and investments in infrastructure could be withdrawn at any time. As observers noted, accepting this Gulf aid package "could add to the turmoil" as its conditions are unpopular in Jordan, an innocent bystander to the GCC dispute.[33]

The MENA: Neither Regionalized nor Globalized

Intense regionalization, including the virtual civil war in which the MENA is presently engaged, poses profound obstacles to effective regionalism that would foster economic interaction and growth. Even in the absence of negative regionalization, however, building effective regional integration associations in the MENA would be an uphill task in the face of less than enthusiastic support from its nation states. These limited access orders are by their nature protectionist, committed to defending the privileges of regime insiders. Any significant economic opening, whether at the regional or global level, would threaten the political and economic foundations upon which these regimes rest.

It is no coincidence that the MENA is not only poorly regionalized, but also comparatively weakly integrated into the global economy. According to the UN's 2016 *Arab Human Development Report*, for example, "The region is one of the most protected in the world. The movement of goods, people and capital is subject to tight restrictions. The behind-the-border barriers that generate trade frictions are more pervasive in the Arab region than elsewhere."[34] A 2013 World Bank report notes that "Limited integration has stifled the MENA region's ability to tap into its significant potential for economic growth and job creation. The MENA region is among the least integrated in the world economy." Drawing on data available at that time, the report observed that the MENA had 5.5% of the world's population, 3.9% of the world's GDP, but only 1.8% of global non-oil trade, as exports of oil and gas accounted for three-quarters of the MENA's total exports. Non-oil exports from the MENA are one-third the amount predicted by comparative country characteristics.[35] As for the MENA's contribution to the global service sector, it has hovered between 2 and 3%, with travel and transport comprising almost 80% of it, as compared to, say, South Asia, where technology and financial services comprised 55% of service exports. Intra-regional exports of goods have remained at some 8% of total MENA exports for years, as compared to 25% in ASEAN countries and 66% in the EU.[36] Another World Bank report pointed out that "the level of MENA countries' participation in vibrant global production networks could be described as negligible. Intra-industry trade is low, reaching just 20% of manufacturing in countries such as Egypt—far below the 70% share found in China and other East Asian countries." The report adds that trade in manufacturing components is minimal, "reflecting the low technology content of the region's imports and exports," with the result that "the MENA region has been unable to benefit from the knowledge spillovers that tend to occur in global production networks."[37]

The MENA has poured more effort into building regional integration associations with fewer substantive results than any other developing region. Driven primarily by regionalization impulses stimulated by widespread popular support for Arab nationalism, as well as by tactical inter-state alliances, but not by fundamental commitments guided by a long-term strategy of integrated economic development, the MENA has witnessed since the 1960s the signing of almost 300 preferential trade agreements. Lack of proclaimed ambition has not been their weak point, as indicated by pledged written commitments to common markets and an economic union. In 1997, for example, 18 Arab states formed the Pan Arab Free Trade Area, the purposes of which were to coordinate policy, stimulate inter-member and global trade, establish a uniform customs policy, and coordinate tax and duty legislation. Twelve years later, with those objectives having at best been only partially met, the Arab League agreed to establish an integrated Arab Customs Union to be fully operational by 2015, a deadline that, like so many others, has come and gone without substantial progress having been made.[38]

Flexible protectionism

During the period of rapid globalization from the late 1990s to the global economic crisis of 2007–8, the MENA did, however, achieve some formal progress in reducing barriers to trade. Between 2002 and 2009 average tariffs in the MENA fell from 15% to 6%, making it the region in which tariffs decreased the most. They nevertheless remained high by global standards, with only South Asia having higher levels of tariff restrictiveness on the Tariff Only Trade Restrictiveness Index.[39] But while tariffs declined, non-tariff barriers to trade remained unaffected, in some cases actually increasing. By 2012 non-tariff measures—such as border closures, lengthy clearance and inspection processes, excessive numbers of required documents and signatures, and discretionary application of health and phytosanitary regulations—when included in the Overall Trade Restrictiveness Index, rendered the MENA "the most restrictive region in the world."[40] A 2018 study of non-tariff barriers imposed in Morocco in the wake of a preferential trade agreement with the EU revealed

148

not only that they were raised precisely because actual tariffs were lowered by that agreement, but that "politically connected businesses ... received disproportionately higher levels of non-tariff protection," thereby illustrating the typically discretionary application of trade and other policies in limited access orders.[41]

Reluctance to open service sectors to competition was similar to that regarding tradeable goods. "Services sectors in the region are liberalized, but only to a limited extent. Governments tend to retain control, leading to a lack of transparency and excessive discretion in how restrictions are applied." As a result, trade in vital service sectors, including finance, retail, telecommunications and transport, "appears noticeably more restricted in the MENA than in other countries at comparable income levels."[42]

Paradoxically, "more progress has been made in implementing preferential trade agreements between MENA countries and other regions of the world than in implementing those among countries of the region."[43] Rather than having positive effects, however, the more effective implementation of these agreements with partners external to the MENA appears neither to have stimulated exports or FDI, nor led to deeper, structural reforms that impact national trade policies and practices, such as exchange and interest rate and competition policies. Instead, these preferential trade agreements, whether with the EU, the US or East Asian countries, have stimulated rapid growth of imports, thereby "widening trade imbalances," which have not been compensated for by European, American or Asian originating FDI, for within the MENA it remains overwhelmingly dominated by capital from GCC countries.[44]

Sub-regional trade agreements

The once bright but ultimately vain hopes for creating broad, inclusive regional integration associations in the Arab world, to say nothing of the MENA, have in recent years given way to more limited ambitions in the form of sub-regional preferential trade agreements, coupled with the spontaneous growth of sub-regional trade. The GCC stands out as having achieved the greatest integration of trade between its member states, which overall constitutes 75% of all their intra-Arab trade, a result driven in significant measure by the reduction of its common external tariff to 5% overall and to nothing on a list of 400 "essential items" imported from neighboring GCC countries, even if such common commitments have been honored as much by the breach as the practice.[45] Intra-GCC trade grew fortyfold in the first 32 years of the organization's existence, but still amounted to only about 8% of member states' total trade at that time.[46] Karen Young attributes the failure of the GCC to achieve greater sub-regional economic integration to the protection of local agents through commercial agency laws governing representation of a foreign principal and restricting that representation to nationals who are given monopolies over that foreign principal's imports.[47]

Following close behind the GCC in sub-regional integration are the member states of the Arab Maghrib Union, formed in 1989 by Algeria, Libya, Mauritania, Morocco and Tunisia, which, despite the region's turmoil and frequent border closures, managed to grow their shared trade to almost two-thirds of their total trade with Arab states. The Mashriq states, by contrast, not linked by any functioning sub-regional integration association and beset by even more political divisions, conduct only one-third of their Arab trade with their sub-regional neighbors. Whether it is the comparative success of sub-regional as opposed to region-wide economic integration, or just complete despair at achieving the latter, the accepted wisdom has become that "Regional cooperation may be best pursued on an à la carte, bottom-up pragmatic basis—as opposed to relying on the type of trade agreements that have been the focal point to date in the region and largely failed to deliver ... Such bottom-up efforts will by their nature involve subsets of countries and may well be limited to bilateral cooperation."[48] The intensification of regional political conflict since those words were written has rendered them even more relevant.

Direct and Opportunity Costs of MENA States' "Grand Isolation"

Inadequate globalization and regional integration have raised direct costs to the MENA's producers and consumers, undermining the region's economic competitiveness. It exports fewer goods and services than predicted by its overall GDP, per capita GDP, and population size. For more than two decades studies have estimated gains in trade that would accrue from reduced tariff and non-tariff barriers, ranging from 10–15% in a liberalized Arab environment, to 147% for the MENA as a whole.[49] A 2017 study reported that "a typical MENA country under-trades with other countries: exports to the outside world are at only a third of their potential."[50] Excluding oil, MENA exports are half the world average.[51] As for specific sectors, a 2014 World Bank study estimated that if restrictions on air traffic competition were lifted, intra-regional passenger traffic would rise by 30%.[52] The World Bank also forecast savings of up to $25 billion for the Arab world if electricity trade were opened up, whereas the Gulf Cooperation Interconnection Authority estimated in 2018 that by 2038 its six member states would save $24 billion were that to happen. According to APICORP Energy Research, "chronic technical, institutional and political barriers are major impediments to (electricity) trading in the region, whose networks are expected to remain amongst the most under-utilized in the world for this purpose."[53] As for intra-regional gas trade in the MENA, it is "one of the lowest in the world despite the region's vast and uneven distribution of gas reserves."[54]

Proportionate to GDP per capita, the MENA's military expenditures are the world's highest, so savings achieved through integration in this sector alone would be substantial. Yet, the example of the GCC, the sub-region that has achieved the greatest integration to date, illustrates how much remains to be done to achieve such savings. Despite efforts to integrate the armed forces of the six member states of the GCC, including weapons procurement, waste and duplication remain widespread. The most expensive weapons systems are aircraft, their cost dramatically escalated by the absence of common procurement of fighter airplanes. Saudi Arabia and Qatar fly Boeing F-15s; Qatar and the UAE fly Dassault Mirages; Kuwait flies Boeing F-18s; and Lockheed F-16s are flown by the UAE, Oman and Bahrain. Personnel costs are increased by duplication of educational and training facilities, with each GCC country having its own military academies, staff colleges and, for the most senior officers, war colleges. According to an American expert on GCC militaries, "there simply are not enough serving officers in the GCC militaries outside of Saudi Arabia to provide the throughput for this system and to justify the mission and expense."[55]

The opportunity costs of inadequate globalization coupled with limited regional integration include those hypothetically incurred not only from the narrow definition of economic integration, which is the reduction or elimination of tariff and non-tariff barriers to the movement of goods, services, capital, labor and technology, but also the profits forgone from deeper economic integration which would include improvement of transport and logistics, harmonization of regulations and practices, and removal of obstacles to business activity, such as inappropriate exchange rates and restrictions on competition. Such benefits would accrue in the domestic economy as well as in government policy and firm behavior. According to the World Bank, "By setting standards for good institutional practice, regional integration can contribute to good governance and accelerate institutional transformation."[56] Since direct and opportunity costs from the MENA's lackluster globalization and tepid embrace of regionalism are well known and substantial, the question of why such little economic integration has been achieved naturally arises.

Obstacles to Economic Integration

Structural obstacles

Structural, regional, economic and domestic political obstacles stand in the way of more effective Arab and broader MENA integration, of which the most important are the consequence of domestic political factors. The key structural obstacle has been the relatively slow development of intra-regional transportation, communication and energy infrastructure. The fraught history of railways in the MENA provides just one example of the broader problem. The Ottomans, primarily with German technical assistance, had by WWI created a railway network that linked Istanbul to many of the empire's present and former provinces, ranging from Egypt in the west, to what is now Iraq in the east, and to Yemen in the south, with a reasonably dense network of intermediate connections in the Levant that made rail travel within and between Lebanon and Syria and then on to Iraq possible and comparatively pleasant. Much of this extensive network was destroyed in WWI. What remained became hostage to subsequent intra-regional conflict and strife, resulting in the closing and even destruction of lines connecting Palestine—now Israel—to the rest of the Arab world, thereby ending rail travel from Egypt to the Levant, and of the links between Syria, Iraq, Saudi Arabia, and Yemen, as well as that between Egypt and Sudan. Some sections of those lines continued to operate through the 1980s, such as that between Beirut and Zabadani in Lebanon, but more as touristic curiosities than serious transportation. Remaining Lebanese employees of the railway, including ticket takers, continue to receive salaries, even though no trains have run for decades. Despite repeated commitments by various Arab states and organizations, including the

Arab League, to reconnect the Arab world by reconstructed and newly built rail lines, virtually nothing has been done. As a result, passengers and freight are conveyed within the MENA primarily by road and air, the regional networks of which remain comparatively poorly developed. The long-discussed freeway linking Egypt to Morocco along the North African coast through Libya, Tunisia and Algeria, for example, remains at the discussion stage, primarily because of various political conflicts within and between these countries. Roads linking Lebanon, Syria and Iraq have been badly degraded by years of conflict and inadequate maintenance, as have those between Saudi Arabia and Yemen. Those linking Qatar to Saudi Arabia have been closed since 2017 as part of the boycott imposed by the latter. As already noted, the inadequacy of regional air connections constitutes a substantial drag-effect on intra-regional travel, while regionally underdeveloped hydrocarbon and electricity networks drive up energy costs. Although air and energy connections are being improved, the overall state of regional infrastructural linkages is well below what would be predicted by the MENA's relative wealth. On the World Bank's "trading across borders" index, a measure primarily of logistics reported in its *Doing Business* rankings, Jordan was in 2018 the best performing of MENA countries, placing 53rd out of 189 ranked countries. Seven of the bottom 20 performers were MENA countries.[57]

Regional political obstacles

Inadequate region-wide infrastructure is both cause and effect of inadequate regionalism, as a brief revisiting of the key regional obstacle to integration suggests. That main obstacle is the level of political competition and conflict between MENA nation states, one negative side effect of which has been to destroy existing infrastructure and to delay the construction of new road, rail, water, air, energy and other linkages. In 2017, for example, all air connections between Qatar and its GCC neighbors were severed as a result of the boycott just mentioned. Most GCC–Iran air links have been severed intermittently or permanently since the outbreak of the Iran–Iraq war in 1980. The Moroccan–Algerian border has been closed since 1994 as a result of tension resulting from conflicting claims in the Western Sahara. Both Tunisia and Egypt have ramped up border surveillance and controls on their frontiers with lawless Libya. Visa-free travel between various Arab countries—such as that between Iraq and

Egypt during the Saddam Hussein era, or between Egypt and Syria during the Nasser era's United Arab Republic, or between Egypt, Sudan and Libya during the brief "union" of those three countries under Sadat, or between all of the GCC countries—is now notable in its almost entire absence as states become ever more concerned with security threats. As for general relations between MENA Arab and non-Arab states, they are yet worse. An Israeli stamp in a passport, for example, is sufficient in most Arab countries without peace treaties with Israel to forbid a third party national from entering, while formal meetings by their citizens with Israelis constitutes a crime. The Turkish–Syrian and Turkish–Iraqi borders have not only been closed intermittently since the 1970s, but have been heavily fortified, including by minefields.

In this atmosphere of mutual distrust and open conflict it is virtually impossible for responsible authorities to enter into meaningful negotiations over the nuts and bolts of integration. Steps toward integration that are taken result primarily from short-term political calculations derived from ever-shifting alliances. The transfer of Egypt's Sanafir and Tiran Islands to Saudi Arabia in 2018, or the agreement between Saudi Arabia, Jordan and Egypt to allow the newly envisioned Saudi mega-city of NEOM to spill over into the territory of the latter two countries, are examples of this phenomenon. Saudi Arabia in these cases is seeking to aggrandize territory in return for its backing of King Abdullah in Jordan and President Sisi in Egypt, both of whom are willing to cooperate even in the face of stiff domestic opposition. One can predict with confidence based on previous experiences that when and if the relevant bilateral relations deteriorate, or the heads of state depart, the agreements will be rolled back and facilities that have been constructed with Saudi capital will be nationalized by Jordan and/or Egypt. To the extent that regional integration occurs, it is driven by short-term political calculations, not by long-term commitments to broad, sustainable economic growth or political integration, as was the case for example with the EU, a project which from the outset sought both deeper economic and political integration.

Economic obstacles

Economic obstacles to regional integration are numerous and interconnected. As compared to other, more economically integrated regions, such as East Asia, Europe and North America, MENA national economies are relatively incompatible. Some three quarters of MENA exports are in the form of hydrocarbons, while its share of non-oil world trade is less than 2% and its share of the global services trade less than 3%. The overall MENA economy is thus one that exports oil and gas and imports food, manufactured goods and a range of services. MENA countries are not major purchasers of oil and gas, nor are they significant producers of food or manufactured goods, so exports generally leave the region and imports overwhelmingly come from outside of it. Economic diversification which would have taken the form of increased production of tradeable goods and services has been retarded by the Dutch Disease. According to De Melo and Ugarte, between 1980 and 2010 only Iran and Yemen within the MENA did not have overvalued currencies in most years, resulting in non-competitive, underdeveloped manufacturing and service sectors.[58]

With the passage of time the task of upgrading those sectors has become ever more challenging as global competition intensifies. Bangladesh, thanks largely to Chinese investment which has helped to make it the world's second largest garment exporter after China itself, exports almost double the value of Turkish, four times the value of Morocco's, and some 15 times Egypt's garment exports, the MENA's three largest clothing exporters. In India, information and communication technology makes up 55% of service exports, compared to the MENA where technological services comprise a miniscule portion of service exports, which are dominated by travel and tourism that constitute 78% of such exports.[59] Most countries of the MENA can reasonably be termed "late, late developers," having missed opportunities to climb up production ladders in the immediate post-colonial era and then in the globalization era of the 1990s through 2008. FDI that would drive industrial upgrading is in the MENA devoted overwhelmingly to hydrocarbons, tourism and real estate, to say nothing of originating primarily within the region and being less than in comparable global regions. The MENA thus faces the challenge of economic diversification when that has become more difficult and dependent upon imported capital and technology, neither of which the region attracts in sufficient magnitude or appropriate type. The poorly diversified MENA economies thus generally do not produce goods and services competitive with those originating outside the region, while prospects for effective diversification fade in the face of ever intensifying global competition.

Hydrocarbon dependence causes other incompatibilities of national economies in addition to that of their being insufficiently diversified to contribute effectively to intra-regional trade. Of these incompatibilities, the most profound are those of micro and macro inequalities. The extreme range of national GDP per capita, corrected for domestic costs by using purchasing power parity (PPP), illustrates the magnitude of inequality. Qatar, for which in 2017 the figure was $128,000, was ranked by the World Bank as the richest country in the world. Yemen, the poorest MENA country with a GDP per capita of $2,300, ranked 171st out of 198 countries.[60] Kuwait and the UAE were in 2017 also among the ten richest countries in the world. The average GDP per capita of those three MENA countries of some $90,000 was more than six times greater than that of Egypt, at $13,000, the 94th ranked country. While other regions that have achieved significant economic integration, including North America, Europe and East Asia, do have unequal national per capita incomes, none has them in such magnitude as the MENA. NAFTA members the US, Canada and Mexico, for example, rank 13th, 25th and 68th on global GDP per capita, respectively, with Americans' incomes being approximately three times those of Mexicans, compared to Qatar's being more than 50 times greater than Yemen's.

Moreover, successful economic integration tends to equalize incomes. In East Asia, for example, Japan's GDP per capita in purchasing power parity in 2017 was approximately three times that of China's, the gap between the two having been halved since 1960.[61] By contrast, disparities in national income in the MENA have increased substantially over much of that period. Oman, for example, the only GCC country for which the relevant World Bank data is available as far back as 1970 and which is the least wealthy of the GCC countries, had in that year a GDP per capita of $9,239, compared to Egypt's of $792 or Sudan's at $786. By 2017 Oman's per capita GDP had grown to $16,144, while Egypt's increased to $2,785 and Sudan's to $1,959. So, while Omanis in 1970 enjoyed GDPs per capita some $8,450 more than Egyptians and Sudanese, by 2017 the gap had widened to $13,360 between Omanis and Egyptians and $14,185 between Omanis and Sudanese. The absence of regional integration has thus been associated with widening national income disparities in the MENA, which in turn renders the task of integration all the more difficult.

A myriad of challenges confronts attempts to integrate very rich and very poor economies, ranging from profound differences in consumption patterns and national physical and human capacities, to fears of pressure for wealth transfers among those in richer countries. Paradoxically, the large MENA middle-income countries that cluster around the midpoint of global per capita income rankings, which include Turkey at $14,933 in 2017 at the top end and Egypt at $2,785 at the bottom, with Morocco, Iran, Iraq and Algeria spread out between them, are no more integrated than the more unequal MENA economies. This may be due to their geographical dispersion, except in the case of Iraq and Iran, which have the most de facto if not de jure integrated economies. It is also likely due to their endemic competition for leadership roles in the MENA. Relative equality thus appears insufficient by itself to drive regional integration, while inequality poses a substantial obstacle to it.

A final economic factor impeding MENA integration is the significant difference in the degree of globalization, which reflects varying exposures to and orientations toward global "others" and transactions with them, so is also a measure of the relative openness of domestic political economies. The KOF Swiss Economic Institute overall index of globalization is based on economic, social and political measures, including current economic flows, economic restrictions, information flows, personal contacts and cultural proximity. Globalization is defined by the KOF "as the process of creating networks of connections among actors at multi-continental distances, mediated through a variety of flows including people, information and ideas, capital and goods. It is a process that erodes national boundaries, integrates national economies, cultures, technologies and governance and produces complex relations of mutual interdependence."[62] "Overall globalization," in short, is not confined to economic transactions, but includes the social and political contexts that shape those transactions.

In 2018, of the MENA countries listed among the 209 total countries on the KOF overall globalization index, the six GCC countries were all in the most globalized half, as they also were on its strictly economic globalization dimension.[63] Heavy dependence upon hydrocarbon exports, reinforced by longstanding connections to Western powers coupled with small populations typically exposed by travel and communications to the outside world, and led politically by reasonably legitimate monarchies, thus appear supportive of the GCC's overall globalization. By contrast, the most populous Arab states, including Egypt, Algeria, Morocco, Yemen, Iraq and Syria, are in the bottom halves of both the overall and the strictly economic indices of globalization, as is Iran. Turkey is the fifth most overall globalized MENA country, but only the 11th most economically globalized. The highest-ranking large population Arab country on the economic globalization index is Morocco, which ranks 107th out of 201 countries. Iraq, Sudan, Syria, Egypt and Algeria rank between 145th and 162nd. Population size is thus inversely correlated with globalization in the MENA, while per capita national income is positively related. This implies that not only are the vast majority of Arabs not highly globalized, but that different socio-political orientations characterize those living in these respective two categories of countries, to say nothing of the significant material differences in their national economies. In sum, MENA countries are characterized by a bifurcated pattern of overall and strictly economic globalization. This divide poses additional obstacles to their effective integration, ranging from varying orientations toward and relations with the world beyond the region, to a host of different economic traits, key of which is the magnitude of barriers to trade.

Domestic political economy obstacles

Political obstacles to regionalism at the nation-state level result from characteristics of both states and societies and relations between the two. All MENA states, except Israel, are limited access orders. The insiders of these orders seek to deny both political and economic elite access to outsiders in order to preserve power and material benefits for themselves. Denial of access applies not only to perceived domestic political and economic competitors, but also to regional and even global ones. Political economies organized around the principle of incumbent elites excluding domestic outsiders naturally also include barriers against non-national outsiders. This latent consequence is reinforced by the active calculations of incumbent elites, who because of the MENA's intense regionalization fear that their domestic challengers might seek to make common cause with regional or even global allies in pursuing demands for access to the political economy. The obvious strategy for incumbents seeking to prevent such alliances, therefore, is to replicate barriers against national competitors to also deter regional and global actors, while admitting a select few who make political or economic side payments. Incumbents thus derive political and material benefits from their power to filter political and economic access by regional and global actors to the domestic political economy. An example of this filtering is provided by barriers to trade, erected selectively to benefit elite insiders and thus deprive outsiders of equal opportunities, unless they provide side payments.

Studies of the causes and consequences of insider/outsider divisions of MENA political economies include investigations of trade protectionism. Adeel Malik and Ferdinand Eibl, for example, seek to explain why "the MENA surpasses all world regions in terms of trade protection" and why in particular it has "the highest level of non-tariff barriers in the world."[64] Their answer to both queries is in a nutshell that "regulatory rents created through trade policy closure can be used to reward connected business elites and elicit their political support." Non-tariff measures have become more important barriers to imports than tariffs as international agreements—including those negotiated within the framework of the WTO and those between the MENA and the EU—have steadily reduced tariffs but done little to reduce non-tariff barriers, which in the MENA have escalated dramatically in tandem with tariff reductions. Globally 70% of trade protection is now attributed to non-tariff measures.[65] The evidence Malik and Eibl attest is from North Africa, where three states—Egypt, Morocco and Tunisia—rank among the world's top six in non-tariff protection. Their evidence pertains to "whether sectors with prior exposure to political cronies disproportionately benefitted from higher levels of non-tariff protection after the EU agreements." The key finding is that the more sectors were dominated by political cronies in the pre-tariff-reform period, the more they "witnessed systematically higher levels of non-tariff protection in the post-reform period than the politically unconnected sectors."[66] Non-tariff measures are in fact more useful for targeted generation of rents than are more categorical tariffs. In Egypt, for example, 88% of technical barriers to trade "were all related to measures that required close administrative oversight and were susceptible to selective enforcement."[67] These barriers thus enabled the regime to channel rents to cronies, many of which, including a significant number of retired military officers, emerged from the state itself. As for the impact of non-tariff measures on regionalism, Malik and Eibl conclude that they "act as a significant barrier to the expansion of regional trade among Arab economies ... and afforded crony sectors a level of trade protection that was higher than the pre-reform period."[68]

The overwhelming majority of MENA states are dominated by elites who view trade and its control primarily as a means of generating rents to sustain their power and only secondarily as a way to grow national wealth. Unlike developmental states described by Chalmers Johnson and Peter Evans as organized around the principle of state support to develop export capacity, most MENA states are organized around the principle of preserving the power and privileges of incumbent elites, virtually whatever the cost to the national economy.[69] Degrees of commitment to developmentalism

159

as opposed to political power preservation do, however, exist in the MENA. Amr Adly's comparative study of the Turkish and Egyptian states revealed how the former, prior to Recep Tayyip Erdogan's consolidation of power, was impelled by the democratic calculation of attracting votes to increase national wealth by promoting exports with numerous state-supported reforms. In Egypt, by contrast, the authoritarian state had no electoral incentive to cultivate broad constituencies, so its export promotion measures were few, ineffective and typically for the benefit of incumbent elites and their cronies.[70]

As for MENA economies, their character is shaped by their rent-seeking states. Most MENA economies share four characteristics associated with limited access orders. The first is the presence of comparatively well capitalized, modern, frequently export-oriented businesses dominated by cronies, typically benefitting not only from selective protection, but by subsidized inputs, as well as preferential access to credit and state contracts. These businesses, however, are relatively few in number and constitute a small proportion of the overall economy and labor force. The second characteristic is the so-called "missing middle," which refers to the relatively small number of medium-sized enterprises, attesting to the difficulty of growing small businesses in limited access orders that tilt economic playing fields against them. The relatively high age of MENA businessmen and the low rates of business creation and bankruptcy point to the stagnation of business in general and of medium-sized enterprises in particular. The third characteristic is the very high proportion of micro and small enterprises. The portion of MENA enterprises that have fewer than ten employees exceeds 90% in most of its economies. In Egypt the average number of employees per firm has varied between two and three for the past decade. The final characteristic of economies in MENA limited access orders is informalism, reflecting a policy environment that is inhospitable to economic competition in general, so creates barriers, largely in the form of excessive direct and indirect costs, to formalization of businesses. The typical response by entrepreneurs is to avoid business registration, which in turn denies them access to credit and other benefits, so inhibits growth. Estimates of the proportions of MENA economies that are informal are high, with informal non-agricultural jobs constituting just under half of all employment in the MENA and some two thirds if the GCC countries are not included. In Morocco, over three quarters of the labor force is employed informally and in Yemen, some 90%.[71]

In sum, the structure of MENA economies reflects the purposefully limited access to them. At the top a comparative handful of insiders control relatively large, highly capitalized and profitable firms. Spreading out below them are a larger number of struggling business-people seeking to grow their firms into medium-sized, modern ones; and at the base are the vast number of citizens involved in micro and small enterprises, the great majority of which are informal, hence facing bleak prospects for expanding.

The obstacles economies with these characteristics pose to regional integration are large and may be insurmountable. The big, well-connected firms, which are politically much the most powerful, generally oppose regional integration, benefitting as they do from monopolized markets created and sustained by protectionism, or from comparatively limited inducements to export. Owners of these firms are generally regime insiders or those closely connected to them, so have a disincentive to rock political boats. They dominate business organizations and use their control of them to deter organized pressure for change. The shared interest of cronies is to preserve the status quo of isolated national economies, hence to resist regional integration. The "missing middle" of medium-sized businesses, the most natural self-interested sub-group in regional integration, is too limited in numbers and influence to impact policy. The mass of micro and small business owners, most of whom are informal, operate entirely locally, so have little awareness of or interest in the potential benefits of regional integration. In Europe, North America and East Asia, by contrast, both formal and informal integration of economies was driven primarily by business interests in turn supported by states keener to enhance national wealth than to protect the economic and political power of cronies.

Prospects for Reform

Recent writings on MENA integration are rightly pessimistic about the prospects for its thoroughgoing, region-wide realization. Some, however, are optimistic that progress can be made at sub-regional levels and in specific sectors.[72] Both the logic of geographical proximity and relevant data provide some support for this proposition.

The MENA as a whole is a huge geographic area, spreading some 6,000 kilometers from Morocco in the west to the Iranian–Afghan frontier in the east, and over 3,000 kilometers from either Sudan or Yemen in the south to Turkey in the north. It is the world's most arid region possessing the largest desert on the globe, which among other things has rendered travel parlous and difficult. Demographically it is fragmented along numerous dimensions, including those based on geography, nationality, wealth, ethnicity, religion, language, and so on. The MENA's sub-regions, on the other hand, are considerably more homogeneous along these various dimensions and tend to have more shared histories of interactions than the region as a whole. Those sub-regions include North Africa and the eastern littorals of the Mediterranean and the Gulf, with Iraq connected to both of these latter sub-regions. It is understandable, therefore, that both the broad type of integration described and measured by the KOF index of overall globalization and the narrower index focused on economics are easier to achieve in these sub-regions. And indeed, the history of integration efforts bears out this hypothesis. The Arab Maghrib Union, formed in 1989 by Algeria, Libya, Mauritania, Morocco and Tunisia, is one such example, even though it has been rendered largely impotent as a result of tense Algerian–Moroccan relations and the collapse of Libya. The GCC formed in 1981 groups together the Arab states of the Gulf littoral and achieved greater economic and overall integration than any other such effort in the MENA prior to its fracturing in 2017. In the decade following the formation of a GCC customs union in 2003, intra-GCC trade grew fortyfold, reaching some $90 billion.[73] Northeast Africa comprised of Libya, Sudan and Egypt has witnessed numerous attempts at integration, dating back to Egypt's colonization of the Sudan in the nineteenth century and including temporary unions under both Nasser and Sadat. In the Levant significant de facto integration has long characterized Syrian–Lebanese and Jordanian–Palestinian relations, while under the Ba'th Party from the 1960s to the 1980s Syria and Iraq were intermittently committed to formal unification. As for strictly economic integration, data on trade and financial flows demonstrates that they are greater within these sub-regions than they are within the MENA as a whole.[74]

It makes good sense, therefore, for integration efforts to build on sub-regional linkages, as is urged by numerous analysts.[75] Such efforts can further benefit from sectoral linkages, such as shared electricity grids, gas and oil pipelines, port facilities, transportation networks and even urban amenities, as is envisioned by plans for the new super-city NEOM, financed by Saudi Arabia and spreading across its frontiers with both Jordan and Egypt. Pragmatism based on proximity, in other words, can provide a stronger, more enduring basis for regionalism than Arab nationalism, Islamism, or any other ideologically inspired grand design for region-wide integration.

This begs the question as to whether sub-regional integrations, were they to proceed apace, would in turn serve as building blocks for broader regional integration, or would further fragment the MENA. While actual experience has yet to provide sufficient data to truly test these alternative hypotheses, experts on regional integration associations tend to believe that something is better than nothing and that favorable experiences at sub-regional levels can encourage widening to the broader region.[76] It is also argued that when and if MENA economies diversify, their then greater mix of products and services will facilitate both sub-regional and regional integration efforts.[77]

But is the MENA so conflict-ridden that its internal divisions will swamp pragmatic, sub-regional integration efforts? Conflictual environments do polarize actors, but they also instill searches for allies. Turkey and Egypt, for example, were pulled together economically in a variety of ways, with significant investments by the former in the latter, including some production linkages in the textile and garment industries, when both were ruled or heavily influenced by Islamists between 2011 and 2013. The overthrow of President Mursi by the Egyptian military, however, terminated that nascent economic integration. Potentially more profound economic linkages could result from Israel's direct engagement with at least some Arab countries, primarily because of the greater compatibility between national economies. The marriage of Israeli technology and Arab capital and labor could be highly productive, as some examples indicate. In the wake of the 1979 Egyptian–Israeli peace treaty, for example, numerous Israeli firms and technicians became involved in upgrading Egyptian agriculture, most notably by provision of irrigation and associated agricultural technologies. Subsequently the Qualifying Industrial Zones (QIZs) that linked the two countries, as well as Israel and Jordan, by virtue of providing duty-free access for their products into American markets, contributed to the upgrading of textile and clothing industries in the two Arab countries. Negotiations for the recently developed Israeli gas fields in the eastern Mediterranean to pipe their production to LNG facilities on the Mediterranean coast in Egypt may result in Egypt becoming an "energy hub" linking the MENA primarily to Europe. Israeli firms have been involved in upgrading the electronic capacities of several Gulf countries. And yet, all of these joint economic undertakings operate in the shadow of political tensions between Israel and many Arab countries and most Arab publics. The fear that these tensions could escalate at any time limits the degree of commitment of parties on both sides to economic undertakings, causing them to focus on activities with rapid returns on investments.

The potential payoffs of more economic integration in the MENA, in sum, are substantial, even if primarily at the sub-regional level. Unfortunately, political conflicts of various sorts impede integration at both levels. They even deter quite pragmatic, non-ideological integration efforts that cross sub-regional borders, whether those between Israel and neighboring Arab states or between, say, Egypt, Saudi Arabia and Jordan, or Qatar and Bahrain. MENA integration thus seems to be stuck in limbo. The days of broad Arab or Islamic integration driven by one or another Arab nationalist or Islamist ideology seem to have ended in failure. The prospects for the successful return or emergence of some new ideological driver of integration are remote. A transition to pragmatism, however, has yet to be effected. Sub-regional and regional conflicts remain too intense for integration driven by the narrow logic of economic efficiency and confined to specific sub-regions or sectors to proceed very far. The nature of MENA political economies, based as most are on rent extraction impelling and sustaining limited access orders, means that national political elites fear truly effective economic integration as it would threaten their control and extraction of rents. Those elites thus remain at best verbal champions of integration, neglecting the political and economic infrastructure required for sustained and effective integration. Counter-elites are too fragmented and too driven to extremism by repression and the nature of their ideologies to formulate coherent policies for integration that could attract wide appeal. Regionalism, in short, is likely to remain piecemeal, intermittent and subject to reversals, whether at the sub-regional or MENA level, while regionalization continues to inspire hopes for integration while paradoxically rendering it yet more difficult to achieve.

9

SURVIVAL STRATEGIES
IN WEAKER MENA STATES

Thoroughgoing, sustainable development of MENA political economies would require their transition from limited to open access orders. In no country of the region is such a profound change currently being contemplated by its rulers, nor is such a transformation likely. It would involve meeting several "doorstep conditions," of which the most demanding are establishing the rule of law, especially in the form of legal, routinized accountability of and control over elites; providing for "perpetually lived organizations," meaning among other things extension of universal citizenship rights including freedom of speech and assembly; and institutionalized civilian control of militaries and security forces. Even Douglass North and his colleagues who coined the term predict that "open access is not just around the corner" and is not a "likely outcome of a revolutionary struggle."[1] Instead, the transition depends on enough elites and organizations concluding that their interests are better served not by extracting rents, but by establishing open competition and access to organizations, combined with "the rule of law to hold society together and to limit violence."[2] These developments in turn depend on stable pacts between competitive elites and the "eventual emergence of enough organizations to create a new equilibrium that can sustain an Open Access Order."[3]

Such a transition in the MENA seems more distant now than in the period leading up to and during the Arab Spring of 2011. The political tumult of those uprisings shook the Arab world to the core, destroying several states, weakening others, and causing surviving states to batten down political hatches, preparing to meet anticipated future political storms. Even the non-Arab MENA states moved in similar, repressive directions. In the wake of the alleged 2016 coup attempt, Turkey's President Erdogan, working through the AK Party and its newly established authority over security forces and the judiciary, succeeded in establishing near dictatorial control over the political system, eroding institutional and legal legacies of prior political freedoms. His counterpart in Iran, Ayatollah Ali Khamanei, unleashed the Basij paramilitary forces and its mother organization, the IRGC, against participants in the June 2009 popular reaction against what was seen as being a forged outcome to that month's presidential election, dubbed the "green revolution" or "Persian Spring." The outcome was similar to that of the Arab Spring in Egypt and Bahrain, with leaders being jailed, others fleeing into exile, and still other participants imprisoned, tortured and killed. Severe constraints on opposition political activity established in Iran in 2009–10 remain in place, and have even intensified. Israel, having all but abandoned attempts to negotiate a two-state solution with the Palestinians, has resorted to ever greater violence against them, especially in Gaza, while cultivating a chauvinist, intolerant Jewish nationalism within Israel itself, steadily restricting the political space for expression of alternative views, most especially if they are put forward by Palestinians, including even those serving in the Knesset, Israel's parliament.

The dilemma which MENA incumbent elites face is how to engineer reforms that will energize their flagging economies without also opening up the closed political systems over which these elites preside. Their initial instinct, when faced with the region-wide challenge posed by the Arab Spring, was to repress real and imagined oppositions, both domestic and regional. As the immediate political threat began to recede it was followed in short order by economic pressure resulting from the 2014 downturn in oil prices, thereby causing incumbent elites to seek new sources of revenue, reduce entitlement allocations to their populations, and accomplish both without relaxing their tight grip on politics.

The combination of these immediate political and economic challenges arose against the backdrop of a growing awareness of the non-sustainability of the region-wide rentier economy in which virtually all states of the region are enmeshed. The basic, ominous math of rapidly expanding populations coupled with stagnating, even declining earnings from direct and indirect hydrocarbon exports was becoming increasingly apparent to all, including incumbent elites. The MENA population increased fivefold from 1950, when it was 110 million, to 569 million in 2017. By the end of this century, despite predicted declines in total fertility rates in the MENA, so-called "population momentum," resulting from a high proportion of women of child-bearing age, will have driven the MENA population to over a billion people, more than China and double Europe's population. Fully half of the MENA population will be concentrated in three countries—Egypt, Iraq and Sudan, with 200 million, 156 million and 137 million respectively—two of which are among the region's poorer countries. Well before that time the age distribution of the MENA population will have shifted from having an economically beneficial youth bulge to one beset with an aging population with its inevitable economic drag effect. In Tunisia, for example, the old age dependency ratio, which was 6.9% in 1980, will be 15% in 2025 and 54% by 2100.[4] These demographic trends bode ill for the region's economic sustainability, including its basic sustenance. It is already the world's largest importer of basic foodstuffs, absorbing one third of the global total. Rapid population growth in the region's two major river systems, the Nile and the Tigris-Euphrates, will place additional downward pressure on the region's aggregate agricultural production, which for years has been falling further behind increasing consumption driven primarily by population growth.[5]

The formula for the region's sustainability over the past half century—trading oil for food and other goods and services—is of ever diminishing utility as population expands, thereby driving up the need for imports and depressing agricultural output, at least on a per capita basis. If calculations also include stagnating or possibly declining gross hydrocarbon export revenues, let alone per capita revenues, their implications become dire. The projections of major forecasters, public and private, for oil and gas, are for their prices to remain more or less flat for several years, with no anticipated major price increases into the foreseeable future under the most likely demand scenarios. Possessing half the world's known oil reserves, the biggest exporter of that commodity and the one whose GDPs, private sectors and governmental budgets are most dependent upon those exports, the MENA will be particularly hard hit as oil earnings fall ever further behind expanding revenue needs. The International Energy Agency's prediction for MENA oil earnings until 2040, based on the assumption that demand for oil will be constrained by environmental concerns and the development of new technologies, is that oil revenues will not return to 2014 levels at any time through the end of the forecasting period.[6] The fiscal oil break-even price for each MENA producer differs as it is the price at which their budgets are in balance, so not only variable between but also within countries. In 2017, with oil forecast for the year to cost $52.50 per barrel, Fitch

Ratings estimated fiscal break-even prices for the major MENA oil exporters at between $60 and $84 per barrel, with Saudi Arabia at $74 and Kuwait at the MENA's lowest with $45, it being the only major exporter to be able to balance its national accounts with its earnings from oil. And indeed, since 2015 most major MENA oil exporters have run budget deficits, covering shortfalls by drawing down their sovereign wealth funds or by borrowing, increasingly from foreign lenders. It is not anticipated that the oil fiscal break-even price for any MENA country other than Kuwait will drop below the actual price for the foreseeable future, condemning the major exporters to significantly reducing spending, increasing revenues from other sources, or incurring budget deficits to be covered by borrowing. As for the external break-even oil price, which is the price at which the current account balance is 0, the IMF predicted in light of anticipated import reductions that in 2018 the break-even price would range from a low of $39 per barrel for Iran, to $54 for Saudi Arabia, to $55 for Iraq, $70 for Algeria and $75 for Libya.[7] The average price OPEC exporters received per barrel in 2017 was as Fitch predicted, $52.50, suggesting that only Iran was able to cover its import needs entirely from oil export revenues.[8]

With these gathering economic clouds increasingly visible to MENA political elites, they recognized the immediate need to trim governmental expenditures while expanding revenues, as well as the longer term need to render their economies more sustainable. Virtually every MENA country thus adopted fiscal reform packages that included some mix of subsidy reductions, lower costs of public employment combined with increased employment in the private sector and, on the revenue side, some or more taxation, typically concentrated on indirect taxes, especially of the value-added type. Stepped up repression applied more or less simultaneously with these reforms was undertaken out of fear of negative public reactions to these stringency measures which amounted to the most significant departure ever from the social contracts which had underpinned these economies since independence.

Innovative as these reforms have been, they have done little if anything to address the primary underlying cause of increasing fiscal deficits, which is the region's pervasive limited access orders generating rents for incumbent elites and those connected to them, while discouraging independent private economic activity. Squaring the circle of maintaining control of the political economy while simultaneously encouraging it to generate more employment, profits and taxes, is the daunting challenge incumbent elites face. Not surprisingly, the methods they have adopted to resolve this dilemma reflect the underlying characteristics of the political economies over which they preside, which are in turn products of their path dependencies since prior to the colonial era. In this and the following chapter we shall investigate the strategies characteristic of the categories of MENA states produced by their particular path dependencies, which are failed and fragile states, authoritarian republics, monarchies and outliers. For each category at least one representative state will be investigated in more detail to exemplify the larger set.

Failed and Fragile States

Failed states in the MENA include Libya, Yemen and Syria, all of which have been devastated by civil wars which are yet to be conclusively resolved. Fragile states include two countries recovering from civil wars coupled with invasions—Iraq and Lebanon—as well as Sudan, which lost the southern portion of its country through an internationally imposed agreement resulting from civil war; and Palestine, which is not only occupied by Israel, but divided as a result of a brief civil war in June 2007 between the rule of Hamas in Gaza and that of Fatah and the Palestine Authority on the West Bank. Any one of these fragile states could dissolve again into civil war, again with devastating consequences. Physical rebuilding of the three failed states, when and if uncontested national authority is re-established, will take hundreds of billions of dollars and a generation or more, judging by the example of much more compact Lebanon, the first MENA country to confront post-civil war reconstruction. As for socio-political and economic recovery, the scars preventing both are so deep that neither is imaginable until a subsequent generation manages to come to power and begins to heal them.

The path dependency shared by these failed and fragile states is that all are the products of the colonial era, none other than Yemen having had any substantial pre-colonial experience of statehood. Yemen's pre-colonial statehood was so fractured geographically, socially and by virtue of foreign occupation that very little stateness emerged there prior to the end of colonial rule, nor much after that either. The capacities of the failed and fragile states are the lowest of any of the categories of MENA states. They preside over the most fragmented of the region's national societies. These countries have throughout their modern histories experienced more internal political violence and external interventions than others in the MENA. Their governments, with the exception of profoundly fragmented Lebanon, have been the region's most authoritarian, possessing the lowest levels of infrastructural power because their rule through dictatorial power has distanced their societies from their states. These then were the MENA states most likely to fail or nearly so when external and/or internal pressures intensified after their creations under colonial tutelage. Lebanon, being subjected to internal and external pressures simultaneously, was the first to do so, beginning with its mini-civil war in 1958, followed by its "maxi" civil war from 1975 to 1990, and its continuing fragile condition since that time. While less authoritarian than its fellow failed and fragile states, by virtue of having grappled with failure and the threat thereof longer than they have, Lebanon provides the most useful prototype of the difficult task of state reconstruction in MENA countries not favorably blessed by historical inheritances.

As for the more authoritarian ones, Sudan may be the most fragile, having lost its southern regions, which contain three-quarters of the combined oil output, to the newly created South Sudan in 2011. Since 2003 the western Darfur region of Sudan has been the site of an insurrection against the Khartoum-based government, with its non-Arab population suffering ethnic cleansing at the hands of Arab troops and irregular forces dispatched by Omar al Bashir, the country's President accused in 2008 of genocide, war crimes and crimes against humanity by the International Criminal Court. Al Bashir's ruling National Congress Party came to power by virtue of an alliance between the military and Islamists that overthrew the elected government of Sadiq al Mahdi, who went into exile only to return to Sudan in late 2018 amidst spreading riots in protest against a currency devaluation from 29 Sudanese pounds to the dollar to 47.5 and associated inflation and general economic mismanagement. In the northern city of Atbara "bread" riots that broke out in December 2018 led to numerous deaths at the hands of security forces. Al Mahdi was presumably preparing to contest the scheduled 2020 presidential election, for which al Bashir was not entitled to run because of a constitutional two-term limit. In late 2018, however, parliament commenced procedures to waive that provision, a move contributing to spreading unrest that in April 2019 caused the military to remove al Bashir. Sudan, in sum, having become heavily dependent for governmental revenues on oil exports, which in volume are now only one quarter what they were prior to 2011 and in value less than a fifth, is facing the immediate task of reinventing its political economy to avert total collapse. According to the World Bank it is in "debt distress" with 86% of its debt in arrears.[9]

Douglass North and his "neo-institutional" economist colleagues argue that stable pacts between competitive elites, combined with agreements to permit open political and economic competition, are the two "doorstep" conditions for transition from a limited to an open access order. Post-civil war state reconstruction, as exemplified by the process in Lebanon, illustrates how in the MENA the first condition, that of forging pacts between elites, is more easily achieved than the latter. Relative peace can be achieved by those pacts, so they are favored by nationals and international peace makers. They are based, however, on short-term, mutual elite interests in rent seeking, meaning plundering state resources, rather than on long-term reconciliation accompanied with measures to shift the economy from rent seeking to production by virtue of opening it to fair, regulated competition. Pacts in these cases enable elites to appropriate political and economic power, plundering resources intended for reconstruction to reward themselves and bolster their patronage networks. This in turn entrenches rather than dissolves the socio-political differences that gave rise to civil war. Pacts and the resources transferred to elites by them reinforce the vertical clientage networks that contested the civil war, rather than supplanting them with new, horizonal affiliations made possible by citizenship rights. Elite pacts can bring temporary peace and some reconstruction, but they are unlikely by themselves to pave the way to reconciliation coupled with thoroughgoing political and physical rebuilding. For this the transition from the limited access orders favored by incumbent elites to open access orders beneficial to the country as a whole would be necessary, but that second doorstep condition is precisely the change elites resist.

Lebanon

Three features characterize the Lebanese post-civil war political economy. The first is the low, indeed almost complete lack of elite turnover since even before the civil war, other than through external intervention or aging and death, in which case replacements are the brothers, sons, sons-in-law, grandsons or nephews of the departed. Those who commanded forces in the civil war and its immediate wake are those now in charge of rebuilding the country. The two exceptions to this general rule are the Hariris—Rafic al Hariri, the Prime Minister assassinated in 2005, and his son, Saad al Hariri, who succeeded him—and Hizbullah, headed by Hassan Nasrallah. Their entrance into the political elite is due primarily to foreign backing, the Saudis in the case of the Hariris and the Iranians in the case of Hizbullah. In the absence of that external support neither would be members of the Lebanese political elite. They became the two major poles around which the Sunni and Shi'a communities gathered, exceeding the political stature of competitive Sunni elites, such as the Kararmi and Miqati families from Tripoli, or Shi'a elites, most vital of which is Nabih Berri, inheritor of the Amal Movement created by the Imam Musa Sadr, also with Iranian support, in the early 1970s. The other confessions also have a prominent *za'im* (leader), such as the Druze Walid Junblatt, or two or three competing ones, such as the Maronites Samir Geagea, Michel Aoun and Suliman Frangieh. It has been a generation since a new family has entered this exclusive political club that shares between its members or their clients the positions of President, Prime Minister, key cabinet portfolios and control over a host of governmental instrumentalities. All attempts since the end of the civil war to mobilize politically across confessional lines in opposition to these traditional *zu'ama* (leaders) have failed, as was most recently the case in the 2018 elections, where only two such candidates won seats in the 128-member parliament, one of whom, a prominent female television presenter, did so with only 2,000 votes drawn virtually exclusively from the Armenian community.

The second dominant feature of the Lebanese political economy that has emerged since the guns fell silent in 1989 is that it has become even more narrowly based on rents produced by capital and human linkages to the oil exporting MENA economies. In the wake of the civil war, Lebanon, assisted by Saudi Arabia, sought successfully to consolidate its position as a leading banking center in the MENA. Although challenged by Bahrain and other GCC countries in this endeavor, Beirut was able to capitalize on some advantages, key of which were Saudi desires to bolster Lebanese banks in support of their client Hariri and to have a conduit for flight capital, coupled with the weak Lebanese state ensuring the independence and secrecy of the banking sector. This it managed by its very weakness, by mutual agreement between elites who benefitted from their ownership of banks, coupled with capable management by its sophisticated, if highly secretive, central bank, which has not publicly released an annual financial statement since 2002.

The source of rents other than the movement of capital was the movement of people. Lebanon became a prime supplier of manpower to the oil-rich states, thereby generating remittances that constituted a greater proportion of its GDP and external earnings than most if not all other MENA countries. Human movement in the opposite direction was that by oil-rich Arabs and even by Iranians and Turks, who came to Lebanon not only for banking and tourism, but to invest in real estate and enjoy the fruits of those investments.

It is that economy that is now in retreat, just as the region-wide oil and gas driven rentier economy itself is as a result of the sustained, substantial fall in the rent to population ratios of the primary oil producers. The decline of hydrocarbon prices is driving them to attempt to diversify into more productive, sustainable economic activity. For this they need capital at home, not in Lebanon. And they need to employ nationals, not expatriates, such as Lebanese. Lebanon's two key sources of rent are both taking hits that show no sign of abating.

During the fat years Lebanon did not prepare itself for the present lean ones. It built a consumption-based economy, underpinned by a currency peg to the US dollar that stimulated capital flow into the country by rendering it more secure against devaluation. The peg guaranteed a severe case of Dutch Disease, whereby the overvalued Lebanese pound rendered the production and export of tradeable goods and services non-competitive. The agricultural and industrial sectors stagnated while construction and real estate, along with banking, boomed. Industrial exports, which averaged over $3 billion annually from 2008 to 2015 and which peaked at $3.57 billion in 2012, had by 2016 dropped to some $2.5 billion and fell further in 2017. The service, industry and agricultural sectors constituted 72%, 14% and 4%, respectively, of real GDP from 2004 to 2016. Real estate is the largest service sector, averaging during that period 14% of GDP. For the six years leading up to 2018 the balance of payments was in deficit, with the trade deficit in 2017 amounting to almost $17 billion. Construction, so vital to the economy, is not only primarily a consumption good, it is inherently incapable of significant productivity increases, thereby ensuring the growth of a low-skilled, low-wage labor force, much of which has been Syrian since even before the influx of refugees after 2011. Inadequate investment in and management of public education reinforced the trend of stagnating human skills and productivity, further reinforced by the emigration of educated and skilled Lebanese. In 2018 Lebanon ranked 105th out of 137 countries on the Global Competitiveness Index, outperforming only Yemen in the MENA.

As for the vitally important banking sector, it too failed to adjust to new realities as it was also harnessed to consumption. While the state was not strong enough to subordinate that key sector directly, the interests of the elites who have captured that state lay in gaining control over banks and ensuring their profitability. That they did, with the Lebanese banking sector being dominated by locally owned enterprises, unlike much banking elsewhere in the region. Most foreign-owned banks simply gave up in the face of what became a closed system, whereby high interest rates attracted domestic and regional deposits that could then be lent on to the government of Lebanon at eye-watering interest rates. The private sector was crowded out, its portion of bank credit falling to only about one third of the total, or half the public sector's share.

In this fashion Lebanon accumulated the world's third highest public debt as a proportion of its GDP, a proportion that now hovers around 150% and is forecast by the World Bank to reach 165% in 2020. The public debt in 1993 was $3 billion, but by 2018 had risen to $84 billion. This financial house of cards can only be kept upright by continued deposits in banks, by provision of public foreign assistance to the government of Lebanon, and by implicit guarantees provided by GCC states, key of which is Saudi Arabia. Domestic production has no chance of playing an important role. The massive public debt was accumulated not for the purpose of investment in fixed capital assets, but for the private gain of the elites who captured the state and the banking sector. Since 2007 public spending on capital projects has averaged less than 2% of GDP, significantly below comparator countries. That the public is now being held responsible for servicing that debt poses what thus far has been a politically impossible task, as reflected in Lebanon's very low total and especially low income tax revenues as a percentage of GDP. So fiscal policy can only nibble at the edge of deficit reduction, while the elite continue to hope that the system can be salvaged with more international bailouts, maybe made more likely by increasing oil prices and European fears of uncontrolled migration, especially of some of the more than 1 million Syrian refugees in uneasy exile in Lebanon.

But salvation is not at hand. The capital available in the West for bailouts of financially beleaguered MENA states, which include Egypt, Jordan, Tunisia, Syria, Yemen and possibly others, is not enough to go around. Lebanon is not of the geo-political significance of several of those states, so not a likely candidate to receive large shares of public foreign assistance. Private investments have been lagging for some years now, as reflected by the steady decline in FDI, not only into Lebanon, where in 2017 greenfield FDI was less than 1% of GDP, but into the entire MENA. It is in most countries now about half of what it was prior to 2007. Rising global interest rates are particularly threatening to Lebanon's fiscal sustainability given its profound debt and already high debt servicing costs which absorb about 40% of total public expenditure. The World Bank observed in 2018, while expressing concern about Lebanon's Net Foreign Asset position, that "Since 2011, there has been a discernable slowdown in deposit growth, the bulwark for financing internal and external imbalances."[10] An upsurge of FDI and even of bank deposits and direct purchases of government bond and T-bill issues would require not only dramatic improvements in Lebanon's unstable political conditions due partly to spillover from the Syrian war, but a thorough-going overhaul of the political economy, the most central feature of which would be the emergence of a responsive, accountable, transparent, capable state able to impose macroeconomic stability while upgrading human and physical infrastructure. Even were such a state to emerge it would be many years before such accomplishments could be achieved and begin to have positive effects.

The long-simmering crisis is thus reaching boiling point with no indication that a steady hand will emerge to reduce the heat. Successive World Bank reports and the data contained in them suggest mounting concern and frustration. Fear of the collapse of the ability to sustain the currency peg, thus of associated runaway inflation, dramatically escalating interest rates and pound denominated public debt, is reflected in the documents and data. Inflation rose from less than 1% to 4.4% between 2016 and 2017 and to 6.2% in 2018, suggesting that worse may be in store unless demand collapses due to impoverishment. And not surprisingly the Lebanese have indeed become poorer over the past five years and are predicted by the World Bank to grow poorer still. Real GDP per capita fell by 4% annually from 2013 to 2015, by 1.6% in 2018, and is forecast to fall by about that amount through 2020. Remittances are not picking up the slack in the domestic economy. They were lower as a percentage of GDP in 2018 than in any of the preceding five years and are predicted to stagnate or fall through 2020. The budget deficit has remained stubbornly high since 2013 at around 8% of GDP but is predicted to rise to 8.9% in 2019 and 9.2% in 2020.

The third feature of the increasingly dysfunctional Lebanese political economy is plundering by the political elite of the state for personal gain and for bolstering the clientage networks upon which their political power rests. The plundering takes two forms, both of which are profoundly deleterious for the state's capacities. One is outright corruption, reflected in Lebanon's ranking 143rd out of 180 countries on Transparency International's Corruption Perception Index, with only the other failed and fragile MENA states of Iraq, Syria, Yemen, Libya, Sudan and South Sudan being perceived as more corrupt. The only other "state" in that category, Palestine, is not included in the rankings.[11] Related to spreading corruption is increasing disparity of wealth. According to the most thorough and recent study, "income is extremely concentrated, with the top 1 and 10% of the adult population receiving 25 and 55% of national income on average, placing Lebanon among the countries with the highest level of income inequality in the world."[12]

The other form plunder takes is utilization of the civil service and public sector to provide patronage positions for clients, a practice that pre-existed the ending of the civil war but which was intensified subsequently as part of the grand bargain tacitly agreed between elites to mutually sustain their political dominance, whatever the cost to the country. This practice directly violates formal provisions of the Ta`if Accords reached to end the war, as they stipulated that confessional-based recruitment would be restricted to only first grade positions in the bureaucracy and public sector, and that those positions would be divided equally between Christians and Muslims but would not be specifically allotted to any particular confession. But these restrictions on confessionalism, hence clientelism, were ignored as "not only first grade positions, but also second, third, fourth and fifth ones were sectarianized ... Recruitment to the public sector became part of a complex ensemble protecting the political, economic, and security prerogatives of the sectarian elite and their cronies." The result was that "state institutions consequently emerged as strategic sites in the postwar political elite's vast clientelist ensemble undergirding the political economy of sectarianism." As Bassel Salloukh concludes, it was transformed into "a veritable 'allotment' state', or *dawlat al-muhasasa*."[13] It is not surprising, therefore, that the vast majority of Lebanese believe that the confessional system aggravates rather than ameliorates inter-sectarian tensions, so does not perform the primary function for which it was designed. A poll conducted by the US Department of State in October 2018, for example, found that "86% overall say Lebanon's confessional pact aggravates sectarian tensions, up substantially from 51% in 2013." The poll results also indicated almost universal pessimism among the Lebanese, with 69% overall and 81% of Christians saying that the general political and economic situation will worsen, with those Lebanese who voted in the May 2018 election substantially more pessimistic than those who did not—74% versus 53%.[14]

The consequences of the debasement of the civil service were not only to undermine what remained of its effectiveness after 15 years of civil war, but to vastly increase its size and cost as it was "preoccupied by predatory rentier practices along sectarian and clientelist lines rather than engineering national unity and implementing policies that serve the public good."[15] The growth of the public sector confirms this assessment. Employing 75,000 in 1974, by 2017 it had expanded to 300,000. About half of all new recruits were hired outside the purview of the Civil Service Board and entirely on the basis of sectarian, rather than meritocratic considerations. As for first grade positions, all of which are selected by the political elite, 27 are affiliated directly with Nabih Berri's Shi'a Amal Movement, 18 with Hariri's Sunni Future Movement, 11 with President Michel Aoun's largely Maronite Free Patriotic Movement, and ten with Walid Jumblatt's Druze-based Progressive Socialist Party. The entire bureaucracy is stove-piped into satraps of one or another of these or other political groupings, so "whole of government" approaches to implementing public policy are out of the question. The Ministry of Higher Education, for example, passes from one political movement to another with changes of government, whereby its Center for Educational Research and Development remains in the hands of the Free Patriotic Movement, while the Directorate of Vocational and Technical Education is a bastion of Amal and the Directorate of Higher Education of Sunnis not allied with the Future Movement. All of these satraps compete for resources and work to undermine the others. The Lebanese University is a battleground between the competing confessional political organizations, struggles between them determining selection of students, choice of deans and professors.[16] Overstaffing reaches absurd levels, such as in public education, where there is an average of 7.37 students for each teacher, with 88 public schools having an average of three or less students per teacher. Every student in public school costs the state $4,000 annually in teachers' salaries. Public sector salaries and wages in 2018 consumed 38% of the government budget and were estimated by the head of the central bank to swallow up 35% of GDP. The proportion of public sector employees of the total labor force climbed from 12.5% in 2004 to 25% in 2017. Public sector pensions alone in 2017 cost 15% of total state revenues. In 2018 a series of new indirect taxes and fees were imposed in order to pay for dramatic public sector wage increases legislated in 2017, thereby further damaging the already ailing business climate, to say nothing of imposing yet greater hardships on a population of whom 30% are living in poverty on less than $4 per day.[17]

Iraq

Lebanon represents the most elaborate, longstanding case of conflict avoidance and statehood preservation through elite "pacting," whereby intra-elite agreement on a ceasefire is coupled with arrangements for generating and sharing rents to preserve incumbents' political and economic power. But the defective Lebanese model is broadly representative of post-conflict agreements in MENA failed and fragile states. Indeed, for Iraq it served as an explicit model for US decision makers when stitching together a post-Saddam constitutional order in the wake of their invasion in 2003. Confessionalism, meaning the division of governmental posts on the basis of sectarian identities, was enshrined in Iraqi constitutional and legal procedures and political practice, supplanting longstanding Iraqi traditions of Sunni pre-eminence ameliorated somewhat by some political inclusion of Shi'i, Kurds and Christians, although not on any formulaic or citizenship rights basis.

As in Lebanon, coupling peace making with confessionalizing all of government became in Iraq a recipe for elite capture of the state, underpinned by clientelism extended throughout the political economy. And just as in Lebanon, the inevitable consequences were elite rent seeking driving corruption, a vast expansion of the civil service, and inevitable administrative and economic deterioration. The only significant difference between the two countries was that whereas in Lebanon rents have been generated through the banking system, in Iraq they have been produced by oil exports. And again, just as Lebanon has become steadily more dependent upon the banking sector to sustain government revenue and foreign currency inflows as other sectors suffered from Dutch Disease effects, so in Iraq has dependence on oil become steadily greater as the agricultural, industrial and non-governmental service sectors have shrunk, sectors which the previous Ba'thist regime of Saddam Hussein had with some success encouraged. As the World Bank observes, "Iraq is the world leader today in terms of dependence on oil, with the hydrocarbon sector accounting for 58% of the country's GDP, 99% of its exports, and more than 90% of central government revenue."[18]

The World Bank also notes that "in addition to undermining the quality of the civil service, the dramatic rise in clientelistic hiring since 2003 has contributed to a ballooning of public sector employment and of the wage bill."[19] Between 2003 and 2015, the civil service alone, so not including state-owned enterprises (SOEs), grew from less than 1 million to over 3 million employees, making it far and away the country's largest employer, providing 42% of all jobs. If SOE employment is included the public sector as a whole accounts for more than half the country's jobs with some 3.5 million employees.[20] Between 2004 and 2016 expenditures on civil service salaries rose by 940%, with their share of the government budget rising from 7% to 44%, at which point they consumed 18% of GDP.[21] The Bank's index of meritocracy versus favoritism in public sector hiring places Iraq at the bottom not only of upper-middle-income countries, but of MENA countries as well, concluding that "in Iraq merit matters far less for promotion and social mobility than ... networks and favoritism."[22] But even the massive increase in government jobs could not contain the rise in unemployment, which reached 16% in 2018.

The drag effects of converting the civil service and SOEs into patronage swamps include its drain on government revenues, its undermining of administrative capabilities and the performance of SOEs—of which only some 25% are profitable and in which about half of employees represent "excess labor"—while also increasing corruption, and paradoxically, political instability coupled with authoritarianism, the very curses that the confession-based clientelistic system was intended to overcome. One of the best measures of administrative capacities is public financial management (PFM), which refers to the government's ability to track spending during the various phases of the budget cycle. The World Bank's assessment of PFM in Iraq suggests profound deficiencies, as "line ministries and affiliated agencies often lack reliable data on the availability of funds ... cash management is weak and the government often has insufficient cash available to meet its financial obligations as they fall due."[23] So-called "ghost workers" are another indicator of poor PFM, with at least 50,000 of them having been identified in only two ministries during a search for such ghosts in 2015.[24] Interestingly Iraq scores next to Lebanon on the Open Budget Index, 11th and 12th from the bottom of 100 countries, respectively, with both scoring 3 out of 100 possible points and both being characterized by the International Budget Partnership as having "scant or no information available."[25] Iraq ranks 169th out of 180 countries on the

179

Corruption Perception Index, worse than Lebanon's 143rd ranking, but not as bad as several other failed or fragile MENA countries, including Libya, Syria, Yemen, Sudan and South Sudan, which rank from 171 to the very bottom rank of 180. The administration of justice is similarly deficient, with Iraq ranking at the bottom of all MENA countries on rule of law indices and in the bottom 10% worldwide.[26] According to the 2018 *Doing Business* report, Iraq ranks 171 out of 190 countries overall, with its scores on enforcing contracts and resolving insolvency, the two dimensions that most directly reflect the quality of administration of justice, being in the bottom half of scores on the nine dimensions that comprise the overall index.[27] Partly because of inadequacies in the administration of justice, as well as the pervasiveness of corruption, Iraq ranks at the bottom of MENA countries in proportion of domestic credit going to the private sector. As in Lebanon, the government uses banks primarily to provide itself with funds, not to extend credit to businesses or individuals.

It is hardly surprising that Iraqis are profoundly dissatisfied with their government and the quality of services it provides. Only 30% of Iraqis are satisfied with educational services, 20% with health services and 15% with security services; 52% do not trust the government "much or at all," and 39% consider its performance "bad or very bad." The World Bank concludes from this survey data that "the feeling of exclusion is reflected in the data: Iraqis have a higher impatience for reform than the populations of comparator countries."[28] An October 2018 poll conducted by the US Department of State revealed the toll taken on public support even among Shi'a for political parties nominally representing them. The Iranian-backed Badr Organization, Kata'ib Hizballah and Asa'ib Ahl al-Haq all suffered from diminished public support since the last poll conducted two years previously. The decline was due primarily to growing disaffection among Shi'a. The vast majority of Sunnis and Kurds had been from the outset opposed to these militias cum political parties. In the 2018 poll, for example, just 28% of Shi'a said they supported the Badr Organization, down from 88% in early 2016, with Shi'a support for the other two organizations falling similarly. Support for Hadi al-Amiri and Abu Mahdi al-Muhandis, the two principal Shi'a militia leaders, fell by half or more over the same period. The only Shi'a militia cum party which received substantial support in the 2018 poll was Muqtada al-Sadr's Saraya al-Salam, with 52% of Shi'a supporting its goals and activities. The gap between Sadr and his Shi'a political competitors is most probably due to his more pronounced pro-Iraqi positions, as evidenced in his criticism of Iran's influence in Iraq, coupled with his calls for reform and stopping corruption.[29]

But reform, despite its widespread appeal, is not imminent. The consequence for politics of this limited access order based on rent-seeking clientelism and failing to provide adequate governance to citizens is not to lay the bases for positive change, but to destabilize politics as elites struggle to garner rents. For good reason, Iraqis are fed up with those who have ruled them, so are looking for alternatives, but constrained in so doing by virtue of the confession-based clientelistic system erected since the US invasion. Cross-confessional, horizontally based political organization, as in Lebanon, competes ineffectively with vertical, clientelistic ties cemented by material resources, presided over by powerful elites. Political contestation is thus primarily between those commanding confessional clientelistic networks, thereby rendering politics an intensely personal struggle for resource control associated with governmental positions.

As in Lebanon, Iraqi cabinet formation is a fraught process, virtually whatever the election outcome. Coincidentally both countries held parliamentary elections in May 2018, and as of December of that year neither had managed to form a government. In both cases leading political figures contested control of key ministries and refused to compromise, exacerbating political and economic crises in both countries. And in both cases, outside influences, chiefly Iran and the US in Iraq, sought to steer the outcome. While in Lebanon the primary conflict pitted Shi'a-based Hizbullah against Saad al Hariri's Sunni-based Future Movement, in Iraq the key contestants were both Shi'a as that sect comprises more than 60% of the population so is more dominant than it is in Lebanon. Saaroun, headed by Muqtada al Sadr, and al Fatah, headed by Hadi al Amiri and backed by Iran, were split over cabinet choices in general and that of the Minister of Interior in particular, vital as that post is to the country's overall security policy and its implementation. Al Sadr threatened to resort to street protests to block al Amiri's nominees, a threat which may have also been related to the killing of one of the commanders of his Saraya al Salam militia. The incumbent Prime Minister, Adil Abdul Mahdi, like his four predecessors since the 2003 invasion, had insufficient power to impose his will on the contestants. In the meantime, the Iraqi economy continued to deteriorate, with total government debt climbing steadily upward from 31% in 2013 to an anticipated 63% at the end of 2018, with GDP per capita falling from over $7,000 to around $5,000 over that five-year period.

Lebanon and Iraq thus both illustrate the perils of elite pacting in limited access orders as a means to end violent national conflicts. Unless coupled with measures to ensure accountability of those elites to citizens adequately empowered, the elites will plunder national resources to ensure their tenure, key of which are provided through the state in the form of rents and clientelistic networks. Both are inimical to growth and political inclusion. But the inappropriate Lebanese and Iraqi model may be replicated in other failed and fragile states because it is preferred by both domestic and external actors to continued violence, who see no other possible model for stopping it. These are countries in which path dependency has not led to states with sufficient capacities to govern well, to adequate inclusion of their populations, nor to incumbent elites willing to open up the limited access orders over which they prevail. Facing the problem of declining national resources per capita, all these states are hard pressed to avert returns to or continuations of political violence.

Authoritarian Republics: Algeria, Egypt, Iran and Turkey

These authoritarian republics have fared better in recent years than the failed and fragile states just discussed, attesting to their more favorable path dependencies leading to superior state capacities. Egypt, Iran and Turkey are three of the MENA countries with venerable traditions of statehood. They manifest more state capacity than Algeria, which, like the failed and fragile states, was essentially a colonial creation, although it had a limited tradition of statehood along portions of its Mediterranean coast. While these four authoritarian republics have greater state capacities than the failed and fragile states, they have less than the monarchies or the "outliers," Israel and Tunisia. They have been strong and cohesive enough to survive national and regional tumult since the early 1990s, but they have been shaken to the core by it.

An Islamist-led insurrection swept through Algeria following a coup in the wake of the 1991 electoral victory by the Islamic Salvation Front (FIS). Lasting throughout the decade of the 1990s the insurrection resulted in between 50,000 and 200,000 deaths, but the government grimly hung on, as in Sudan resorting to a "dirty war" to liquidate opponents. That experience, combined with subsequent terrorist attacks launched by Islamist extremists, chief of whom were in al Qaida of the Islamic Maghrib (AQIM), appeared to politically numb much of the population. But when President Abd al Aziz

Bouteflika announced in early 2019 his intention to run for a fifth term, the street suddenly awoke, with protests initially led by students swelling as they had some eight years previously in Cairo and other Arab capitals. And as in Egypt the military distanced itself from the President, initially announcing that he would not be a candidate, then standing by as demonstrations for his resignation intensified, causing him to tender it in early April as the military sought a replacement and so to preserve its grip on power.

Egypt, Iran and Turkey have not faced civil wars as has Algeria, but they have had to deal with popular uprisings, violent conflict and coups. Egypt's Arab Spring demonstrations culminated in the removal of President Husni Mubarak by the military, which then staged a coup in June 2013 against the elected Muslim Brotherhood President, Muhammad al Mursi. Since that time an Islamist insurrection has bubbled away in the Sinai Peninsula, occasionally boiling over into other regions of the country.

Iran faced its own popular uprising in June 2009, which the regime brutally suppressed. It continues to confront violent opposition on the periphery of the central plateau that has always provided the core of the Persian state, most notably in the southwest region of Khuzestan, where an Arab separatist movement flourishes. Intermittent protests in rural and poor areas throughout the country in 2018 reflected broad dissatisfaction with the regime and the corruption within it.

After the 2002 parliamentary election won by the Islamist AK Party, Turkey was the site of an underground struggle between the Kemalist security state based primarily on the military and, originally, the Islamist movement generally, but this ultimately became a triangular struggle between the AK Party led by Erdogan, the Gulenist movement and the military. The failed coup attempt in 2016 led to massive arrests and purges of not only the military but the entire state apparatus, accompanied by a severe crackdown on all political freedoms and a new constitution that endowed the President with dictatorial powers.

The going has thus not been easy for any of these states, but they have survived. To do so they relied ever more heavily on coercion and repression, as manifested by the ascending power of the military and security services in all of them, with the former having assumed more direct power in Algeria and Egypt. Along with security services, militaries in Iran and, to a lesser extent, Turkey, have come to exercise significant power under authoritarian Islamist leaders, the mullahs led by Supreme Leader Ali Khamenei in Iran and President Erdogan and his AK Party in Turkey. In that latter case, however,

183

the network of Islamist civil society organizations and businesses provides a substantial base for the regime, hence a counterbalance to all coercive institutions.[30] The authoritarian republics are thus either military or Islamist party led dictatorships—limited access orders in which ruling elites are fearful of providing space in which autonomous political or economic actors might operate and accrue political or material resources.

The World Bank's governance indicators provide an insight into their comparative state capacities. In 2017, the most recent year for which data are available, all except Turkey scored below the MENA average on all six indicators, and those three countries also scored below the average of the Latin American and Caribbean (LAC) region, in GDP per capita the closest region to the MENA. The LAC region's average score across the six indicators is above 50, some ten points higher than the MENA average score. The average score of OECD countries is in the 80s, about double the MENA average. As for Turkey, it outperforms the MENA average on all of the six indicators other than "political stability and the absence of violence." On the two measures most directly reflective of state capacity, "government effectiveness" and "regulatory quality," Turkey's scores of 55 and 57, respectively, place it several points above the average of upper-middle-income countries and 11 and 15 points, respectively, above the MENA average on those two indicators. By way of comparison to a fragile authoritarian state, Sudan's average score on all six indicators is just over 5, indicative of its comparatively very weak state capacities, whereas Turkey's leading average score similarly suggests its superior state capacities, further reflected in the fact that it has the highest GDP per capita of the authoritarian republics.

Turkey is the most successful of the authoritarian republics, with the other three more or less equal in total across the six indicators of governance quality, with Egypt slightly outperforming Algeria and Iran, which are virtually tied. Interestingly this ranking reflects what their historical legacies would predict, with Turkey at the top as the core of the most institutionalized imperial order in the MENA's modern history and as a state having enjoyed for some half century at least partially competitive democratic politics. Colonial creation Algeria is at the bottom but not as far down as it would have been absent the substantial oil and gas wealth that enabled it to outperform levels predicted solely by path-dependency consequences for state capacities.

Rankings on the Resource Governance Index produced by the Natural Resource Governance Institute are less inclusive of MENA states, but those they do rank are generally in the same order as they are on the World Bank's Governance Indicators. Of the 89 countries ranked, Sudan and Libya at 86 and 87, respectively, and Yemen at 78 are the MENA countries with the poorest management of their natural resources, meaning oil in their cases. They are described by the Institute as having "almost no governance framework to ensure resource extraction benefits society. It is highly likely that benefits flow only to some companies and elites."[31] Egypt, Iraq and Iran score 60, 61 and 62, respectively, suggesting in their cases that there are "some minimal procedures and practices to govern resources, but most elements necessary to ensure society benefits are missing." Other than Saudi Arabia at 69, all the other listed MENA states, including Morocco, Tunisia, the UAE, Oman and Kuwait rank between 54th and 26th. In other words, the evaluated authoritarian republics do better on average than the failed or fragile states, but not as well as the monarchies or Tunisia.

There is substantial variation in the political economies of the authoritarian republics, with Turkey's being the best performer, in large part because the onset of authoritarian rule there is comparatively recent. The differences may therefore narrow as they all appear to be becoming more authoritarian, coupled with greater governmental intervention into their economies. A closer look at the internal dynamics of the political economy of one of these states, that of Egypt, will thus serve as an example for the group. It will be briefly compared to Algeria to illustrate differences.

Limited access orders within the authoritarian republics

The Egyptian military abandoned President Mubarak in 2011 out of its institutional interests, one of which is reflective of similar interests in the other authoritarian republics. That interest was control of rents, especially from hydrocarbons and the energy derived therefrom, which increasingly under Mubarak had been captured by cronies associated with the presidency. Once it gained absolute power by virtue of the 2013 coup, the military removed remaining Mubarak cronies or subordinated them to military-owned and operated enterprises or to the Armed Forces Engineering Authority, the body charged by the high command with controlling virtually all major public construction ranging from the as yet to be named new administrative capital to nuclear reactors purchased from Russia to the expanding network of bridges and freeways. Crony capitalists had first emerged in the Sadat era, in part to serve the President's desire for a counterbalance to the military, and in part because of the broader liberalization of the political economy due initially to Sadat's pivot to the West. Subsequently, accelerating globalization combined with the decline of oil prices from the mid-1980s caused most MENA countries to embark on hesitant liberalizations, thereby opening further space for crony capitalists.

Contestation for rents has also characterized the relationship in Algeria between the military, the security services and an expanding group of crony capitalists. Just as in Egypt, the regime's liberalization in the 1980s—a defensive strategy propelled primarily by falling oil prices, hence inability to service the social contract—included relaxation of control over private sector economic activities. This provided the opening for cronies, many of them being the sons and relatives of officers in the military and security services or officials in the ruling party, the FLN, to commence business dealings. When the civil war wound down in the late 1990s and the civilian Abdel Aziz Bouteflika was brought in as President by the military to symbolize reconciliation, the economic and political roles of those cronies began to expand. President Bouteflika, like Sadat and Mubarak, needed them as a counterbalance to the military. The cronies in turn provided resources with which Bouteflika and others could service their clientage networks and finance their election campaigns. The military did, however, undermine one of the key cronies supported by the President and security services, one Rafik Khalifa, the son of a former FLN leader who, with backing from Bouteflika and elements in the security services, had acquired a personal empire including a bank, an airline, a TV station and a football club, worth in total more than $1 billion. The uneasy ruling alliance between Bouteflika, the FLN, the military and the security services, below which cronies jockeyed for position and attachments to powerful political figures above them, was ruptured by widespread protests in 2019 that caused the military to dump Bouteflika. Simultaneous with his removal, numerous prominent cronies were reported by the military as having been apprehended while seeking to flee the country, very reminiscent of the Egyptian military's actions in 2011.

The Algerian economy, in sum, has been at the mercy of key actors in the deep state comprised first and foremost of the military, secondarily of the presidency and security services, and below them, various cronies. And just as in Egypt and most MENA countries, despite its rapaciousness, economic mismanagement and oppression of civil liberties, the military remains far and away the most popular institution in Algeria. The Arab Barometer Survey of 2017 reported that 75% of Algerian respondents said that it was the institution in the country they most trusted, as compared to parliament and political parties, which were trusted by only 14% and 17%, respectively.[32] The primary difference between Egypt and Algeria's limited access orders is that in the former the military since 2013 has asserted absolute power, subordinating the security services and cronies to its will, whereas in Algeria the presidency and security services retained some autonomy, while cronies floated between these protectors, thus enjoying some independence themselves. This fluidity and multiplicity of competing power centers within the elite wrought havoc with public policy, especially that for the vital energy sector. In the last round of bidding for oil and gas licenses, for example, in 2014, only four of 31 blocks on offer were awarded. Production of oil and gas, which accounts for 95% of the country's foreign currency earnings and 40% of its budget, has steadily fallen while domestic consumption, driven by subsidies, has skyrocketed. The failure to attract bids by international oil companies and thus to enhance production is due, according to a London-based energy analyst, to "the political structure of the Algerian regime, which is divided into factions and patronage networks with different clienteles ... It is a minefield."[33] Whether the removal of President Bouteflika will result in a more centralized, militarized regime, as in Egypt, remains to be seen.

Turkey and Iran have different configurations of relationships between the key actors within their ruling orders. Turkey's AKP and Iran's mullahs and their fellow travelers play more important roles than Algeria's FLN or Egypt's regime-allied but weak parties. In Iran the IRGC shares power with the mullah establishment, but in Turkey the one-time Kemalist military has been reconfigured by the AKP, so is yet to assert significant autonomous power in Erdogan's new order. The relative independence of the Turkish economy reflects greater political competition historically and the current relative weakness of the military. The network centered on the "Anatolian Tigers" that Erdogan is now rewarding with state contracts and thereby enlarging his patronage, suggests that if he continues to consolidate his personal power, the autonomy of economic actors will be reduced.

Egypt as exemplar of military reconsolidation

In Egypt the consolidation of military power has proceeded the furthest, with the most profound impacts on the economy, which has been harnessed to the military's will. Central to that will is to demonstrate the institution's and, by implication, the country's power. This is manifested in a project-based approach to economic development, such that economic policy consists of large engineering projects, all of which are under the military's control and implemented by itself, by companies owned directly by it, or by sub-contracting firms, most of which are owned by retired officers. The civil service, the civilian public sector and most private crony capitalists have been brushed aside, although some of the last have been patronized by the military because of their expertise, their external connections and/or their willingness to provide kickbacks to their officer patrons.

What most of these overgrown state projects have in common is that they are touted by President Sisi and the military as being the world's, the MENA's or Africa's largest or highest. The list of such projects is long and growing. In December 2018 it was announced that the Bahr al Baqar (cow's sea) water drainage treatment system would be built, which would process 5 million cubic meters of wastewater daily, sufficient to irrigate more than a quarter of a million acres in the Sinai desert and including the largest desalination plant in the MENA. In that month the Armed Forces Engineering Authority announced a delay in the opening of the world's longest tunnel, which it had begun building in 2017, running under the Suez Canal and linking Cairo to Sharm al Sheikh. In 2016 the Authority commenced construction of the world's largest archeological museum, costing $1 billion, at which time the government borrowed $2.5 billion from Swiss and German banks to have Siemens construct the world's largest power plant in Beni Suef. In March 2018 Cairo announced it would be spending $3 billion from China to build 20 skyscrapers in the new administrative capital, including the tallest in Africa, while in the preceding month it announced it was building in Musturad the largest oil refinery in the MENA, at a cost in excess of $4.1 billion. In December 2018 Sisi also announced that Egypt would "enter the list of the best countries in the world in agriculture" at a launch of the "world's largest date farm" in a suburb of Cairo.[34] Previous projects commenced under Sisi include an $8 billion upgrade of the Suez Canal, a $21 billion nuclear power station on the Mediterranean coast, reclamation of 1 million acres of desert, construction of a network of new freeways, and so on. Insofar as can be determined, no economic cost/benefit studies of any of these projects has been undertaken. No such information at least has been made publicly available. The $8 billion upgrade of the Suez Canal was not followed by a substantial increase in traffic through it or revenues from it.

The new administrative capital has been estimated to be costing $40 billion. From 2014 to 2018, according to the Stockholm Peace Research Institute, Egypt was the world's third largest purchaser of weaponry on world markets.

The immediate and pressing question is from where does Egypt acquire the funds to finance these projects and its profligate military expenditures, especially since it had to obtain a $12 billion emergency bailout loan from the IMF in November 2016. The funds do not come from private investments, which in 2017 amounted to only 6% of GDP, the lowest proportion since 1970.[35] The answer is that it has borrowed them, principally in foreign currencies, as its national savings rate is very low—just over 10% of GDP in 2017 compared unfavorably to Turkey's 25% and even Sudan's 13%, to say nothing of Singapore's at 48%.[36] This in turn raises doubts about the country's future solvency in the face of what was already an $83 billion foreign debt as of May 2018. Egypt's debt crisis is substantially worse than Turkey's, the indebtedness of which attracted negative worldwide attention in mid-2018. Canada's National Bank Financial, for example, noted that "Turkey is especially exposed ... as its $195 billion in debt is a stunning 23 percent of GDP."[37] The Egyptian government's foreign debt stood at 36.8% of GDP at the end of June 2018, having increased over the year by 11.6%. Egypt's domestic debt is also proportionately larger than Turkey's, reaching 86.8% of GDP. On world rankings of debt/GDP ratio, Egypt is 13th, whereas Turkey is not in the top 50 proportionately most indebted countries. Of the 12 countries more indebted than Egypt, all but three are OECD members, hence far less threatened by inability to repay their debt.

Egypt's crushing debt burden is reflected by the high cost of servicing it. In 2018 interest payments absorbed some 35% of the budget, eating up "almost 55% of all government revenues."[38] Three factors will continue to drive debt servicing costs upward in the foreseeable future. The first is globally rising interest rates combined with increasing distrust in the value of the Egyptian pound, so causing domestic interest rates to remain extraordinarily high and probably to rise further. In 2018 Egypt was paying over 6% interest on its 12-year Eurobonds and some 20% on its Egyptian pound denominated T-bills, with the proportion of foreign investors in the latter having dropped so sharply during 2018 that the central bank stopped reporting their relative purchases. In contrast, the average for the 31 countries in the Bloomberg Emerging Market Local Sovereign Index saw a rise of only 13 base points to 4.73%, about one quarter of the Egyptian rate, far and away the highest on that Index. Second,

Egypt's external debts are set to continue to mount. The country is scheduled to float another 7 billion worth of Eurobonds in 2019 and, according to the Ministry of Finance, just under $23 billion in additional euro and dollar bonds by 2021.

The third factor that will continue to drive up the cost of debt servicing is that the borrowed funds are not being wisely invested, so are not generating adequate returns, especially in foreign currencies. The key ratio is the nation's gross fixed capital investment as a proportion of GDP. Despite the grandiose projects, that proportion sank to one of the world's lowest, from 24% in 2014 to 15% two years later and in 2018 to about 12%. In Turkey, by contrast, gross fixed capital investment as a proportion of GDP was over 29% in 2016, almost double Egypt's.

Egypt, in other words, is now borrowing mainly to cover the costs of previous loans and current consumption. The white elephant projects—ranging from the new administrative capital, to the widening of the Suez Canal, to the 2018 contract signed with Russia for the $21 billion nuclear power plant, of which Egypt paid 15% on signing with the balance taking the form of an interest bearing loan, along with the associated burden of Egypt having to invest $18 billion over five years to upgrade the electricity transmission network[39]—all attest to Sisi's profligacy and the crushing financial burden it is imposing on his country.

Egypt's people are ill-equipped to face high inflation, it being some 20% at the end of 2018, after having exceeded 35% in the wake of the IMF mandated devaluation in 2016. Wages and salaries have not kept pace with inflation. Reductions in energy and food subsidies have driven up household expenditures. About 40% of the population now lives on less than $2 daily. Their margins of subsistence are so narrow that a new bout of inflation would have dire economic and potentially explosive political consequences. A poll of Egyptians taken in September 2018 by Zogby Research Services reflects their increasing concerns and dissatisfaction. Only one in five said they were better off than they were five years previously, with 64% saying they were worse off. In June 2013, 68% of respondents in a similar poll said they were optimistic that the country was on the right track, a proportion that dropped to 41% in a follow up poll at the end of 2014, and then to 19% in September 2018, when 55% said Egypt was moving in the wrong direction. Support for the military also dropped precipitously over this period, from over 90% in June 2013, to 70% by the end of that year, to 40% in September 2018, a drop of 50 points in five years.[40]

As Egypt becomes progressively more indebted to pay for its sustenance and mega-projects of dubious economic value, so does its population expand ever more rapidly, placing yet greater strain on public services and the budget to pay for them. The recently deceased former Secretary General of the UN, Boutrus Boutrus-Ghali, once sagely observed that "Egypt with a population of 20 million people could have been a Mediterranean country, a Greece or Portugal. Egypt with 70 million people will be Bangladesh."[41] Egypt now has 100 million people and, indeed, more closely resembles South Asian than northern Mediterranean countries. In another 30 years, with a population projected to be 140–150 million, Egypt will be more populous than either Russia or Japan. In 2008, 2.1 million children were born, while by 2012 more than 2.6 million were being born annually, the largest number by far in Egypt's history.[42] Every four years the size of the class entering primary school increases by some 28%, placing huge additional pressure on an educational system already struggling to cope with a crushing student load.[43]

Given this population explosion the challenge of educating the country's youths has become ever more pressing. How the military-dominated government is responding to that challenge is illustrative of its more general approach to human resource development and economic management. It appears to hope to have its cake and eat it too, with "reforms" designed to both mitigate public criticism of the quality and expense of education, as well as to produce disciplined youths supportive of military rule.

The government in 2018 launched three initiatives to achieve these seemingly contradictory objectives. The first is broad reform of public primary, preparatory and secondary education, which includes some 20 million students in about 60,000 public schools. Supported by a World Bank loan of $500 million, the new program is to expand kindergarten education for 500,000 children, create 50,000 new teaching jobs and provide up to 1.5 million digital-learning devices to high school students and teachers. Laudable as these reforms are, they are unlikely to rapidly transform the abysmal quality of Egyptian public education, currently ranked by the World Economic Forum as 130th out of 137 in the world, with primary education ranking 133rd, Egypt's lowest ranking on the almost 100 indicators from which the Global Competitiveness Index is constructed. Although some 90% of the Ministry of Education's budget is allocated to personnel salaries, teachers are very poorly paid so typically moonlight or extract fees for private tutorials from their students, the latter of which have resulted in household expenditure on education exceeding that of the government. The hurdles to be overcome, in short, are high and require budgetary outlays beyond those currently, or in the foreseeable future, likely to be made. The 2014 constitution stipulates that public education receive 4% of government expenditures, a proportion yet to be reached since the constitution was ratified. Government expenditure as a proportion of GDP has fallen steadily since the 1960s, at 10% now less than half of what it was then.

The government's second educational initiative is to privatize as much education as possible at all levels. About 10%, or some 2 million of the country's 18–20 million (the figures vary) primary and secondary students, are in private schools. Of the country's 50 universities, 26 are private. While encouraging privatization, the government is simultaneously bringing private schools and universities under more direct, obtrusive control. As for pre-tertiary private schools, the big change is the Arabization of the first six years of teaching, including mathematics and science, with English being taught only as a second language during that period, including in the so-called "language schools," which have always taught in English and whose share of age cohorts has been steadily increasing since the Mubarak era. This move has been strongly criticized by parents and teachers, but to no avail. What seems a related change is a new requirement "agreed" between the Ministry of Education and the chairman of the International Schools Association, that international schools "teach school subjects that are related to the national identity in line with the international curricula."[44]

These changes, reminiscent of similar ones in the Nasser era, are presumably intended to promote Egyptian nationalism. They are, moreover, connected to the broader, third educational initiative, which is to induce discipline and loyalty, especially to the military, while opening a recruitment channel into the military-controlled elite. An anecdotal example of this initiative was provided by a visit by the governor of Qalyubiya Province to a kindergarten, where he spied images of Disney characters, including Mickey Mouse, on the walls. He immediately decreed that they be replaced by drawings of "military martyrs, so that children will look up to them as role models. These characters are US made, whereas we have our own noble figures who can deepen children's patriotism and love of country." The Ministry of Education immediately echoed the theme, announcing the formation of a committee to implement the order.[45]

A more systematic initiative was the launching of 79 of what is ultimately intended to be 200 "Japanese schools" in the 2018 school year, which more than 30,000 students are now attending. Supported by the Japanese International Cooperation Agency, the declared purpose of the schools, according to the Japanese Ambassador to Egypt, is to "teach students the main principles of discipline, commitment, and respect for time." The special curricula and teaching method is referred to as Tokkatsu, which is intended to produce a "balanced development of intellect, virtue and body by ensuring academic competence, rich emotions and healthy physical development." Education Minister Tariq Shawky declared at the opening of one of the schools that "the goal of the new educational system is to build a new, different Egyptian generation." The schools will teach the Egyptian curriculum but include "distinctive features of Japanese education," including "cleanliness and self-reliance."[46]

As with the civil service and the private business sector, the military appears also to have decided that it can educate better than others, so has become an education service provider in competition with both public and private schools. As part of its counter-terror campaign, it opened four new primary schools in north and central Sinai under the control of the Commander of the East of the Suez Canal Counter-Terrorism Forces. The jewel in the crown of the military pre-tertiary educational system is the Badr International School, opened in a military zone on the outskirts of Cairo in 2015, two years after the then defense minister, Abd al Fattah al Sisi, issued the order for its creation. A reporter who visited the school observed that its "managers and staff see their role not only in educational terms, but as a patriotic duty, holding themselves responsible for enhancing the image of the military and introducing activities that develop the nationalistic sentiments of the students."[47]

This third educational initiative, focused on patriotism, discipline and loyalty to the military and the President, begs the question of its origins. What were the sources that inspired the military to directly sponsor and operate schools? The Badr School is remarkably reminiscent of the so-called Napola, the acronym for Nationalpolitische Lehranstalt (National Political Institution of Teaching), which were secondary schools established by the German National Socialists after they took power in 1933. The main task of what ultimately became 43 such schools, educating at least 6,000 pupils at any one time by 1945, was "education of national socialists, efficient in body and soul for the service to the people and the state."[48]

Another possible and contemporary source of inspiration for the Badr School—and for some of the new curricular and language impositions on both public and private schools intended to instill patriotism and possibly even distrust of foreign language speaking outsiders—is East Asia. The new Japanese Schools are explicit copies of that East Asian model, while the elite schools under the Chinese Communist Party, intended to educate party cadres and prepare them to rule, may just have informed Egyptian leaders when making their recent choices about changes to the educational system. Again, the emphasis on discipline, physical training, patriotism and elitism are common to both.

The tripartite educational reforms currently underway in Egypt are driven by both profound popular discontent with the lamentable state of the country's entire educational system, as well as by the desire of the military-dominated regime to recruit and train loyalist implementors of regime policies, while simultaneously reinforcing Egyptian nationalism throughout the entire system. These are top down, not bottom up reforms, hence depart profoundly from best practice in educational reform, which emphasizes the need for broad stakeholder participation by parents, teachers, students, administrators, and so on, for reforms to be effective. Combined with the lack of adequate financial support for the public educational system now dealing with some 20 million students, and with new interventions into the private sector that will restrict the autonomy of schools and universities and probably undermine the quality of their offerings, these decreed initiatives are likely to perpetuate, even intensify, the problem of a woefully inadequate educational system, rather than cure its ills. "Reform" of the educational sector reflects the broader approach of the Egyptian regime to other public services and indeed to public policy in general. Healthcare delivery, for example, is driven by the same objectives of reducing costs through privatization, combined with direct military involvement in the sector, such as through military hospitals and clinics. The entire economy is indeed now honeycombed with military-owned enterprises or those established by retired officers, while the state is similarly penetrated by former members of the officer corps now serving as public servants in central and local government, as well as in the key regulatory agencies. Since 2013 the state and economy have been converted into extensions of the military and its interests, with the civil service and private sector actors being sidelined. None of the other authoritarian republics has witnessed such thoroughgoing militarization, but depending on the outcome of the Egyptian experiment, they might be tempted to follow suit, especially in the case of the Algerian military, which is already the closest to the Egyptian model. But the Egyptian case is simply the extreme example of what prevails in the others, which is the assumption of ever greater political power by coercive agencies charged with providing national security, and then their extension into the economy and state. They have no conception of infrastructural power based on interaction with civil society. Their modus operandi is military style, top down authoritarian control, dictating policy from above, and increasingly implementing it by themselves.

The nuances of macroeconomics and their consequences are of little if any interest to these coercive institutions and those who serve or who have served in them. So long as they can obtain resources to implement their projects, they will proceed to do so. In all cases then, the danger of macroeconomic mismanagement becomes ever more profound, with the obvious manifestation being the accumulation of heavy debt burdens. The two exceptions to that rule are Iran, essentially unable to borrow abroad, and Algeria, which has since 2014 covered budget deficits primarily by drawing down its sovereign wealth fund which in that year was some $179 billion. It has been extracting at least $20 billion annually from it since that time.[49] Egypt and Turkey are dangerously close to being caught in debt spirals that continue to drive high interest rates coupled with downward pressure on their currencies, coupled with yet more foreign borrowing to cover existing commitments. While the authoritarian republics have survived, they have not prospered and have become yet more authoritarian in their effort to hold on to power.

10

SURVIVAL STRATEGIES IN STRONGER MENA STATES

Grouping Jordan and Morocco together with the GCC monarchies at first thought seems inappropriate, as those two monarchies are not oil rich and a state's form of government is presumably less vital than other factors, including its socio-political base. Among the GCC states Oman and Bahrain have substantially less oil and gas revenues than Saudi Arabia, the UAE, Kuwait and Qatar, so on strictly economic grounds even the GCC is not itself a coherent category. But the reason for considering all monarchies conjointly is not only that they are ruled by royals and typically their families, which has some consequences as noted previously, but for other reasons as well. First, their similar rankings on governance indicators suggest they constitute a distinctive type of MENA state. Second, they all have close relations with the West, which has profoundly impacted their regimes and broader political economies. In the case of the GCC states and Jordan, their governments were for the most part established by Britain and since that time have been at least partially staffed at the higher levels by Western expatriates. In Morocco's case the close relationship with France has served to connect the country to Europe as much as to the Arab world. Only Israel of the MENA states has had such close connections to the West.

Third, with the exception of Morocco, they have similar histories that do not involve much if any pre-colonial stateness, even in Saudi Arabia, which was not directly colonized. But in those states Western tutelage seems to have substituted for traditions of stateness. In structure, policy content and even in personnel their states were partially imported, partially locally produced, with the imported components more substantial and lasting than in other MENA countries. Morocco, by contrast, has drawn upon its comparatively impressive history of stateness in building capacities that have in turn enabled its reasonably effective economic performance, at least by MENA standards. In all cases the monarchies have had greater capacities for economic management than the states considered in the preceding chapter.

Fourth, all MENA monarchies are more actively struggling with the challenge of diversifying their economies from oil and gas rents, whether derived directly or indirectly, than most other MENA states. Jordan and Morocco, indirect beneficiaries of hydrocarbon rents accrued directly by most other monarchies, have also derived geo-strategic rents, in the case especially of Jordan, and from phosphate exports, in the case of Morocco, the world's largest exporter possessing the world's greatest reserves of that mineral. Six percent of its second largest non-oil GDP in the Arab world, after Egypt's, is generated by phosphates, which account for a fifth of total exports. In all cases other than Morocco's phosphates, the rent to population ratios have been becoming less favorable for several years. Necessity is thus the mother of invention for all the monarchies, but more compelling for those with lower hydrocarbon rent to population ratios, hence a greater need to diversify their economies. Jordan's dependence on its strategic position as a buffer state in the Arab–Israeli conflict and as a policeman for hire in the region is becoming as untenable as dependence on hydrocarbon rents because the centrality of the Israeli–Palestinian conflict is receding in the MENA and because other militaries are becoming more capable. By contrast, Kuwait and Qatar have no compelling need to diversify their economies given their high oil and gas production and reserves, respectively, and small populations which result in the region's most favorable hydrocarbon rents to population ratios. Bahrain was the first GCC state that confronted the need to diversify away from oil earnings, while Oman is also now facing exhaustion of its limited oil reserves so its always relatively low rent to population ratio continues to decline. The UAE is divided between Abu Dhabi, which is in the same category of high hydrocarbon endowment and low population as are Kuwait and Qatar; Dubai, which is the region's great success story of diversification driven by necessity as it never had substantial hydrocarbon exports; and the other five, much poorer emirates that have for all intents and purposes become bedroom communities of Dubai and Abu Dhabi. Abu Dhabi underwrites in greater or lesser measure the other six emirates, which along with competition with Dubai provides an incentive to diversify even its very oil-rich economy. This leaves Saudi Arabia, which is the second most populous of the monarchies after Morocco, with only some 3 million less inhabitants, so despite being the world's largest oil exporter, has seen its rent to population ratio deteriorate at a rate that dramatically accelerated in 2014 and seems set to continue to decline. Saudi Arabia is thus the real test case of diversification, an inherently more difficult task in a country both large in land area and population, to say nothing of it being one of the world's longest and most thoroughly established rentier states, so one with a bureaucracy created and sustained more for the purpose of distributing resources than administering or guiding development.

In sum, the MENA monarchies are similar in their state capacities and the important role played by Western countries in developing them; in their status as rentier states dependent directly or indirectly on hydrocarbon exports or, in the case of Jordan and Morocco, substitutes for them; and in the challenge they now face to diversify those rentier economies away from direct or indirect hydrocarbon dependence.

The rentier character of the monarchies is revealed by their rankings on World Bank governance indicators. The two principal features of that character are authoritarianism coupled with relatively capable economic governance focused on rent extraction and distribution. With the exceptions of Morocco, Jordan and Kuwait, institutionalized political participation in the form of political parties, legislatures, elected local governments and NGOs is limited to non-existent. Personalism and clientelism are intended as substitutes for those formal means of inclusion, rendering them, at least in the eyes of the monarchs, redundant. Rankings of the monarchies on the World Bank's voice and accountability indicator reflect the weakness of formal political participation. Only Morocco, Jordan and Kuwait score above the MENA mean of 25 out of 100 on this indicator, with Saudi Arabia at 6 being the lowest ranked MENA country. Saudi Arabia also is the worst performing monarchy on the Press Freedom Index, on which it ranks 169th out of 180 countries. But all the other monarchies, including the three most "liberal" ones, also score in the bottom half of countries on that scale, with Kuwait at 105 having the most press freedom. By contrast, on the Economic Freedom Index compiled by Freedom House, all the MENA monarchies except Saudi Arabia and Oman score in the upper half, with the UAE, Bahrain and Jordan in the upper third of all countries. Similarly, on the World Bank's Ease of Doing Business scale, which ranks 190 countries, six of the monarchies are in the upper half, with only Kuwait and Jordan in the lower half. These results suggest that the monarchies are limited access orders in which political exclusion is matched with considerable although not as great restrictions on independent economic activity. As for governance quality, the four most relevant World Bank indicators are government effectiveness, regulatory quality, rule of law and control of corruption. On these indicators all the monarchies score above the MENA mean, which averages 43 across the four. It is also worth noting that except for Kuwait and Morocco on the government effectiveness indicator, Morocco on the regulatory quality and rule of law indicators, and Morocco, Bahrain and Jordan on the control of corruption indicator, they all score above the LAC mean across all the four indicators. Similarly, on the Resource Governance Index, of the six ranked monarchies, all except Saudi Arabia rank above the six other ranked MENA countries. The quality of governance in the MENA monarchies thus appears to be bipolar, being very low on political inclusion and comparatively high on administration and economic management.

It is precisely this governance bipolarity that both reflects the nature of these rentier monarchies and poses the chief obstacle to their diversification. Having relied upon social contracts in which political acquiescence was exchanged for material rewards made possible by an abundance of rents, the monarchies face ever intensifying material challenges to sustain their end of that bargain. The states they constructed are misshapen between weak input and stronger output sides. The choices thus seem to be to develop the input side by facilitating the emergence of participatory institutions and organizations, along the lines laid out by Douglass North and his colleagues in their mapping of transitions from limited to open access orders; to step up repression to counter political reactions to declining patronage; to generate more resources to service social contracts; or some mix of these three approaches. What the monarchies have attempted thus far is primarily the third option in the form of diversifying economies in order to create more governmental resources and patronage, coupled with increased repression. No effort has been made to facilitate greater political participation and very little to increase private sector activity and autonomy. The monarchies, with the partial exception of Morocco, are doubling down on the rentier approach, hoping that economic diversification will miraculously generate sufficient rents to sustain the patronage lifeblood of their political economies. The case of Saudi Arabia, the biggest of the monarchial economies and the country with the greatest potential impact on all the others, to say nothing of the MENA and world as a whole, illustrates the general approach and its likely prospects.

Saudi Arabia Exemplifies Difficulties of Reform

Many MENA monarchies have drafted blueprints for economic diversification, most bearing the name of "vision" coupled to a year by which it is to be realized, such as Vision 2035 in Kuwait, Vision 2030 in Abu Dhabi and Qatar, Vision 2025 in Jordan, or Vision 2020, which then became Vision 2040 in Oman. Emulating the monarchies, Egypt launched a Vision 2030 in 2016, promising that "The new Egypt will possess a competitive, balanced and diversified economy, dependent on innovation and knowledge."[1] The introduction of Qatar's 2030 vision is similar, stating that, "Economic development is an essential part of the Qatar National Vision 2030, as the engine that drives progress by providing better opportunities and a better way of life for the country's citizens. Achieving that objective hinges on Qatar's ability to create a balance between an oil-based and a knowledge-based economy, helping diversify the country's economy and guaranteeing a stable and sustainable business environment."[2]

Saudi Arabia's "Vision 2030" was launched in April 2016 by the ambitious new Crown Prince, Muhammad bin Salman. Among the commonalities of these monarchial visions—all drafted with substantial input from Western consulting firms, chief of which has been McKinsey—is first and foremost that none were formulated with the participation of stakeholders outside ruling elites, other than the Western consulting firms, which typically arranged implementation roles for themselves.[3] As for the declared objectives, they include decreasing dependence on oil resources, which has been repeatedly stated as a governmental goal in Saudi Arabia since the 1970s; developing alternative sources of governmental revenue from taxes, fees and income from sovereign wealth funds; reducing the dependency of citizens on public entitlements such as subsidies and government employment; reducing unemployment by increasing private sector hiring; and enhancing the contribution of the private sector and the "knowledge economy" to the GDP. These objectives are to be achieved in Saudi Arabia in association with enhancing its status as the "heart of the Arab and Islamic worlds," emerging as a "global investment powerhouse," and becoming a "hub connecting the 3 continents (Asia, Europe, Africa)." Specific targets include among others expanding cultural activities and entertainment, drawing more women into the labor force, improving governmental effectiveness and attracting FDI.

Key to the success of the plan is the vital financial and supervisory role of the Public Investment Fund (PIF), the formerly rather staid SWF founded in 1971 which in March 2015 was shifted from the Ministry of Finance to the Council of Economic and Development Affairs, chaired by the Crown Prince himself, who in turn appointed himself as head of the PIF, which immediately became, according to some commentators, "a parallel state."[4] Its effort to attract foreign investment in support of Vision 2030 in its "Davos in the Desert" in October 2018 misfired as most of the prominent global actors scheduled to attend withdrew in the wake of the killing by the regime of Saudi journalist Jamal Khashoggi shortly before the scheduled gathering. This posed to the world investment community the vital questions of whether a regime as repressive as that of Saudi Arabia could implement a development plan as ambitious as that of Vision 2030 and what role, if any, external actors should play in it.

Available information suggests that in the case of Saudi Arabia and probably the other monarchies—with the possible exception of Morocco, already the most diversified of the monarchial economies—the plan embodied in Vision 2030 is overly ambitious and beset with internal contradictions. The most important of those contradictions are, first, that a transformation of the political economy of this magnitude, involving fundamental changes to the rentier system which has structured the lives of all Saudis for more than two generations, is to be accomplished without public consultation, to say nothing of participation in decision making. Connected with that flaw is the assumption that the notoriously weak Saudi bureaucracy, in the absence of a fundamental overhaul presumably involving some engagement of the citizens who work in it and are served by it, is capable of implementing this wide-ranging plan entailing such profound change. Indeed, observers of the PIF have noted that even this flagship financial enterprise of that bureaucracy lacks managerial capacity and is little more than "a one-man investment vehicle" for the Crown Prince.[5]

A second contradiction is contained in the assumption that yet further expansion of the rentier state will stimulate a fundamental change in the private sector, which will absorb ever increasing numbers of Saudis while producing rising shares of GDP. Within two months of the marred rolling out of Vision 2030 at "Davos in the Desert," King Salman announced measures to increase the flow of benefits from the state to Saudi citizens, including cost of living allowances for civil servants and soldiers, contained within a record annual budget representing a 7% increase in government spending in 2019. Revenues to cover some of the increased expenditures were to be derived from further drawdowns of reserves, increased revenues from the newly imposed VAT, and foreign borrowings, but the deficit was nevertheless projected to be the sixth in a row and the largest of them all. Saudi borrowings in 2016, the first year it had turned to foreign lenders, were $17.5 billion, while in the following year they sold internationally another $23.5 billion in debt.[6] In the year ending in mid-2018 government spending had increased by 34% over the previous year, primarily because of increases in the public sector wage bill, which accounts for nearly half of government spending.[7] Among other negative impacts on the private sector of continued public expenditure of this magnitude is it being crowded out of credit markets by stepped up state borrowings, and private sector salaries being rendered yet less competitive than those paid in the civil service. The spending has also had profoundly negative consequences for macroeconomic balances. The budget deficit in 2017 was 9% of GDP, which drove the fiscal break-even price for oil up to $87 according to the IMF, and consumed yet more of the country's once prodigious foreign currency reserves, of which some 40% of the 2014 figure of $700 billion had been drawn down by mid-2018.[8]

A third apparent inconsistency in Vision 2030 and the associated reforms announced by Muhammad bin Salman is the liberalization of the cultural environment, especially for youth, such as by allowing women to drive, opening cinemas and staging concerts, and fostering internal tourism, all without fear of intrusion by the now disbanded *mutawin*, the formerly dreaded religious police. Cultural liberalization has been coupled with intensified restrictions on any form of unauthorized political participation. Just as women were allowed to drive, for example, several of those who had protested against the now lifted ban were jailed. The brutal killing by Saudi security agents of journalist Jamal Khashoggi—once a media advisor to Prince Turki bin Faysal, former Saudi ambassador to the UK and US and brother of the long-serving Foreign Minister—signaled a tightening of already severe restrictions on political expression. Isam al Zamil, for example, an economist critical of the planned initial public offering of Aramco shares, was sentenced to a year in jail on trumped up charges of membership in a terrorist organization and "meeting foreign diplomats."[9] How young Saudis, liberated from historic restrictions on cultural freedom, will react to tightened ones on political expression is the paradoxical question facing the Crown Prince and his allies now in charge.

A fourth contradiction is Vision 2030's dependence on foreign capital for its implementation, but the government doing little to encourage and a lot to discourage it. Recent results reflect this unfavorable balance. The planned initial public offering of 5% of shares of the state oil company Aramco had to be cancelled because of investor resistance in light of the lack of clarity surrounding the rights of potential shareholders given the absence of authoritative information released by Aramco or the government about matters central to valuations, such as reserves, production costs, royalties and taxes paid to the Saudi government, emoluments to princes, and so on. Weak rule of law was illustrated graphically in November 2017, when some 300 princes, tycoons and former government officials, including a prominent minister of the economy, Ali Faqih, were detained by the newly formed anti-corruption committee in Riyadh's Ritz-Carlton Hotel until they transferred cash and assets to the government.[10] Reflecting these uncertainties and threats, FDI into the country collapsed from $7.45 billion in 2016 to $1.42 billion a year later. As one foreign banker commented in the wake of the Khashoggi killing, "you've got risks coming at you from all angles."[11] Apparently wealthy Saudis are frightened by these risks, as suggested by capital flight, which JP Morgan estimated in 2017 at $80 billion and in 2018 to be $65 billion, a staggering 8.4% of GDP. This is in addition to $14.4 billion in outward portfolio investment into foreign equities in only the first quarter of 2018, the largest amount since the crisis of 2008.[12] The decade-old effort to launch the King Abdullah Financial Center in Riyadh to compete with Dubai in attracting foreign clients and investments has essentially failed, and the $10 billion worth of buildings there remain largely vacant. The problem with this initiative, according to Mark Yeandle, the lead author of the Financial Centers Index, is lack of trust, as "there is a sense of being an untried centre, which in a pretty autocratic country is beholden to their leader."[13] That Saudi Arabia is not alone among GCC countries in experiencing capital outflows rather than inflows is indicated by Kuwait, where foreign capital invested in local projects fell from $419 million in 2017 to $301 million in 2018, whereas FDI outflows rose from $4.5 billion to $8.1 billion.[14]

Yet another issue with Vision 2030 and its key financial instrument, the PIF, is the choice of investments, which seem overwhelmingly to favor foreign enterprises coupled with domestic mega-projects that have in the past been prone, like the King Abdullah Financial Center, to become white elephants, having done little if anything to stimulate employment of Saudis, or indeed even to survive. Nuanced, well-designed support for activities that would assist small and medium enterprises and even job creating activities of large ones are notable in their almost total absence from the PIF portfolio. Among the mega-projects touted by the PIF are the aforementioned NEOM, a $500 billion futuristic city replete with robotics and artificial intelligence to be built at the confluence of Saudi Arabia, Jordan and Egypt, and a $200 billion solar project with Japan's SoftBank, both of which were scaled back drastically by the end of 2018 as a result of investor disinterest. Foreign acquisitions include a $2 billion, 5% stake in Tesla, $400 million in Endeavor, a Hollywood talent and event manager, a 55% stake in a South African property management firm, and significant holdings in Uber, Magic Leap and various joint ventures with the investment firm Blackstone.[15] As PIF funds were flowing into mega-projects and to overseas companies, even owners of the largest Saudi companies were "hurting, and they are telling the crown prince how."[16] These businessmen feared that the direction of investments away from them was a purposeful act by the Crown Prince, who, "a person familiar with the royal court noted", "regards the traditional private sector—much of which depends on government contracts—as a 'leech that does not deliver value, just sucks money out and takes no risk'."[17] This reported sentiment is strikingly similar to that of Egypt's President Sisi and the military that brought him to power, presumably in part because both the Saudi and the Egyptian leader neither want to be constrained by their private sectors, nor to share state largesse with them. How to square that attitude with the need to encourage private investment, however, remains a puzzle.

A final paradox embodied in Vision 2030 is that it is intended to stimulate private sector employment of Saudis while reducing that of expatriates and also of Saudi public sector workers. In reality, however, it has reduced private sector employment overall while increasing that in the public sector. The centrality of job creation to all monarchial "vision" plans reflects the absolute importance of that objective, the difficulty of attaining it, and the different strategies for achieving it, none of which has been notably successful. Half of the GCC states, for example, have abandoned the *kafala* (sponsorship) system, while Saudi Arabia, Kuwait and Oman have retained it. Among other consequences of the system was to endow the *kafil* (sponsor), typically a member of the relevant royal family or someone connected to it, with the rent resulting from his virtually total control over a migrant worker, including entrance into and departure from the country as well as place of work while in it. The basic divide in the GCC over foreign employment has become one between those states that continue to encourage it, most notably the UAE, and those that are actively seeking to discourage it, such as Saudi Arabia with its Saudization policy. The former strategy is predicated on a broader acceptance of globalization and the idea that more engagement with the world will benefit the economy, while the latter is based on a more nationalistic approach that views hydrocarbon rents as the primary source of national income, hence to be reserved as much as possible for nationals. Thus far in practice there is little evidence to suggest the results differ profoundly depending on the strategy, with the main factor driving expatriate employment being the price of hydrocarbons. Dubai, for example, the most open of the emirates to foreign employment, residence, property ownership and so on, has been witnessing a significant outflow of non-nationals, who comprise 90% of the population, as its economy has slumped in tandem with falling oil prices. Its stock market fell 20% from 2017 to 2018, making it the worst performing in the MENA. Emaar Properties, Dubai's biggest developer, lost 38% of its value in 2018. Bankruptcies, including that of the Abraaj Group, the largest firm in the Dubai International Financial Center, have added to factors dragging down job creation, resulting in shrinking employment for the first time in the emirate's history. The government's response has been to provide more incentives for foreigners to keep them in Dubai, including longer term visas, fewer restrictions on business ownership and a freezing of private school fees.[18]

Saudization takes the opposite approach by trying to squeeze non-nationals out of the labor market, thereby making room for nationals. What has occurred might be considered a vindication of the more open Dubai approach. While the foreign labor force dropped by 1.5 million between 2016 and early 2019, during that period the number of additional Saudis employed in the private sector and the civil service increased by less than 50,000.[19] Shrinkage of the overall labor force results from the broader downturn of GCC economies, in turn the result of lower hydrocarbon-based revenues. By 2018 unemployment of Saudi nationals had reached almost 13%, with youth unemployment double that proportion and some four times it for women, all the highest levels on record.[20] Banning expatriates from January 2018 from holding jobs selling watches, eyeglasses, medical equipment, electrical appliances, auto parts, confectionaries and various other items raised questions not only about why these jobs were targeted, but also about whether or not Saudis would fill them. In the majority of cases of the hundreds of thousands of foreigners evicted from such employment, the jobs themselves were terminated because the owners of the largely small and medium enterprises that employed them could not afford to hire Saudis.[21] The most noteworthy economic consequence was to further depress demand as total employment fell, thereby exacerbating the recession that had commenced in 2017.

The net results after two years of implementation of Vision 2030, including Saudization, appeared more negative than positive for the economy, with few prospects of dramatic improvement in the near future. Possibly the close association of the Crown Prince with the plan caused him to allay the apprehensions of his thousands of fellow princes by increasing their monthly stipends, which in 1996 had ranged from a low of $800 to a high of $270,000, with the total increase in 2018 costing the state some $2 billion.[22] This in turn increased resentments of such privileges by other Saudis, rendering the Crown Prince's task of managing reform of the political economy yet more challenging.

Observing the stalled reform, Saudi specialist Steffen Hertog commented that Saudi Arabia is "going back to what has been tried and tested. They are going back to meat and potatoes."[23] By that he meant the Saudi leadership was more or less abandoning efforts to shift from an allocation rentier state to a diversified, production-oriented economy. The revised strategy involved reduced hopes for expanded private sector employment of Saudis or for substantial economic diversification. Instead the focus was to be on the tried and proven oil sector, seeking to expand its upstream and downstream components, with the latter receiving greater attention. It consisted of several interconnected value-adding undertakings, such as increased refining capacities, both in Saudi Arabia and in Asia, combined with expanding petrochemical production and downstream processing of those feedstocks, again both in Saudi Arabia and abroad. The Crown Prince, not dissuaded by the failure of his PIF to attract foreign investment, mandated Aramco to purchase for $70 billion the Fund's shares in SABIC, the primary SOE involved in petrochemical production, thereby killing two birds with one stone—the PIF's need for capital and Aramco's desire to expand downstream activities.

A further component of the strategy of returning to "meat and potatoes" is increased economic relations with Asia, especially China, reflective of shifts in the Gulf, the MENA and, indeed, the world more generally. The GCC states by 2018 were the largest suppliers of oil and second largest of gas to China, with Chinese exports to GCC countries by 2020 anticipated to be $135 billion and tourist arrivals 2.5 million.[24] The MENA and China are thus witnessing dramatically increasing interactions of goods, capital and people, at the core of which are GCC countries, especially Saudi Arabia. Aramco and SABIC are entering into partnerships to build new refineries, petrochemical plants and end user processing facilities for petrochemicals with China's Sinopec, China North Industries Corporation and other Chinese SOEs. For its part, China is investing heavily in infrastructure, especially ports, in the Gulf and throughout the MENA. Clearly the pivot to Asia of the "meat and potatoes" strategy cannot stimulate substantial employment in Saudi Arabia or elsewhere in the GCC. Downstream refining and processing are particularly capital rather than labor intensive. Chinese infrastructural investments are accompanied with Chinese laborers. Nor will the pivot to Asia diversify GCC economies. It will generate greater returns from oil and gas and presumably, therefore, yet more dependence on hydrocarbon extraction, export and processing. Whether this is advisable in the face of uncertain long-term demand, to say nothing of the future use of petrochemical feedstocks in plastic manufacture when that commodity is under pressure because of its adverse environmental effects, are relevant queries when a nation's and indeed sub-region's future look set to become ever more dependent upon them. The strategic and possibly economic consequences of intensified relations with Asia in general and China in particular are other open questions to which answers might not be favorable, especially in light of Chinese exploitation of political economies with which it has engaged, ranging from Pakistan to Ecuador.[25] So what appears to be a conservative strategy of avoiding the risks associated with bolder moves to diversify the economy, Saudization, and subjecting the state to greater scrutiny by international investors and possibly also Saudi citizens, ultimately may entail yet greater risks, the most obvious of which is falling under unfavorable Chinese influence.

A final constraint on reform of the Saudi political economy is public opinion in the Kingdom. The 2017–18 Arab Opinion Index reported that 49% of Saudis either did not know or had no answer to a question asking them to define democracy, compared to an average of 14% of nationals in the other ten Arab countries who responded in that fashion. Only 5% of Saudis polled defined democracy as "equality and justice for all citizens," compared to 21% of the overall Arab sample. The poll suggested similarly conservative attitudes among Saudis about religious issues: 57% disagreed, strongly disagreed, refused to answer or "did not know" in response to the statement "no religious authority is entitled to declare followers of other religions to be infidels"; 32% of respondents in the ten other Arab countries chose those options, while 68% agreed or strongly agreed, compared to 43% of Saudis.[26] A poll taken in Saudi Arabia in November 2018 as reported by David Pollock "demonstrates only minority support for the official initiative of Islamic reform."[27] Three quarters of respondents disagreed, 39% "strongly," to the statement that "we should listen to those among us who are trying to interpret Islam in a more moderate, tolerant, and modern direction." As for views on economic reforms, 63% of respondents agreed that the government was still doing "too little in reducing the level of corruption in our economic and political life"; 41%, a plurality, agreed that "Saudi officials are not doing enough to share the burden of taxes and other obligations to the government in a fair manner."[28] A private poll taken shortly before indicated the obstacle public opinion may pose to reducing public entitlements. Only 26% of respondents supported introducing a VAT, and 16%, 13% and 12% cutting fuel, electricity and water subsidies, respectively; 38% favored a slower pace of social reforms, compared to 31% who wanted a faster one.

While Saudi Arabia is more conservative than most if not all the monarchies and has what has become among the most institutionalized allocation states, none of the other monarchies has succeeded in diversifying away from rents as the prime government resource, from their allocation as the chief means of interacting with publics, or in creating a citizenry that feels empowered and capable of facing the challenges of globalization. Dubai is the most globalized, but remains dependent upon oil revenues from Abu Dhabi as a key driving force for its economy and as guarantor of its economic well-being. Morocco has diversified its economy more effectively than the GCC states and the Arab republics such as Egypt and Iraq, but there is still much to be done. In 2017 it was exporting some 42 products per million inhabitants, compared to 55 for Turkey and 160 for Malaysia. Manufactured goods comprised only 13% of exports, compared to 25% for middle-income countries as a whole. Of those manufactured exports, by 2015 only 3.5% were high technology, compared to more than 11% in 2000.[29] Exerting a drag effect on Moroccan economic diversification are its relatively poorly developed human resources, a prime cause of which is persisting inequality. Bahrain, the most diversified of the GCC economies, incurred a budget deficit of 15% in 2017–18 while running up its public debt to 90% of GDP. So Saudi Arabia is not a unique case as suggested by "star" performer Morocco's comparatively poor performance by global standards and diversified Bahrain's sagging public finances. All the MENA monarchies face the challenge of adjusting to declining rents per capita, and none of them has yet developed a successful strategy for so doing. Real GDP per person in most countries of the GCC has been "flat or in decline for decades," and productivity, "the underlying source of long-term growth, has been stagnant." Public sector jobs continue to pay about three times more than private sector ones, and oil on average still provides 80% of GCC government revenues.[30]

Outliers: Israel and Tunisia

The "outlier" category and the two states in it are non-obvious other than that neither state fits into the other three categories. But together they do share some similarities that account for their relative uniqueness. The first and most important is that both have strong historic and contemporary ties to the West. Israel was created as a Zionist settler colony cum state, so is a European implant into the MENA, with which it continues to share relatively little in common and indeed is frequently not included in the MENA region as categorized by many international organizations. Israel's stateness thus derives more directly from European prototypes than from a dialectical encounter with colonialism, as in the case of Tunisia, even though the most radical Zionist nationalists did militarily challenge British power in mandate Palestine. But as Clement Henry so cogently argued, Tunisia's colonial dialectic was the most complete of those in North Africa and, indeed, in the Middle East.[31] Unlike others it produced three "moments" or generations of nationalists, the one that ultimately succeeded in gaining independence being a civilian synthesis of European and local political beliefs and practices. From its national birth Tunisia was thus heavily influenced by Europe in the sense that its successful national movement was led by a civilian political party that subordinated the means of coercion to its control, and that it did not rely upon Islam as a tool of political mobilization. Indeed, Habib Bourguiba, leader of the Neo-Destour Party, was the most secular of Arab nationalist leaders to then become President of an independent state, and unique among Arab leaders in the immediate post-colonial period in calling for a termination of fasting at Ramadan and refraining from taking strident anti-Israeli positions. Tunisia was economically, socially and even politically then somewhat schizophrenic, oriented toward both Europe, especially France, as well as the Arab world, from whose internal conflicts it sought to keep a discreet distance.

A second similarity is the recent history of Israel's and Tunisia's political economies. Both were enamored of the import substitution industrialization model during their independence struggles and in the immediate post-colonial period, associated as it was with socialism and nationalism. But both subsequently abandoned that model and its associated left-leaning ideology in favor of a more open embrace of globalization, neo-liberalism and export-led growth, which in the case of Israel has fundamentally transformed the country into one of OECD status, with a GDP per capita approaching $40,000 derived in substantial measure from hi-tech exports supported by one of the world's most dynamic start-up financial and technical environments. Were it not for its subordination of the Palestinians, Israel could serve as an exemplar of how the transition from a limited access order—dominated by "insider" Labor Zionism prior to 1977—to a competitive, open access order can stimulate economic growth. It is, however, growth that has come at the price of relative equality, as reflected in the highest level of poverty in the OECD. State capacity has also suffered, as reflected in declining public investment and deteriorating infrastructure. Israel's roads are the OECD's most crowded, for example, while its hospitals provide only 1.8 beds per 1,000 people, which, as *The Economist* notes, "is well below the rich-country mean."[32]

Tunisia has not enjoyed Israel's level of mixed success, but in 2017 its total trade as a proportion of GDP was 99%, outperforming all MENA economies, including Israel at 57%, other than Bahrain, Oman and the UAE.[33] Tunisia's is thus by MENA standards an outward oriented, non-hydrocarbon-based economy, reflecting the country's more general, longstanding orientation toward and engagement with the West, and the necessity for it to diversify due to the lack of substantial oil deposits, both also characteristics of Israel. The relative strength of its private sector is reflected by the recovery of investments in it as a proportion of GDP, which reached 18% in 2018, 5% more than five years previously and almost exactly the proportion in the US.[34]

A third similarity is that both are flawed democracies, albeit Israel's democracy is more longstanding than that of Tunisia, the real launching of which was not under Bourguiba or Ben Ali, both of whom maintained authoritarian control, but in the wake of the 2011 Arab Spring, which itself commenced in Tunisia. The primary flaw in Israel's democratic system lies in the country's treatment of Palestinians. Those living in Israel proper are relegated to second-class status, while those resident in Gaza or the West Bank are subject

210

to draconian controls and intermittent violence of an especially brutal nature in the case of the former, as Operation Cast Lead, which resulted in the deaths of 1,400 Gazan Palestinians in 2006, reflects.[35] Failure to reach an accommodation with the Palestinians undermines Israeli democracy by elevating security both conceptually and operationally; by driving the country ever further to the chauvinist, religious right; and by impeding relations with the surrounding region, thereby reinforcing the emphasis on security as well as the sense of being isolated and surrounded, which in turn feeds chauvinism. The MENA civil war, in which many Arab states and Israel find themselves facing a common enemy in Iran, combined with the attractiveness of Israeli technical exports and expertise, have reduced its isolation by causing various Arab states, especially those in the GCC, to engage in at least economic and security relations with it. Oman, for example, has relied heavily on Israeli technology in its drive for economic diversification and has reached out politically as well, inviting Prime Minister Binyamin Netanyahu to visit Muscat in October 2018.[36] But more intense and formal political and economic relations are still hostage to the Palestinian issue and settlement of it. Arab publics remain strongly anti-Israeli, thereby limiting the degree of engagement Arab leaders can politically afford.

Tunisian democracy is struggling not only because it is novel, but because it faces several challenges simultaneously, the most important of which is stimulating economic growth. After reaching an historic high of $4,310 GDP per capita in 2008, it commenced a more or less steady slide to $3,490 in 2017.[37] A survey taken in Tunisia in September 2018 points to the negative impact of this flagging growth on the population and its political attitudes: 59% of respondents said they were worse off than they had been five years previously, only 21% saying they were better off; 69% observed that their country was "headed in the wrong direction." Their confidence in national institutions was also low, led by the military in which 33% of respondents expressed confidence, followed by only 25% in parliament, 15% in the religious establishment and 10% in the media.[38]

The second major challenge confronting Tunisia is dealing with the institutional and political residues of authoritarianism since independence in 1956, significantly intensified after Ben Ali's coup in 1987. The vital intelligence services upon which both Bourguiba and Ben Ali had relied heavily, in large measure to serve as a counterbalance to the military, remain independent of institutionalized, effective civilian control, as does the politically less obtrusive military. Nidaa Tunis, the ruling party, led de facto by 92-year-old President Muhammad Beji Caid Essebsi, elected in 2014, is, like Essebsi himself, a remnant of the ancien regime, in cabinets of which he served. The actual party head is Essebsi's son Hafedh, who clearly hopes to succeed his father but has managed to drive away about half its MPs since 2014. The profoundly different orientations of those such as Essebsi and his son, who rely on residues of the previous state, including the security services, to exercise power, on the one hand, and reformist elements on the other, became particularly manifest in relation to Tunisia's equivalent of South Africa's Truth and Reconciliation Commission. Due to submit its final report in late 2018, the Truth and Dignity Commission, which commenced its work in June 2014, interviewed nearly 50,000 witnesses, or about one Tunisian for every 230 citizens, in its televised investigations of possible political and economic crimes committed as far back as 1955, but with a primary focus on the period 1987 to 2011. The government, however, intervened to obstruct the work of the Commission, with both the Ministry of Interior and military courts—backed by the President, who has spoken repeatedly of "letting go of the past"—refusing to hand over relevant files. In March 2018 Essebsi's government voted to end the Commission's mandate, but was overruled by a court decision. This struggle over the Commission reflects the intensity of the broader political conflict that has rendered yet more difficult the task of governing effectively and fostering more rapid economic growth.[39]

A third challenge is similar to the second, only in this case it is the divide between Islamists and secularists which has plagued Tunisia since the fall of Ben Ali. Rached Ghannouchi's Ennahda Party won a plurality in the country's first free election held in 2011 and formed a government, but was forced by a secularist backlash to step down three years later. The divide has if anything intensified since then, with Ennahda remaining in the political wings as intermittent acts of Islamist-inspired violence reflect the continuing appeal of the extreme elements of that movement.

The performances of Israel and Tunisia on the World Bank's governance indicators reflect similar features of these two MENA outliers. The lowest score for both is on the indicator of political stability and absence of violence and terrorism, on which Israel's score is 17 and Tunisia's 14, compared to the MENA average of 26 and the LAC region's of 58. Both countries do much better on the most direct indicator of degree of democracy, which is that of voice and accountability. Whereas the MENA mean on that indicator is

26, Israel scores 70 and Tunisia 53. On the four indicators related to state capacities, Israel averages 80, not much behind the OECD average of 87, and Tunisia 50, which is the same as Morocco and 7 points ahead of the MENA average of 43. In sum, these indicators suggest that the two states have comparatively well-developed capacities but are struggling to establish full democracies in that both face unresolved issues of profound importance that contribute to their relative destabilization and violence, which in the case of Tunisia can be attributed to the difficulties of transition from authoritarianism in a divided polity. Israel has far and away the highest state capacities in the MENA, approaching OECD levels, while Tunisia's are better than average for the MENA, equivalent to those in the comparatively well-governed monarchy of Morocco.

Survival is at Stake

All four types of MENA states face serious challenges, with the failed and fragile ones confronting the mortal one of continued national existence. Consumed with either trying to restore statehood by asserting control over all national territory, or preventing it from collapsing, those states, profoundly deficient in capacities, do not have the collective will or the ability to conceive and manage effective economic growth strategies. The most populous MENA states, which are the four authoritarian republics, have responded to increasing political opposition with stepped up repression, diverting attention from stimulating economic growth while typically also subordinating ever more of the economy to control by elements within their deep states. The monarchies, most dependent upon rents so most in need of diversification of their economies, have yet to make substantial headway in that quest. The outlier Israel has sought its economic future largely out of the MENA, while the other outlier Tunisia is caught up in dealing with the political and economic challenges of transition from authoritarianism, which has consumed most of its energies. MENA states, in sum, confront challenges that could be mortal in that unless they are met, ultimately those states will succumb to ever mounting pressures of population growth, stagnating rents, lack of alternative sources of economic growth, environmental degradation and external interventions.

CONCLUSION

This book has drawn upon literatures in three fields—political economy, new institutional economics and historical sociology—to formulate a framework within which to understand contemporary MENA political economies. The key ideas taken from these disciplines are the paramount importance of politics for understanding economic outcomes; the centrality of states and their institutions to those politics; the division of states into those presiding over limited as opposed to open access orders; and finally, that while elite policies and the nature of societies are important to understanding the performance of states, absolutely crucial is their capacity to interact with civil society in the formation and implementation of public policies—their infrastructural power. Based on these ideas the book has explored how MENA political economies came to be limited access orders as a result of their histories, the centrality of hydrocarbons to the regional economy, and their penetration by regional and extra-regional state and non-state actors. The path dependency through which the MENA's states developed their varying capacities was explored in their pre-colonial, colonial, post-colonial and post-post-colonial periods, the principal finding being that countries with significant histories of stateness prior to colonial encounters emerged with greater capacities, the primary exceptions being those states that were transplanted directly from the West—Israel—or which were built in close relationship with it—the monarchies.

Those capacities were divided into two basic types: those relevant to managing populations and those for managing economies. The former type was in turn conceptualized as inclusion—integrating citizens into public decision making—and as developing human resources through provision of educational and health services. Inclusion was measured by comparative institutional performances of bureaucracies and representative bodies, as well as by pervasiveness of e-government. MENA administrations suffer from the maladies of over-centralization, absence of merit-based recruitment and promotion, excessive size and stove-piping. On the most relevant global indices of administrative performance, the Government Closeness Index and the World Bank's Global Indicators of Regulatory Governance, the MENA performs extremely poorly, suggesting that those administrations fail adequately to include citizens by extending public services to them in effective, impersonal fashion, as opposed to through clientelistic networks. As for representative bodies, the Parliamentary Powers Index reveals MENA parliaments to be the world's weakest, while the Arab Democracy Index reports a profound gap between formal legal provisions and their implementation, reflecting the inability of MENA parliaments to compel implementation of the laws they enact. In relation to the most recently developed means of facilitating inclusion of citizens in public policy decision making, which is that of e-government, the World Bank's recent assessment of digital infrastructure in the MENA notes that it "lags that of other emerging regions."[1]

Provision of education and health services parallels and reinforces these deficiencies in inclusion. Based on standardized global tests, the gap between actual years of school and learning adjusted years, on average about three, is greater in the MENA than any other region. On the newly developed Human Capital Index educational attainment and personal health in all MENA countries falls below levels that should be attained based on their relative wealth. Not surprisingly, dissatisfaction with the quality of public services is profound in the MENA, causing comparative life satisfaction to sharply decline and political resentment to increase. The impacts of inadequate human resource development on economic performance are negative, as reflected in the declining Total Factor Productivity of even the richest MENA countries.

Economic management capacities include extracting resources, maintaining fiscal balances and directing credit appropriately, supervising the financial sector to prevent capital flight, deterring corruption, promoting financial inclusion and curtailing informality. These capacities are not well developed in most MENA states. Resource extraction through taxation and particularly direct taxes on incomes and profits is low by global standards, to say nothing of being inefficient. The region has suffered from the Dutch Disease of overvalued currencies since the first oil boom of the early 1970s. Lack of fiscal responsibility has resulted in cumulative budget deficits that annually average almost 8% of the MENA's total GDP, a staggeringly high proportion and one that has led to accumulating public debt, of which the median level for the most populous MENA countries is now almost 90% of GDP. A growing proportion of virtually all MENA state budgets is devoted to recurrent expenditures, thereby eroding fixed capital investment. Budgetary procedures are inefficient and opaque. Allocation of credit is determined more by political connections than by economic rationality, which among other consequences has deterred the emergence of equity markets. Financial inclusion, as reflected by the MENA's ranking on the Global Findex Survey, is the lowest in the world, largely because its residents do not trust financial institutions. Islamic finance has not addressed that gap, while illicit financial flows and corruption have flourished. Failure to induce formalization of vital sectors, including housing and private business, has served as a brake on MENA economic growth.

In no case has any MENA state demonstrated an unambiguous capacity to confront the key challenges facing it. Most importantly, other than Israel and Tunisia, no MENA regime has manifested the intent to open the limited access order over which it prevails. These closed orders impede not only national economic development, but also obstruct the formation of effective regional integration associations that would assist MENA economic growth and facilitate its globalization. The MENA is highly regionalized in the sense that its peoples interact socially and politically across borders more than those of other emerging regions. That regionalization, however, now exacerbated by what is in effect a regional civil war, has impeded rather than facilitated the formation of effective institutionalized regional economic ties. In the absence of meeting doorstep conditions to transition to open access orders, MENA regimes are unlikely either to promote regional integration or to be able to mobilize state and societal resources to weather the gathering economic and political storms facing the region. These are driven by population explosion, environmental degradation, a region-wide civil war and human and physical infrastructural capacities below levels in comparator countries.

The survival strategies of MENA states vary according to their type—failed and fragile, authoritarian republics, monarchies and the regional outliers of Israel and Tunisia. None of the strategies guarantees success and each suffers from what appears to be a fatal flaw. Failed and fragile states are consumed with the need to establish order and security, but do so by promoting state capture and clientelism under the authority of contending elites unable to agree on coherent government policies. Authoritarian republics have all doubled down on repression as the best means to combat popular dissatisfaction, typically under military leadership. Most monarchies have signed up to one or another version of a "vision" plan, concocted by Western management consulting firms with no input from local citizens whose acceptance and active participation is vital to their success. Israel is beset with the problem of failing to accommodate the Palestinians, while the semi-democratic Tunisian government has yet to establish firm control over remnants of the Ben Ali deep state.

Thus far unable to make observable progress in meeting their particular challenges, incapable of continuing to service the social contracts that underpinned their regimes since their foundation, and unwilling to open limited access orders, ruling elites in the MENA have chosen instead to repress populations yet more, further undermining their already limited capacities to deal with these challenges. The MENA, in sum, is facing a multifaceted crisis which has already undermined the viability of its most fragile states and threatens that of others. While one or more states may undertake the reforms necessary to save themselves and their peoples, it is by no means clear this will be the case.

SELECTED READINGS

Comparative and Theoretical

Adly, Amr, *State Reform and Development in the Middle East: The Cases of Turkey and Egypt*. London: Routledge, 2012.

Brynen, Rex, Pete W. Moore, Bassel F. Salloukh and Marie-Joelle Zahar, *Beyond the Arab Spring: Authoritarianism and Democratization in the Arab World*. Boulder: Lynne Rienner, 2012.

Cammett, Melani, Ishac Diwan, Alan Richards and John Waterbury, *A Political Economy of the Middle East*, 4th edition. London: Routledge, 2013.

Clark, Janine A., *Local Politics in Jordan and Morocco: Strategies of Centralization and Decentralization*. New York: Columbia University Press, 2018.

Diwan, Ishac, Adeel Malik and Izak Atiyas, *Crony Capitalism in the Middle East: Business and Politics from Liberalization to the Arab Spring*. Oxford: Oxford University Press, 2019.

Fawcett, Louise, ed., *International Relations of the Middle East*, 5th edition. Oxford: Oxford University Press, 2019.

Henry, Clement M. and Robert Springborg, *Globalization and the Politics of Development in the Middle East*, 2nd edition. Cambridge: Cambridge University Press, 2010.

Kamrava, Mehran, *Inside the Arab State*. London: Hurst, 2018.

Kandil, Hazem, *The Power Triangle: Military, Security, and Politics in Regime Change*. Oxford: Oxford University Press, 2016.

Mcnally, Robert, *Crude Volatility: The History and Future of Boom-Bust Oil Prices*. New York: Columbia University Press, 2017.

Moore, Pete W., *Doing Business in the Middle East: Politics and Economic Crisis in Jordan and Kuwait*. Cambridge: Cambridge University Press, 2004.

Noland, Marcus and Howard Pack, *The Arab Economies in a Changing World*, 2nd edition. New York: Columbia University Press, 2011.

Stepan, Alfred, *Democratic Transition in the Muslim World: A Global Perspective*. New York: Columbia University Press, 2018.

Arabian Peninsula

Al-Rasheed, Madawi, *Salman's Legacy: The Dilemmas of a New Era in Saudi Arabia*. Oxford: Oxford University Press, 2018.

Brehony, Noel and Saud al-Sarhan, eds, *Rebuilding Yemen: Political, Economic and Social Challenges*. Berlin: Gerlach Press, 2015.

Carapico, Sheila, *Civil Society in Yemen: The Political Economy of Activism in Modern Arabia*. Cambridge: Cambridge University Press, 1998.

Davidson, Christopher, *Dubai: The Vulnerability of Success*. New York: Columbia University Press, 2008.

Davidson, Christopher, *Abu Dhabi: Oil and Beyond*. New York: Columbia University Press, 2009.

Freer, Courtney, *Rentier Islamism: The Influence of the Muslim Brotherhood in Gulf Monarchies*. Oxford: Oxford University Press, 2018.

Gray, Matthew, *The Economy of the Gulf States*. New York: Columbia University Press, 2019.

Haykel, Bernard, Thomas Hegghamer and Stephane Lacroix, eds, *Saudi Arabia in Transition: Insights on Social, Political, Economic, and Religious Change*. Cambridge: Cambridge University Press, 2015.

Herb, Michael, *All in the Family: Absolutism, Revolution and Democracy in the Middle Eastern Monarchies*. Albany: State University of New York Press, 1999.

Herb, Michael, *The Wages of Oil: Parliaments and Economic Development in Kuwait and the UAE*. Ithaca: Cornell University Press, 2014.

Hertog, Steffen, *Princes, Brokers, and Bureaucrats: Oil and the State in Saudi Arabia*. Ithaca: Cornell University Press, 2011.

Hertog, Steffen, Giacomo Luciani and Marc Valeri, eds, *Business Politics in the Middle East*. London: Hurst, 2018.

Kamrava, Mehran, ed., *The Political Economy of the Persian Gulf*. London: Hurst, 2018.

Krane, Jim, *Energy Kingdoms: Oil and Political Survival in the Persian Gulf*. New York: Columbia University Press, 2019.

Lackner, Helen, *Yemen in Crisis: Autocracy, Neo-Liberalism and the Disintegration of a State*. London: Saqi Books, 2017.

Niblock, Tim, with Monica Malik, *The Political Economy of Saudi Arabia*. London: Taylor and Francis, 2007.

Ulrichsen, Kristian Coates, *The Gulf States in International Political Economy*. London: Palgrave Macmillan, 2015.

Valeri, Marc, *Oman: Politics and Society in the Qaboos State*. Oxford: Oxford University Press, 2017.

Wehry, Frederic M., *Sectarian Politics in the Gulf: From the Iraq War to the Arab Uprisings*. New York: Columbia University Press, 2016.

North Africa

Abul-Magd, Zeinab, *Militarizing the Nation: The Army, Business and Revolution in Egypt*. New York: Columbia University Press, 2018.

Adly, Amr, *Cleft Capitalism: Understanding Failed Capitalist Transformation in Egypt*. Palo Alto: Stanford University Press, 2019.

Bogaert, Koenraad, *Globalized Authoritarianism: Megaprojects, Slums, and Class Relations in Urban Morocco*. Minneapolis: University of Minnesota Press, 2018.

Cammett, Melani Claire, *Globalization and Business Politics in Arab North Africa: A Comparative Perspective*. Cambridge: Cambridge University Press, 2007.

Chorin, Ethan, *Exit Gaddafi: The Hidden History of the Egyptian Revolution*. London: Saqi Books, 2012.

Fahmy, Khaled, *In Quest of Justice: Islamic Law and Forensic Medicine in Modern Egypt*. Berkeley: University of California Press, 2018.

Girguis, Laure, *Copts and the Security State: Violence, Coercion and Sectarianism in Contemporary Egypt*. Palo Alto: Stanford University Press, 2016.

Ikram, Khalid, *The Political Economy of Reforms in Egypt: Issues and Policy Making Since 1952*. Cairo: American University in Cairo Press, 2018.

Lowi, Miriam R., *Oil Wealth and the Poverty of Politics: Algeria Compared*. Cambridge: Cambridge University Press, 2009.

Santini, Ruth Hanau, *Limited Statehood in Post-Revolutionary Tunisia: Citizenship, Economy and Security*. London: Palgrave, 2018.

Schechter, Relli, *The Rise of the Egyptian Middle Class: Socio-Economic Mobility and Public Discontent from Nasser to Sadat*. Cambridge: Cambridge University Press, 2019.

Soliman, Samer, *The Autumn of Dictatorship: Fiscal Crisis and Political Change in Egypt under Mubarak*. Palo Alto: Stanford University Press, 2011.

Springborg, Robert, *Egypt*. Polity Press, 2018.

Israel, Iran and Turkey

Alizadeh, Parvin and Hassan Hakimian, eds, *Iran and the Global Economy: Petro-Populism, Islam and Economic Sanctions*. London: Routledge, 2016.

Buğra, Ayşe and Osman Savaşkan, *New Capitalism in Turkey: The Relationship between Politics, Religion and Business*. Cheltenham: Edward Elgar, 2014.

Del Sarto, Raffaella A., *Israel under Siege: The Politics of Insecurity and the Rise of the Israeli Neo-Revisionist Right*. Washington, DC: Georgetown University Press, 2017.

Gohardani, Farhad and Zahra Tizro, *The Political Economy of Iran: Development, Revolution and Political Violence*. London: Palgrave Macmillan, 2019.

Gürakar, Esra Çevike, *Politics of Favoritism in Public Procurement in Turkey: Reconfigurations of Dependency Networks in the AKP Era*. London: Palgrave Macmillan, 2016.

Maloney, Suzanne, *Iran's Political Economy Since the Revolution*. Cambridge: Cambridge University Press, 2015.

Razin, Assaf, *Israel and the World Economy: The Power of Globalization*. Cambridge, MA: MIT Press, 2018.

Rivlin, Paul, *The Israeli Economy from the Foundation of the State through the 21st Century*. Cambridge: Cambridge University Press, 2011.

Senor, Dan and Saul Singer, *Start Up Nation: The Story of Israel's Economic Miracle*. New York: Council on Foreign Relations, 2009.

Waldman, Simon and Emre Caliskan, *The New Turkey and Its Discontents*. Oxford: Oxford University Press, 2017.

Iraq, Jordan, Lebanon and Syria

Blaydes, Lisa, *State of Repression: Iraq Under Saddam Hussein*. Princeton: Princeton University Press, 2018.
Cammett, Melani, *Compassionate Communalism: Welfare and Sectarianism in Lebanon*. Ithaca: Cornell University Press, 2014.
Gunter, Frank R., *The Political Economy of Iraq: Restoring Balance in a Post-Conflict Society*. London: Edward Elgar, 2014.
Haddad, Bassam S. A., *Business Networks in Syria: The Political Economy of Authoritarian Resistance*. Palo Alto: Stanford University Press, 2012.
Matar, Linda, *The Political Economy of Investment in Syria*. London: Palgrave Macmillan, 2016.
Ryan, Curtis R., *Jordan and the Arab Uprisings: Regime Survival and Politics Beyond the State*. New York: Columbia University Press, 2018.
Safieddin, Hicham, *Banking on the State: The Financial Foundations of Lebanon*. Palo Alto: Stanford University Press, 2019.
Yousif, Bassam, *Human Development in Iraq*. London: Routledge, 2013.

NOTES

INTRODUCTION

1 See https://rulemaking.worldbank.org/en/key-findings.

1 ACCOUNTING FOR DEVELOPMENT IN THE MENA

1 World Bank, *MENA Economic Monitor: Recent Economic Developments and Prospects* (October 2017), p. 6.
2 World Bank, *Jobs or Privileges: Unleashing the Employment Potential of the Middle East and North Africa*, http://www.worldbank.org/en/region/mena/publication/jobs-or-privileges-unleashing-the-employment-potential-of-the-middle-east-and-north-africa.
3 For historical trends of unemployment in the MENA as well as other key indicators, see the World Bank's *MENA Economic Update*, which in 2019 replaced its previous *MENA Economic Monitor*, http://www.worldbank.org/en/region/mena/publication/mena-economic-monitor.
4 Ian Vasquez and Tanja Porcnik, *The Human Freedom Index 2017: A Global Measurement of Personal, Civil and Economic Freedom*. Washington, D.C.: The Cato Institute, 2017.
5 Ha-Joon Chang, *Economics: The User's Guide*. London: Pelican Books, 2014, p. 377.
6 Ibid.
7 The post-Mao economic reform program, dubbed "touching stones to cross the river," drew explicitly on Chinese history and Confucianism in particular. See Peter Nolan, "The China Puzzle: Touching Stones to Cross the River," *Challenge* (January–February 1994), https://public.wsu.edu/~hallagan/EconS391/weeks/week4/chinapuzzle.pdf.
8 Many of Muhammad Ali's reforms, including those to the legal system, synthesized existing and imported models, achieving thereby considerable success. For an in-depth study of such reforms, see Khaled Fahmy, *In Quest of Justice: Islamic Law and Forensic Medicine in Modern Egypt*. Berkeley: University of California Press, 2018.

9 Charles Issawi, *The Middle East Economy: Decline and Recovery. Selected Essays*. New York: Marcus Wiener Publishers, 2010.

10 Charles Issawi, "Introduction," in Issawi, ed., *An Economic History of the Middle East, 1800–1914*. Chicago: University of Chicago Press, 1966, p. 4.

11 Ibid.

12 For reviews of this literature, see Robert Springborg, "Arab Militaries," in Marc Lynch, *The Arab Uprisings Explained: New Contentious Politics in the Middle East*. New York: Columbia University Press, 2014, pp. 142–59; and Robert Springborg, "A Shifting Role of the Military in Arab Politics? Cross-Regional Perspectives and Implications for the Future of Civil-Military Relations in the Region," in Holger Albrecht, Ariel Croissant and Fred Lawson, eds, *Armies and Insurgencies in the Arab Spring*. Philadelphia: University of Pennsylvania Press, 2016, pp. 71–96.

13 Issawi, *An Economic History*, p. 4.

14 Ibid., p. 5.

15 Richard W. Bulliet, *The Camel and the Wheel*. Cambridge, MA: Harvard University Press, 1975.

16 Timur Kuran, *The Long Divergence: How Islamic Law Held Back the Middle East*. Princeton: Princeton University Press, 2010.

17 Ibid., dustjacket.

18 Daron Acemoglu and James A. Robinson, *Why Nations Fail: The Origins of Power, Prosperity, and Poverty*. New York: Random House, 2012.

19 Ruth Hanau Santini, "A New Regional Cold War in the Middle East: Regional Security Complex Theory Revisited," *The International Spectator* (November 2017), pp. 1–19; and Cilja Harders and Matteo Legrenzi, eds, *Beyond Regionalism: Regional Cooperation, Regionalism and Regionalization in the Middle East*. London: Ashgate Publishing, 2008.

20 Santini, "A New Regional Cold War," p. 1.

21 Leon Carl Brown, *International Politics and the Middle East: Old Rules, Dangerous Game*. Princeton: Princeton University Press, 1984.

22 Michael Mann, "The Autonomous Power of the State: Its Origins, Mechanisms, and Results," *European Journal of Sociology* 25:2 (1984), pp. 185–213.

23 *The World Factbook*. Washington, D.C.: Central Intelligence Agency, 2018, https://www.cia.gov/library/publications/the-world-factbook/docs/notesanddefs.html#330.

24 For a review of the data see Adeel Malik and Bassem Awadallah, "The Economics of the Arab Spring," *World Development* 45, c (2013), pp. 296–313. They note that, "in comparative terms, defense spending is high even in resource-scarce countries (e.g., Morocco, Jordan, Syria, and Lebanon) and even after accounting for the large outlay in internal security."

25 Ibrahim Ahmed Elbadawi and Philip Keefer, "Democracy, Democratic Consolidation and Military Spending," Cairo: Economic Research Forum, Working Paper 848 (October 2014), pp. 11–14.

26 Charles Tilly, ed., *The Formation of National States in Western Europe*. Princeton: Princeton University Press, 1975; and Charles Tilly, *Coercion, Capital, and European States: AD 990–1992*. Oxford: Basil Blackwell, 1990.

27 Charles Tilly, "War Making and State Making as Organized Crime," in Peter Evans, Dietrich Rueschemeyer and Theda Skocpol, *Bringing the State Back In*. Cambridge: Cambridge University Press, 1985, pp. 169–87.

28 Figures cited in Nicholas J. Lotito, "Public Trust in Arab Armies," *Sada*, Carnegie Endowment for International Peace (October 30, 2018).

29 See R. P. Cincotta and J. Doces, "The Age-structural Maturity Thesis: The Youth Bulge's Influence on the Advent and Stability of Liberal Democracy," in J. A. Goldstone, Eric Kaufmann and Monica Duffy Toft, eds, *Political Demography: Identity, Conflict and Institutions*. Basingstoke and New York: Palgrave MacMillan, 2012, pp. 98–116.

30 Wolfgang Merkel and Brigitte Weiffen, "Does Heterogeneity Hinder Democracy?," *Comparative Sociology* 11 (2012), pp. 387–421; Jose Montalvo and Marta Reynal-Querol, "Ethnic Diversity and Economic Development," *Journal of Development Economics* 76 (2005), pp. 293–323; and Alberto Alesina et al., "Factionalization," *Journal of Economic Growth* 8, (2003), pp. 155–94.

31 Acemoglu and Robinson, *Why Nations Fail: The Origins of Power, Prosperity, and Poverty*. See especially Chapter 4.

32 Ronald F. Inglehart and Christian Welzel, "Changing Mass Priorities: The Link between Modernization and Democracy," *Perspectives on Politics* (June 2010), pp. 551–67. For more information about the World Values Survey, see the WVS websites, https://www.isr.umich.edu/cps/project_wvs.html and http://www.worldvaluessurvey.org/wvs.jsp.

33 For recent books produced by this team, see Ronald Inglehart and Christian Welzel, *Modernization, Cultural Change and Democracy*. New York and Cambridge: Cambridge University Press, 2005; and Pippa Norris and Ronald Inglehart, *Cosmopolitan Communications: Cultural Diversity in a Globalized World*. New York: Cambridge University Press, 2009.

34 Ronald Inglehart, *Islam, Gender, Culture and Democracy: Findings from the Values Surveys*. Ontario: de Sitter Publications, 2004.

35 Arab Opinion Index, 2015. Doha: Arab Center for Research and Policy Studies.

36 According to the chief economist for the Middle East of the World Bank, "In MENA, manufacturing exports—as a percentage of GDP per year— have been reduced by some 18% over the 1970–1999 period as a result of the region's substantial overvaluation of its currency." The problem has not subsequently been addressed. See Mustapha Nabli et al., "Exchange Rate Management within the Middle East and North Africa: The Cost to Manufacturing Competitiveness." Washington, D.C. World Bank, nd, http://web.worldbank.org/archive/website01418/WEB/IMAGES/AUAEXRAT.PDF.

2 THE ORIGINS OF STATE EFFECTIVENESS

1 Atul Kohli, *State Directed Development: Political Power and Industrialization in the Global Periphery*. Cambridge: Cambridge University Press, 2004, p. 2.

2 Miguel Centeno, Atul Kohli and Deborah J. Yashar, "Unpacking States in the Developing World," in Miguel Centeno, Atul Kohli and Deborah J. Yashar, *States in the Developing World*. Cambridge: Cambridge University Press, 2017, pp. 1–34.

3 Ibid.

4 Ibid.

5 Ibid.

6 See http://info.worldbank.org/governance/wgi/#home.

7 For the argument that only "core" components of governance are really necessary for development, see Musthaq Khan "'Good Governance' an Appropriate Model for Governance Reforms? The Relevance of East Asia for Developing Muslim Countries," in Robert Springborg, ed., *Development Models in Muslim Contexts: Chinese, "Islamic" and Neo-Liberal Alternatives*. Edinburgh: Edinburgh University Press, 2004, pp. 195–230.

8 See http://info.worldbank.org/governance/wgi/#reports.

9 James D. Fearon, "Ethnic and Cultural Diversity by Country," *Journal of Economic Growth* 8:2 (June 2003), pp. 195–222.

10 Khan "Good Governance."

11 Indra Overland, ed., *Public Brainpower: Civil Society and Public Resource Management*. London: Palgrave, 2018.

12 See for example Milan W. Svolik, *The Politics of Authoritarian Rule*. Cambridge: Cambridge University Press, 2012; Sheena Chestnut Greitens, *Dictators and their Secret Police: Coercive Institutions and State Violence*. Cambridge: Cambridge University Press, 2016; and Khan, "Good Governance."

13 MSCI Emerging Markets Index, https://www.msci.com/documents/10199/c0db0a48-01f2-4ba9-ad01-226fd5678111. In 1988, MSCI launched the Emerging Markets Index, which consisted of just ten countries representing less than 1% of world market capitalization. Today it consists of 24 countries representing 10% of world market capitalization.

14 Centeno, Kohli and Yashar, "Unpacking States in the Developing World: Capacity, Performance and Politics," in *States in the Developing World*, pp. 1–34.

15 Orfero Fioretos, Tulia G. Falleti and Adam Sheingate, eds, *The Oxford Handbook of Historical Institutionalism*. Oxford: Oxford University Press, 2016. See also Valerie Bockstette, Areendam Chanda and Louis Putterman, "States and Markets: The Advantage of an Early Start," *Journal of Economic Growth* 7:4 (December 2002), pp. 347–69; and Oana Borcan, Ola Olsson and Louis Putterman, "State History and Economic Development: Evidence from Six Millennia," *Journal of Economic Growth* 23:1 (March 2018), pp. 1–40.

16 See, for example, the papers delivered to a panel on "State Capacity and Economic Development: Historical Experience from China," World Economic History Conference, Boston, 2018, at http://wehc2018.org/state-capacity-and-economic-development-historical-experience-from-china.

17 Ibid.

18 On "stateness" see Clement M. Henry, "'Stateness' and Revolution in the Arab World," unpublished paper, National University of Singapore, 2018.

19 Ibid.

20 Robert W. Stookey, *Yemen: The Politics of the Yemen Arab Republic*. Westview Press, 1978, p. 134.

21 Marc Valeri, *Oman: Politics and Society in the Qaboos State*. London: Hurst, 2nd edition, 2017.

3 Colonialism, Post-Colonialism, Globalization and the State

1 Joseph A. Schumpeter, *Capitalism, Socialism, and Democracy*. London: Routledge, 1994, pp. 82–3.

2 Scholars associated with the World Bank have produced several such studies, the most recent collection of which was presented at the conference on The Political Economy of State–Business Relations in the Middle East, organized by Ishac Diwan, sponsored by the Economic Research Forum and the Paris School of Economics, in Paris, June 21–22, 2018.

3 "Twilight of the Bureaucrats," *The Economist* (March 30–April 5, 2019), p. 52.

4 The term was coined in 1989 by John Williamson and included recommendations to minimize budget deficits, spend public money carefully, reduce tax rates and expand tax bases, adopt market driven interest rates, render exchange rates competitive, reduce barriers to trade, allow in FDI, privatize SOEs, abolish restrictions on competition and guarantee property rights.

5 See https://www.statista.com/statistics/273951/growth-of-the-global-gross-domestic-product-gdp.

6 Giacomo Luciani, "Introduction: In Search of Economic Policies to Sustain Democratic Transitions," *Combining Economic and Political Development: The Experience of MENA*. The Graduate Institute, Geneva, International Development Policy Series 7, 2017, pp. 1–21.

7 Adam Hanieh, *Money, Markets, and Monarchies: The Gulf Cooperation Council and the Political Economy of the Contemporary Middle East*. Cambridge: Cambridge University Press, 2018, pp. 3–4.

8 Bernard Hoekman, "Intra-Regional Trade: Potential Catalyst for Growth in the Middle East," Washington, D.C.: Middle East Institute, Policy Paper 1, 2016, http://cadmus.eui.eu/bitstream/handle/1814/44717/MEI_PP_2016_01.pdf?sequence=1.

9 See https://www.eia.gov/todayinenergy/detail.php?id=35632.

10 "From Zero to Not Much More," *The Economist* (June 4, 2016), p. 46.

4 LIMITED ACCESS ORDERS AND THE RISE OF DEEP STATES

1 Michael Mann, "The Autonomous Power of the State: Its Origins, Mechanisms and Results," 1985, http://www.sscnet.ucla.edu/soc/faculty/mann/Doc1.pdf.

2 Douglass C. North, John Joseph Wallis, Steven B. Webb and Barry R. Weingast, "Limited Access Orders: Rethinking the Problem of Development and Violence," Stanford University (January 25, 2011), https://web.stanford.edu/group/mcnollgast/cgi-bin/wordpress/wp-content/uploads/2013/10/Limited_Access_Orders_in_DW_-II_-2011.0125.submission-version.pdf.

3 Hazel Gray, "Access Orders and the 'New' New Institutional Economics of Development," *Development and Change* 47:1 (2015), pp. 51–75.

4 Janis Nikolaus Kluge, "Foreign Direct Investment, Political Risk and the Limited Access Order," *New Political Economy* 22:1 (2016), pp. 109–27.

5 Ibid.

6 For an overview of this literature and its utilization for assessing labor markets, see Steffen Hertog, "Is There an Arab Variety of Capitalism?," Cairo: Economic Research Forum, Working Paper 1068 (December 2016).

7 Ufuk Akcigit, Salome Baslandze and Francesca Lotti, "Connecting to Power: Political Connections, Innovation, and Firm Dynamics," National Bureau of Economic Research, Working Paper 25136 (October 2018).

8 Ellen Lust, "Governance in Service Delivery in the Middle East and North Africa," Background Paper for World Development Report 2017, World Bank, p. 2.

9 Ibid., pp. 4–5.

10 Ibid., p. 9.

11 For a summary of this literature, see Allen Hicken, "Clientelism," *Annual Review of Political Science* 14 (June 2011), pp. 289–310.

12 "The study shows that the widespread use of wasta adversely affects the business climate in Jordan by making state–business relations inefficient and unfair." Markus Loewe et al., "The Impact of Favoritism on the Business Climate: A Study of Wasta in Jordan," Bonn: German Development Institute, 2007.

13 Ishac Diwan, "The Arab Spring's Second Chance," Project Syndicate (April 23, 2019), https://www.project-syndicate.org/commentary/algeria-sudan-army-power-struggle-by-ishac-diwan-2019-04.

14 Anne Marie Baylouny, *Privatizing Welfare in the Middle East: Kin Mutual Aid Associations in Jordan and Lebanon*. Bloomington: Indiana University Press, 2010.

15 Diane Singerman, *Avenues of Participation: Family, Politics and Networks in Urban Quarters of Cairo*. Princeton: Princeton University Press, 1996.

16 Since the early 1980s the United States Agency for International Development has conducted at least four major decentralization projects in Egypt, investing more than $1 billion in them. Local administration, including its financial and political dimensions, remains as centralized as it was before these activities commenced.

17 The term "info-shy" was coined by Clement M. Henry in reference to Tunisia. For elaboration of it there and in other settings, and of the inadequacy of public accounts in the MENA, see Clement M. Henry and Robert Springborg, *Globalization and the Politics of Development in the Middle East*. Cambridge: Cambridge University Press, 2nd edition, 2010.

18 Hicken, "Clientelism," pp. 289–310.

19 Gabriela Ippolito-O'Donnell, "Political Clientelism and the Quality of Democracy," Paper presented to the annual conference of the International Political Science Association, Fukuoka, Japan, July 9–13, 2006.

20 Jonathan Fox, "The Difficult Transition from Clientelism to Citizenship: Lessons from Mexico," *World Politics* 46:2 (January 1994), pp. 151–84.

21 Nicolas van de Walle, "The Democratization of Clientelism in Sub-Saharan Africa," Paper delivered at the 3rd European Conference on African Studies, Leipzig, Germany, June 4–7, 2009, http://citeseerx.ist.psu.edu/viewdoc/download?doi=10.1.1.536.4738&rep=rep1&type=pdf. (emphasis added).

22 Robert Gay, "Rethinking Clientelism: Demands, Discourses and Practices in Contemporary Brazil," *European Review of Latin American and Caribbean Studies* 65 (December 1998), pp. 7–24.

23 Nazih N. Ayubi, *Overstating the Arab State: Politics and Society in the Middle East*. London: I.B. Tauris, 1996.

24 "What is the Deep State"? *The Economist* (March 9, 2017).

25 According to Dexter Filkins, the Turkish deep state "is a presumed clandestine network of military officers and their civilian allies who, for decades, suppressed and sometimes murdered dissidents, Communists, reporters, Islamists, Christian missionaries and members of minority

groups—anyone thought to pose a threat to the secular order." According to historians, Filkins notes, it has "functioned as a kind of shadow government, disseminating propaganda to whip up public fear or destabilizing civilian governments not to its liking." Dexter Filkins, "Letter from Turkey: The Deep State," *The New Yorker* (March 12, 2012).

26 Robert Springborg, *Egypt*. Cambridge: Polity Press, 2017.
27 Sanam Vakil and Hossein Rassam, "Iran's Next Supreme Leaders: The Islamic Republic After Khamenei," *Foreign Affairs* (May/June 2017), pp. 76–87. For the view of the Iranian deep state as being comprised of the IRGC, see Alex Vatanka, "How Deep is Iran's State?," *Foreign Affairs* (July/ August 2017), pp. 155–9.
28 Jean-Pierre Filiu, *From Deep State to Islamic State: The Arab Counter-Revolution and its Jihadi Legacy*. Oxford: Oxford University Press, 2015, p. 45.
29 Ibid.
30 Ibid., p. 48.
31 Charles Tripp, "Iraq's Dual State: Product of the Past, Very Present," Watson Institute of International and Public Affairs, Brown University (October 22, 2010), https://watson.brown.edu/news/2010/iraqs-dual-state-product-past-very-present. See also Charles Tripp, *A History of Iraq*. Cambridge: Cambridge University Press, 3rd edition, 2007; and Charles Tripp, "Militias, Vigilantes, Death Squads," *London Review of Books* 29:2 (January 25, 2007), pp. 30–3.
32 Tripp, "Iraq's Dual State."
33 Ibid.
34 Joseph Sassoon, *Anatomy of Authoritarianism in the Arab Republics*. Cambridge: Cambridge University Press, 2016.
35 Adeel Malik, "Rethinking the Rentier Curse," in Giacomo Luciani, ed., *Combining Economic and Political Development: The Experience of the MENA*. Leiden: Brill Nijhoff, 2017, pp. 41–57.
36 Mohammed Hachemaoui, "Who Really Governs Algeria?," *Politique Africaine* 142:2 (2016), pp. 169–90.
37 Gregory J. Kasza, *The Conscription Society: Administered Mass Organizations*, New Haven: Yale University Press, 1995, p. 59, cited in ibid., p. 180.
38 "Algeria: Reviving the Land of the Living Dead," *The Economist* (July 1, 2017), p. 42.

5 DEEP STATES: TYPES, RESOURCES AND IMPACTS

1 Tripp, "Iraq's Dual State."
2 Joseph Sassoon, *Saddam Hussein's Ba'th Party: Inside an Authoritarian Regime*. Cambridge: Cambridge University Press, 2012. Lisa Blaydes, *State of Repression: Iraq under Saddam Hussein*. Princeton: Princeton University Press, 2018.
3 Shahir Shahidsaless, "Why Iran's 'Enemy Narrative' is Flawed," Atlantic Council (August 11, 2017), https://www.atlanticcouncil.org/blogs/iransource/why-iran-s-enemy-narrative-is-flawed.
4 Noureddine Jebnoun, *Tunisia's National Intelligence: Why "Rogue*

Elephants" Fail to Reform. Washington, D.C.: The Center for Contemporary Arab Studies, Georgetown University, 2017.

5 Borzou Daragahi, "Former President's Tunisian Crony Capitalism Laid Bare," *Financial Times* (March 25, 2014), p. 6.

6 On Iranian covert support for Shi'a groupings in Lebanon, Syria, Iraq and Yemen, see Phillip Smythe, Tim Michetti and Owen Daniels, *Revolution Unveiled: A Closer Look at Iran's Presence and Influence in the Middle East.* Washington, D.C.: The Atlantic Council (September, 2017).

7 Abdurahman al-Masri and Alexander Corbell, "Hezbollah Re-Ascendant in Lebanon," *Sada*, Carnegie Endowment for International Peace (August 17, 2017).

8 Ibid.

9 Ibid.

10 Ibid. Hassan Nasrallah, Secretary General of Hizbullah, stated in June 2016, in a speech broadcast by the organization's TV station, al Manar, that "We are open about the fact that Hezbollah's budget, its income, its expenses, everything it eats and drinks, its weapons and rockets, come from the the Islamic Republic of Iran." "Hezbollah Brushes off US Sanctions, Says Money Comes via Iran," *al Monitor* (June 24, 2016).

11 "Captured by Captagon," *The Economist* (July 22, 2017), p. 38.

12 Ben Hubbard, "Hezbollah: Iran's Middle East Agent, Emissary and Hammer," *New York Times* (August 27, 2017).

13 Guido Steinberg, "The Badr Organization: Iran's Most Important Instrument in Iraq," *SWP Comments* 26, German Institute for International and Security Affairs (July 2017).

14 Ibid., p. 3.

15 Ibid., p. 5.

16 Ibid., p. 7.

17 Filkens, "Letter from Turkey."

18 Carlotta Gall, "President Recep Tayyip Erdogan of Turkey Replaces Top Military Chiefs," *New York Times* (August 2, 2017).

19 The subterranean battle commenced in earnest in 2007 when military members of the Kemalist deep state tried to block the AK Party's presidential candidate from running. A year later the chief prosecutor sought to ban the party on the grounds that it was anti-secular. So, as in Egypt, Turkey's Islamists had good reason to believe that winning power and then holding it through democratic means would only be possible if it countered the opposed deep state with its own.

20 Since the beginning of the Yemeni civil war in March 2015, the competing deep states have fought for control over the central bank, the oil producing regions of Marib and the Hadhramaut, the supply of fuel to the population, customs, mobile phone networks and smuggling of Qat. Rafat Al-Akhali, "The Battle to Control the 'Commanding Heights' of the Yemeni Economy," #LSE Yemen, Middle East Centre, London School of Economics (March 29, 2017). In Syria Hafiz al Asad depended ever more heavily on his security services, which were allowed to extract resources from the population. This was done through a variety of means, from "blackmail to bribes people paid for 'security approval,' as it is called in Syria. This refers to the security forces' approval of any kind of activity after one's graduation, from opening a barber shop or founding a company, approving someone for a job with

the state, or even holding a wedding." Abdel-Nasser al-Ayed, "Can Syria be Salvaged? The Role of the Military and Security Forces," in Bassma Komani and Nayla Moussa, *Out of the Inferno: Rebuilding Security in Iraq, Libya, Syria and Yemen*. Arab Reform Initiative (August 2017), pp. 70–103.

21 Khaled Yacoub Oweis, "Syria's Society Upended," *SWP Comments* 27, German Institute for International and Security Affairs (July 2017), p. 2.

22 Alex Vatanka, "Rouhani Goes to War Against Iran's Deep State," *Foreign Policy* (May 18, 2017), https://foreignpolicy.com/2017/05/18/rouhani-goes-to-war-against-irans-deep-state.

23 Ibid.

24 Ibid.

25 Sanam Vakil and Hossein Rassam, "Iran's Next Supreme Leader: The Islamic Republic After Khamenei," *Foreign Affairs* (May–June 2017), pp. 76–86; "The Pain of No Deal," *The Economist* (August 11, 2018), p. 35.

26 Bijan Khajehpour, "The Real Footprint of the IRGC in Iran's Economy," *al Monitor* (August 9, 2017), https://www.al-monitor.com/pulse/originals/2017/08/iran-irgc-economy-footprint-khatam-olanbia.html.

27 Monavar Khalaj, "Revolutionary Guards Eye Iran Gasfield," *Financial Times* (March 22, 2019).

28 Muhammad Sahimi, "Iran's 'Deep State' has the Most to Lose from Opening to the West," *The National Interest* (November 10, 2015), https://nationalinterest.org/feature/irans-deep-state-has-the-most-lose-opening-the-west-14297.

29 Mohammed Alsulami, "Rouhani and Iranian Revolutionary Guards: Political Tension of an Economic Nature," Arabian Gulf Center for Iranian Studies (August 18, 2017), https://arabiangcis.org/english/articles/rouhani-and-iranian-revolutionary-guards-political-tension-of-an-economic-nature.

30 The report was prepared by the Peterson Institute for International Economics and is cited in Daragahi, "Former President's Tunisian Crony Capitalism Laid Bare."

31 Ibid.

32 Ibid.

33 Virginie Collombier, "Make Politics, Not War: Armed Groups and Political Competition in post-Qaddafi Libya," in Komani and Moussa, *Out of the Inferno*, pp. 48–69.

34 For a review of the literature relevant to this argument, see Robert Springborg, "GCC Countries as 'Rentier States' Revisited," *The Middle East Journal* 67:2 (Spring 2013), pp. 301–9.

35 Michael Herb, *All in the Family: Absolutism, Revolution and Democracy in Middle Eastern Monarchies*. Albany: SUNY Press, 1999.

36 Sultan Qaboos, enjoying less "natural" legitimacy than the kings of Morocco, has invested more heavily in building a personality cult. See Valeri, *Oman: Politics and Society in the Qaboos State*.

37 Marc Valeri, "Oligarchy vs. Oligarchy: Business and Politics of Reform in Bahrain and Oman," in Steffen Hertog, Giacomo Luciani and Marc Valeri, eds, *Business Politics in the Middle East*. London: Hurst, 2013, pp. 17–42.

38 Ibid., p. 32.

39 "Uneasy Sits Qaboos," *The Economist* (July 8, 2017), pp. 43–4.

40 Ibid.

41 Jomana Amara, "Reality vs. Fantasy: Transforming the Arab States' Military

Force Structure," *Middle East Policy* 24:3 (2017), pp. 104–16. See also http://www.nationmaster.com/country-info/stats/Military/Personnel/Per-capita.

42 Eleonara Ardemagni, "Building New Gulf States Through Conscription," *Sada*, Carnegie Endowment for International Peace (April 25, 2018).

43 "Saudi Royal Decisions ... Bring Prince bin Salman One Step Closer to the Throne," *Rai al Youm* (June 18, 2017).

44 Ben Hubbard, "Saudi Arabia Detains Critics as New Crown Prince Consolidates Power," *New York Times* (September 14, 2017).

45 For a discussion of his coining of the term and its subsequent spread, see Juan Cole, *The New Arabs: How the Millennial Generation is Changing the Arab World*. New York: Simon and Schuster, 2014, pp. 32–3.

46 Roger Owen, *The Rise and Fall of Arab Presidents for Life*. Cambridge, MA: Harvard University Press, 2014.

6 INCLUSION, HUMAN RESOURCES AND STATE POWER

1 Maksym Ivanyna and Anwar Shah, "How Close is Your Government to Its People?: Worldwide Indicators on Localization and Decentralization," *Economics* (January 27, 2014), http://www.economics-ejournal.org/economics/journalarticles/2014-3.

2 Laurie A. Brand, "Review of Janine A. Clark, *Local Politics in Jordan and Morocco: Strategies of Centralization and Decentralization*," *The Middle East Journal* 72:3 (Summer 2018), pp. 522–4. For an assessment of Jordanian decentralization as a strategy to preserve the political status quo, see Grace Elliott, Matt Cieslieski and Rebecca Birkholz, "Centralized Decentralization: Subnational Governance in Jordan," *Middle East Policy* 25:4 (2018), pp. 130–45.

3 See http://rulemaking.worldbank.org/en/key-findings.

4 Melissa Johns and Valentina Saltane, "Citizen Engagement in Rulemaking: Evidence on Regulatory Practices in 185 countries," Policy Research Working Paper 7840. Washington, D.C.: The World Bank, Global Indicators Group (September 2016), p. 2.

5 Hadi Fathallah, "Failure of Regional Governance in Saudi Arabia," *Sada*, Carnegie Endowment for International Peace (July 26, 2018), https://carnegieendowment.org/sada/76928.

6 World Bank, *MENA Economic Monitor* (April 2018), p. 56.

7 World Bank, *Jobs or Privileges*, p. 94.

8 Ibid., p. 95.

9 Adam Harris et al., *Governance and Service Delivery in the Middle East and North Africa*, Gothenburg, Program on Governance and Local Development, 2017, p. 5.

10 M. Steven Fish and Matthew Kroenig, Parliamentary Powers Index Score by Country, https://polisci.berkeley.edu/sites/default/files/people/u3833/PPIScores.pdf.

11 Arab Democracy Index 5 (June 2017).

12 World Bank, *MENA Economic Monitor* (October 2018), p. 45.

13 Ibid., pp. 46–51.

14 Mark Dincecco, *State Capacity and Economic Development: Past and Present*. Cambridge: Cambridge University Press (2018) pp. 14–15.

15 World Bank, *Learning to Realize Education's Promise* (2018), p. 48.
16 Ibid., p. 8.
17 Ibid., p. 39.
18 World Bank, *World Development Report 2019*, p. 62.
19 Ibid., p. 61.
20 World Bank, *Inequality, Uprisings, and Conflict in the Arab World* (October 2015), p. 13.
21 Ibid., p. 22.
22 Ibid., p. 23.
23 Ibid., p. 30.
24 World Bank, *MENA Economic Monitor* (October 2018), pp. 30–2.
25 Ibid., p. 31.
26 For reviews of this literature see Timothy Besley and Torsten Persson, "State Capacity, Conflict, and Development," *Econometrica* (February 8, 2010); and Daron Acemoglu, Camilo Garcia-Jiminez and James A. Robinson, "State Capacity and Economic Development: A Network Approach," *American Economic Review* 105:8 (August 2015), pp. 2364–409.
27 For a discussion of the emergence of the state as the center of political economy analysis, see Acemoglu, Garcia-Jiminez and Robinson, "State Capacity."
28 Michael Mann, *The Sources of Social Power*, Vol. 1. Cambridge: Cambridge University Press, 1986, p. 113.
29 Petros G. Sekeris, "State Power, State Capacity, and Development," *Peace Economics, Peace Science, and Public Policy* 21:4 (2015), pp. 553–60.
30 Mancur Olson, "Dictatorship, Democracy and Development," *American Political Science Review* 87:3 (1993), pp. 567–76.
31 Global Peace Index Report cited at https://www.atlasandboots.com/most-dangerous-countries-in-the-world-ranked.
32 State Fragility Index and Matrix 2019, https://fragilestatesindex.org.
33 Monty G. Marshall and Gabriele Enzinga-Marshall, *Global Report 2017: Conflict Governance and State Fragility*. Center for Systemic Peace, 2018, http://www.systemicpeace.org/vlibrary/GlobalReport2017.pdf.
34 Ibid., p. 13.
35 Ibid., p. 12.
36 Ishac Diwan and Tarik Akin, "Fifty Years of Fiscal Policy in the Arab Region," Economic Research Forum, Working Paper 914 (May 2015), p. 21.
37 The Economist, *Pocket World in Figures*, 2018 edition, p. 83.
38 For comparative figures on military and security personnel, see Gijs Verbossen, *Mubarak's Weakness: A Political Economy of a Structurally Weak Regime*. Unpublished PhD Thesis, Department of Politics and Philosophy, Latrobe University, Melbourne, 2018.
39 Douglass North, John Wallis and Barry Weingast, *Violence and Social Orders: A Conceptual Framework for Interpreting Recorded Human History*. Cambridge: Cambridge University Press, 2009. Cited in Diwan and Akin, "Fifty Years of Fiscal Policy in the Arab Region," p. 21.

7 STATE CAPACITIES FOR ECONOMIC MANAGEMENT

1 Dincecco, *State Capacity and Economic Development*.

2 Besley and Persson, "State Capacity," pp. 54, 56–7.
3 D. S. Acemoglu, S. Johnson and J. Robinson, "Institutions as a Fundamental Cause of Long-Run Growth," in P. Aghion and S. Durlauf, eds, *Handbook of Economic Growth*, Amsterdam: Elsevier, 2005, pp. 1200–1. Besley and Persson, "State Capacity," pp. 61–2, as cited in Dincecco, *State Capacity and Economic Development*, p. 8.
4 Dincecco, *State Capacity and Economic Development*, p. 5.
5 IMF, *Economic Diversification in Oil Exporting Countries*. Annual Meeting of Arab Ministers of Finance, Manama, Bahrain (April 2016), p. 7, https://www.imf.org/external/np/pp/eng/2016/042916.pdf.
6 The Economist, *Pocket World in Figures*, 2018 edition, p. 42.
7 Georgio Cafiero, "Challenges of Saudi Arabia's Vision 2030," in Annalisa Pertaghella, ed., *Saudi Arabia at a Crossroads*. Milan: ISPI, 2018, pp. 35–50.
8 World Bank, *World Development Indicators: Central Government Revenues*, 2018, https://data.worldbank.org/indicator/GC.TAX.TOTL.GD.ZS.
9 *2018 Index of Economic Freedom*. The Heritage Foundation, https://www.heritage.org/index/pdf/2018/book/index_2018.pdf.
10 World Bank, *Doing Business 2018: Reforming to Create Jobs*, p. 33.
11 Cited in Nora Abooushady and Chahir Zaki, "Politics Affect Exports in Egypt," Cairo: Economic Research Forum, Policy Brief 30 (March 2018), p. 4.
12 World Bank, *MENA Economic Monitor* (October 2018), p. 56.
13 The Economist, *Pocket World in Figures*, 2018 edition, p. 56.
14 IMF, *Economic Diversification in Oil Exporting Countries*, p. 15.
15 Diwan and Akin, "Fifty Years of Fiscal Policy in the Arab Region," p. 24.
16 Ibid., p. 25.
17 "Inversions and Aversions," *The Economist* (March 30, 2019), p. 14.
18 Anis Chowdhury and Iyanatul Islam, "Is There an Optimal Debt to GDP Ratio?," CEPR Policy Portal (November 9, 2010), https://voxeu.org/debates/commentaries/there-optimal-debt-gdp-ratio.
19 See https://data.worldbank.org/indicator/GC.XPN.TOTL.GD.ZS?view=chart.
20 World Bank, *Fiscal Policies toward Sustainability, Efficiency and Equity: Vietnam Public Expenditure Review*, 2017, p. 15.
21 Mohamed Zaky, "Egypt Must Strengthen Budget Institutions to Curb Mounting Budget Deficit," Cairo: Economic Research Forum, Policy Brief 23 (May 2017), p. 2. Maged Mandour, "Sisi's Debt Crisis," *Sada*, Carnegie Endowment for International Peace (November 20, 2018).
22 Zaky, "Egypt Must Strengthen Budget Institutions," pp. 1–2.
23 The Open Budget Survey, 2018, https://www.internationalbudget.org/open-budget-survey.
24 These GDP per capita figures are from the World Bank data set at https://data.worldbank.org/indicator/NY.GDP.PCAP.CD?locations=SA.
25 See https://data.worldbank.org/indicator/fs.ast.prvt.gd.zs.
26 Ishac Diwan and Marc Schiffbauer, "Private Banking and Crony Capitalism in Egypt," *Business and Politics* 20:3 (2018), p. 2.
27 World Bank, *Jobs or Privileges*, p. 56.
28 Ibid.
29 Rym Ayadi and Emanuele Sessa, "Micro, Small and Medium Sized Enterprises Development in Egypt, Jordan, Morocco and Tunisia: Structure,

Obstacles and Policies," EMNES Studies 3 (December 2017); and "Assessing the Business Environment and Entrepreneurial Ecosystem in Egypt and Tunisia," Center for International Private Enterprise (October 14, 2014), https://www.cipe.org/blog/2014/10/14/assessing-the-business-environment-and-entrepreneurial-ecosystem-in-egypt-and-tunisia.

30 Ayadi and Sessa, "Micro, Small and Medium Sized Enterprises."
31 "Assessing the Business Environment and Entrepreneurial Ecosystem in Egypt and Tunisia," Center for International Private Enterprise.
32 Ibid.
33 World Bank, *Jobs or Privileges*, p. 21.
34 NRGI, 2017 Resource Governance Index, https://resourcegovernance.org/analysis-tools/publications/2017-resource-governance-index.
35 Ibid., p. 17.
36 See https://www.bti-project.org/en/index/status-index.
37 Nihal Bayraktar, "Measuring Relative Development Level of Stock Markets: Capacity and Effort of Countries," *Borsa Istanbul Review* 14 (2014), pp. 74–93.
38 See https://ac.els-cdn.com/S2214845014000040/1-s2.0-S22148450140000 40-main.pdf?_tid=71c1025d-ff26–40d4-b9af-38d1dbcd1f64&acdnat=1542 901219_648e3bca179bd61159fddd3a924dc030.
39 See the World bank indicators at https://data.worldbank.org/indicator/ CM.MKT.LCAP.GD.ZS.
40 Bayraktar, "Measuring Relative Development," pp. 78–9.
41 Justin Scheck et al., "Saudi Arabia Pumps up Stock Market after Bad News, Including Khashoggi Murder," *Wall Street Journal* (December 13, 2018).
42 Steve Johnson, "Saudi Exchange Takes First Step into Main Global Equity Benchmarks," *Financial Times* (March 19, 2019).
43 Scheck et al., "Saudi Arabia Pumps up Stock Market after Bad News."
44 World Bank, *Bond Market Development Indicators*, https://www.worldbank. org/en/publication/gfdr/data/global-financial-development-database.
45 World Bank, *MENA Economic Monitor* (October 2018), p. 42.
46 Snider cited in Henry and Springborg, *Globalization and the Politics of Development*, p. 80.
47 Ibid., p. 81.
48 Tom Reynolds et al., "The End of Dana Gas Saga?," Trowers and Hamlins, London (June 28, 2018), https://www.trowers.com/resources/articles/ the-end-of-dana-gas-saga.
49 "Appealing to the Umpire: A Court Case Shakes the Foundations of Islamic Finance," *The Economist* (July 1, 2017), p. 65.
50 Global Financial Integrity (April 2017), https://www.gfintegrity.org/issues/ data-by-country.
51 The Economist, *Pocket World in Figures*, 2018 edition, p. 42.
52 Marwa Fatafta, "Rampant Corruption in Arab States", Transparency International (February 21, 2018), https://www.transparency.org/news/ feature/rampant_corruption_in_arab_states.
53 See http://info.worldbank.org/governance/wgi/#reports.
54 Hernando de Soto, *The Mystery of Capital: Why Capitalism Triumphs in the West and Fails Everywhere Else*. New York: Basic Books, 2003.
55 For an example of such work by the IMF, see Leandro Medina and Friedrich

Schneider, "Shadow Economies Around the World: What Did We Learn Over the Past 20 Years?," Washington, D.C.: IMF Working Paper WP/18/17 (January 2018). The flagship report by the World Bank on MENA shadow economies is Robert Gatti et al., *Striving for Better Jobs: The Challenge of Informality in the Middle East and North Africa.* Washington, D.C.: The World Bank, 2014.
56 Gatti et al., *Striving for Better Jobs*, p. 8.
57 Ibid., p. 16.
58 Ibid., p. 18.
59 Medina and Schneider, "Shadow Economies," p. 4.
60 Ibid., p. 58.
61 Ibid., pp. 69–76.
62 Gatti et al., *Striving for Better Jobs*, p 6.
63 "Assessing the Business Environment and Entrepreneurial Ecosystem in Egypt and Tunisia," Center for International Private Enterprise.

8 THE MENA: REGIONALIZED BUT NOT INTEGRATED

1 Giacomo Luciani, "Oil Rent and Regional Economic Development in MENA," in Giacomo Luciani, ed., *Combining Economic and Political Development: The Experience of MENA.* Geneva: International Development Policy, 2017, pp. 211–30.
2 Matteo Legrenzi and Cilja Harders, "Introduction," in *Beyond Regionalism: Regional Cooperation, Regionalism and Regionalization in the Middle East.* London: Palgrave, 2016 pp. 1–17.
3 Brown, *International Politics and the Middle East*, p. 8.
4 Ibid.
5 Arab Barometer, Wave IV, 2016–17, question 901, http://www.arabbarometer.org/waves/arab-barometer-wave-iv.
6 *Arab Human Development Report 2016.* New York: UNDP, Chapter 2.
7 World Values Survey, http://www.worldvaluessurvey.org/wvs.jsp; Pew Global Attitudes and Trends, http://www.pewglobal.org/datasets.
8 Cited in *Arab Human Development Report 2016*, p. 38.
9 Arab Opinion Index 2015, Doha: Arab Center for Research and Policy Studies, https://www.dohainstitute.org/en/lists/ACRPS-PDFDocumentLibrary/Arab_Opinion_Index_2015_Results_in_Brief_REVISED_JUNE_2016.pdf, p. 35.
10 Ibid., p. 15.
11 Ibid.
12 Ibid.
13 *Arab Human Development Report 2016*, pp. 50–2.
14 Ibid.
15 "High Spending Arab Tourists Go on More Diverse Holidays," ITB Berlin (December 7, 2015), https://www.itb-berlin.de/en/Press/PressReleases/News_19843.html.
16 Luciani, "Oil Rent," pp. 211–30.
17 Ibid.
18 *Arab Human Development Report 2016*, p. 84.
19 Hoekman, "Intra-Regional Trade"; Ahmed Galal and Bernard Hoekman,

eds, *Arab Economic Integration: Between Hope and Reality*. Cairo: Egyptian Center for Economic Studies, 2003.

20 See https://publications.iom.int/books/intra-regional-labour-mobility-arab-world.

21 Luciani, "Oil Rent."

22 World Bank, Remittance Inflows, 2017, http://www.worldbank.org/en/topic/migrationremittancesdiasporaissues/brief/migration-remittances-data, and M. I. T. el-Sakka, "Remittance of Egyptian Migrants: An Overview," Middle East Institute (April 2010).

23 "Remittances," *The Economist* (April 28, 2018), p. 81.

24 Luciani, "Oil Rent."

25 *Arab Human Development Report 2016*, p. 16; Gavin Haines, "Six of the Seven Countries on Donald Trump's 'Muslim Ban List' Also Bar Visitors Based on Nationality," *Sunday Telegraph* (January 31, 2017).

26 Mustapha Rouis and Steven R. Tabor, *Regional Economic Integration in the Middle East and North Africa: Beyond Trade Reform*. Washington, D.C.: The World Bank, 2013, p. 33.

27 *Arab Human Development Report 2016*, p. 40; Anthony Cordesman, *The Human Cost of War in the Middle East*. Washington, D.C. Center for Strategic and International Studies (February 3, 2016).

28 Cordesman, *The Human Cost*.

29 Ibid. See also https://data.worldbank.org/indicator/MS.MIL.XPND.GD.ZS.

30 Luciani, "Oil Rent." See also *Tackling the MENA Region's Intersecting Conflicts*. International Crisis Group, Brussels (December 22, 2017).

31 "Iraq Seeks $88.2 Billion for Post-IS Reconstruction," *The New Arab* (February 12, 2018).

32 Karen E. Young, "Self-Imposed Barriers to Economic Integration in the GCC," Arab Gulf States Institute in Washington (August 4, 2017).

33 Rachel Furlow and Salvatore Borgognone, "Gulf Designs on Jordan's Foreign Policy," *Sada*, Carnegie Endowment for International Peace (July 17, 2018).

34 *Arab Human Development Report 2016*, p. 16.

35 Fida Karam and Chahir Zaki, "Why Don't MENA Countries Trade More? The Curse of Bad Institutions," Cairo: Economic Research Forum, Working Paper 1148 (October 2017), p. 6.

36 Rouis and Tabor, *Regional Economic Integration*.

37 *From Political to Economic Awakening in the Arab World: The Path of Economic Integration—A Deauville Partnership Report on Trade and Foreign Direct Investment*. Washington, D.C.: The World Bank, 2012.

38 Hoekman, "Intra-Regional Trade," p. 70.

39 Rouis and Tabor, *Regional Economic Integration*.

40 Ibid., p. 18.

41 Christian Ruckteschler, Adeel Malik and Ferdinand Eibl, "The Politics of Trade Protection: Evidence from an EIU-mandated Tariff Liberalization in Morocco," Paper delivered to the Conference on the Political Economy of State–Business Relations in the Middle East, Paris School of Economics, June 21–22, 2018.

42 Rouis and Tabor, *Regional Economic Integration*, p. 78.

43 Ibid., p. 79.

44 Ibid.

45 Jean-Pierre Chauffour and Jean-Christophe Maur, *Beyond Market Access:*

The New Normal of Preferential Trade Agreements, Washington, D.C.: The World Bank (October 2010), http://documents.worldbank.org/curated/en/638891468326209179/pdf/WPS5454.pdf.

46 Young, "Self-Imposed Barriers to Economic Integration in the GCC."
47 Ibid.
48 Hoekman, "Intra-Regional Trade," p. 75.
49 *The Impact of Regional Trade Agreements and Trade Facilitation in the Middle East and North Africa.* Washington, D.C.: The World Bank, Policy Research Working Paper 3837 (February 2006).
50 Karam and Zaki, "Why Don't MENA Countries Trade More?," p. 2.
51 Ibid., p. 6.
52 Anca Cristea et al., *Open Skies Over the Middle East.* Washington, D.C.: The World Bank, Development Research Group, 2014, pp. 22–3.
53 APICORP Energy Research, 03, 04 (January 2018).
54 Ibid.
55 David B. Des Roches, "GCC Military Cooperation: A Receding Vision," in Zeina Azzam and Imad Harb, eds, *The GCC Crisis at One Year: Stalemate Becomes New Reality.* Washington, D.C.: Arab Center, 2018, pp. 81–90.
56 World Bank, *From Political to Economic Awakening in the Arab World*, p. 3.
57 See http://www.doingbusiness.org/rankings.
58 Jaime De Melo and Cristian Ugarte, *Resource Dependence, Integration, and Diversification in MENA.* Geneva and Clermont-Ferrand: Fondation pour les Études et Recherches sur le Développement International, 2012.
59 Rouis and Tabor, *Regional Economic Integration*, ch. 3.
60 See https://en.wikipedia.org/wiki/List_of_countries_by_GDP_(PPP)_per_capita.
61 See https://data.worldbank.org/indicator/NY.GDP.PCAP.CD.
62 See https://www.statista.com/statistics/268168/globalization-index-by-country.
63 See https://www.kof.ethz.ch/en/forecasts-and-indicators/indicators/kof-global isation-index.html.
64 Adeel Malik and Ferdinand Eibl, "The Politics of Trade Protection in North Africa," in Ishac Diwan, Adeel Malik and Izak Atiyas, eds, *Crony Capitalism in the Middle East: Business and Politics from Liberalization to the Arab Spring.* Oxford: Oxford University Press, forthcoming 2019.
65 Ibid.
66 Ibid.
67 Ibid.
68 Ibid.
69 Chalmers Johnson, *MITI and the Japanese Miracle.* Stanford: Stanford University Press, 1982; and Peter Evans, *Embedded Autonomy: States and Industrial Transformation.* Princeton: Princeton University Press, 1995.
70 Amr Adly, *State Reform and Development in the Middle East: The Cases of Turkey and Egypt*, London: Routledge, 2012; and Sarah Smierciak, *Assembling Egypt's Business–State Relations: Cosmopolitan Capital and International Networks of Exclusion, 2003–2016.* Unpublished PhD thesis, Oxford University, 2017.
71 Martha Chen and Jenna Harvey, "The Informal Economy in Arab Nations: A Comparative Perspective," Paper for Arab Watch Report on Informal Employment in the MENA Region, (January 23, 2017), p. 14, https://www.wiego.org/sites/default/files/resources/files/Informal-Economy-Arab-Countries-2017.pdf.

72 Rouis and Tabor, *Regional Economic Integration*; Sharokh Fardoust, "Economic Integration in the Middle East: Prospects for Development and Stability," Middle East Policy Paper, Middle East Institute (2016); Bernard Hoekman and Patrick Messerlin, "Initial Conditions and Incentives for Arab Economic Integration: Can the European Union's Success be Emulated?," Egyptian Center for Economic Studies, Working Paper 75 (December 2002); Alessandro Romagnoli and Luisa Mengoni, "The Challenge of Economic Integration in the MENA," *Economic Change & Restructuring* 42:1/2 (May 2009), pp. 69–83.

73 Young, "Self-Imposed Barriers to Economic Integration in the GCC."

74 Hoekman, "Intra-Regional Trade."

75 Ibid.

76 Ibid.

77 Karam and Zaki, "Why Don't MENA Countries Trade More?"

9 Survival Strategies in Weaker MENA States

1 Douglass North et al., *In the Shadow of Violence: Politics, Economics and the Problems of Development*. Cambridge: Cambridge University Press, 2013, p. 349.

2 Gray, "Access Orders and the New 'New' Institutional Economics of Development."

3 Ibid., p. 58.

4 This demographic data is taken from Musa McKee et al., "Demographic and Economic Material Factors in the MENA Region," Working Paper 3, MENARA (October 2017).

5 Ibid.

6 Simone Tagliapietra, "The Political Economy of Middle East and North Africa Oil Exporters in Times of Global Decarbonisation," Working Paper 5, Breugel, 2017, http://bruegel.org/wp-content/uploads/2017/04/WP-2017_05.pdf.

7 See https://www.imf.org/en/Publications/REO/MECA/Issues/2018/04/24/mreo0518#Statistical Appendix.

8 See https://www.statista.com/statistics/262858/change-in-opec-crude-oil-prices-since-1960.

9 John Hurley, "How Sudan's Crippling Debt Could Cause a Budget Problem for President Trump," Center for Global Development (July 20, 2017), https://www.cgdev.org/blog/how-sudans-crippling-debt-could-cause-budget-problem-president-trump.

10 *Lebanon Economic Monitor: De-Risking Lebanon 2018*, World Bank (October 2018), p.15.

11 See https://www.transparency.org/news/feature/corruption_perceptions_index_2017?gclid=EAIaIQobChMI9LCEmZ6k3wIVw0PTCh2ssAf4EAAYASAAEgJvCvD_BwE.

12 Lydia Assouad, "Rethinking the Lebanese Economic Miracle: The Extreme Concentration of Income and Wealth in Lebanon, 2005–2014," World Inequality Data Base, Working Paper Series 2017/13 (September 19, 2018).

13 Bassel F. Salloukh, "Taif and the Lebanese State: The Political Economy of a very Sectarian Public Sector," unpublished ms, Lebanese American University, Beirut, 2018.

14 US Department of State, Office of Opinion Research (December 20, 2018).
15 Salloukh, "Taif and the Lebanese State."
16 Information provided by a professor of the Lebanese University and confirmed by another.
17 Salloukh, "Taif and the Lebanese State."
18 World Bank, *Iraq: Systematic Country Diagnostic* (February 3, 2017), http://documents.worldbank.org/curated/en/542811487277729890/pdf/IRAQ-SCD-FINAL-cleared-02132017.pdf., p. 1.
19 Ibid., p. 64.
20 Ibid.
21 Ibid., p. 65.
22 Ibid.
23 Ibid., p. 66
24 Ibid., p. 68.
25 See https://www.internationalbudget.org/open-budget-survey/open-budget-index-rankings.
26 World Bank, *Iraq: Systematic Country Diagnostic*, p. 71.
27 See http://www.doingbusiness.org/en/data/exploreeconomies/iraq#.
28 World Bank, *Iraq: Systematic Country Diagnostic*, p. 80.
29 US Department of State, Nationwide Poll of Iraqi Adults (December 2018).
30 Ayşe Buğra and Osman Savaşkan, *New Capitalism in Turkey: The Relationship Between Politics, Religion and Business*. London: Edward Elgar Publishing, 2014.
31 NRGI, 2017 Resource Governance Index, https://resourcegovernance.org/analysis-tools/publications/2017-resource-governance-index.
32 Cited in Dalia Ghanem-Yazbeck, "Are Bouteflika's Shake-Ups a Sign of Shifting Civil-Military Ties in Algeria?," *World Politics Review* (November 15, 2018). On relations within and between the Algerian political elite, see Amel Boubekeur, "Rolling Either Way? Algerian Entrepreneurs as both Agents of Change and Means of Preservation of the System," *Journal of North African Studies* 18:3 (2013), pp. 469–81.
33 Heba Saleh, "Algeria Energy Crisis Hangs over Economy," *Financial Times* (March 26, 2019).
34 "Egypt Set to be Amongst the World's Best in Agriculture," *Egypt Independent* (December 23, 2018).
35 Diwan, "The Arab Spring's Second Chance."
36 See https://www.theglobaleconomy.com/rankings/Savings.
37 Matt Lundy, "The Dangers of U.S. Dollar Debt," *The Globe and Mail* (August 16, 2018), p. B6.
38 Osama Diab, "The Risks of Egypt's Mounting Debt," Tahrir Institute for Middle East Policy (April 24, 2018), https://timep.org/commentary/analysis/the-risks-of-egypts-mounting-external-debt.
39 "MENA Nuclear Plans Stalled as Challenges Begin to Surface," APICORP Energy Research, 3, 11 (August 2018).
40 James J. Zogby, "Poll has Troubling News About State of Affairs of Tunisia and Egypt," Lobelog (December 26, 2018), https://lobelog.com/poll-has-troubling-news-about-state-of-affairs-of-tunisia-and-egypt.
41 Cited in Onn Winkler, *Arab Political Demography: Population Growth and Natalist Policies*. Eastbourne: Sussex Academic Press, 2009.
42 Caroline Krafft and Ragui Assaad, "Beware of the Echo: The Impending Return

of Demographic Pressures in Egypt," *Policy Perspective* 12 (May 2014), http://www.academia.edu/19463887/Beware_of_the_Echo_The_Impending_ Return_of_Demographic_Pressures_in_Egypt.

43 Ibid.

44 See http://english.ahram.org.eg/NewsContent/1/64/311508/Egypt/Politics-/ Egypt-education-ministry,-intl-schools-association.aspx.

45 See https://www.bbc.com/news/blogs-news-from-elsewhere-45671180.

46 See https://www.egypttoday.com/Article/1/57333/New-Cumulative-Secondary -School-System-to-be-applied-2018-19.

47 See https://madamasr.com/en/2016/09/15/feature/society/the-international- school-of-egypts-military.

48 See https://en.wikipedia.org/wiki/National_Political_Institutes_of_Education.

49 Iriss Jebari, "Can Algeria Ditch Austerity?," *Sada*, Carnegie Endowment for International Peace (September 28, 2016).

10 Survival Strategies in Stronger MENA States

1 See http://mcit.gov.eg/Upcont/Documents/Reports%20and%20Documents_ 492016000_English_Booklet_2030_compressed_4_9_16.pdf.

2 Qatar National Vision 2030, Doha: Ministry of Development Planning and Statistics, http://hdr.undp.org/sites/default/files/qhdr_en_2009.pdf.

3 On the perverse impacts of external advisors on the legitimacy and effec- tiveness of authoritarian rulers, see Calvert W. Jones, "Adviser to the King: Experts, Rationalization and Legitimacy," *World Politics* 71:1 (January 2019), pp. 1–37.

4 Andrew England and Simeon Kerr, "Saudi Arabia: How the Khashoggi Killing Threatens to Overturn the Prince's Project," *Financial Times* (October 22, 2018).

5 Ibid.

6 Simeon Kerr et al., "Saudi Sovereign Wealth Fund in Bank Talks," *Financial Times* (July 31, 2018).

7 Karen E. Young, "Spending to Grow in Saudi Arabia," Arab Gulf States Institute in Washington (August 10, 2018).

8 "Why Gulf Economies Struggle to Wean Themselves Off Oil," *The Economist* (June 21, 2018).

9 Ibid.

10 Subsequently, an advisor to Ali Faqih, Hani Khoja, a partner in McKinsey and Company, the most successful western consulting firm in Saudi Arabia and long-time adviser to Aramco, was arrested and held without trial until at least the end of 2018. Summer Said, Justin Scheck and Bradley Hope, "Former McKinsey Executive Imprisoned by Saudis," *The Wall Street Journal* (December 28, 2018).

11 Ibid.

12 Karen E. Young, "Saudi Arabia's Problem Isn't the Canadian Fight, It's Capital Flight," Bloomberg (August 17, 2018).

13 Elizabeth McBride, "Saudi Arabia is Stumbling in its Effort to become a Global Financial Center," CNBC (August 21, 2018), https://www.cnbc. com/2018/08/21/saudi-arabia-is-backsliding-in-effort-to-build-global-fi- nancial-center.html.

14 Robert Mogielnicki, "The Supply-Side Politics of Kuwait's Industrial Strategy," Arab Gulf States Institute in Washington (October 12, 2018).

15 Sarah Algethami, "What Now for Saudi Arabia's Planned $2 Trillion Fund?," Bloomberg (August 8, 2018).

16 Simeon Kerr and Anjli Raval, "Saudi Prince's Flagship Plan Beset by Doubts After Khashoggi Death," *Financial Times* (December 12, 2018).

17 England and Kerr, "Saudi Arabia: How the Khashoggi Killing Threatens to Overturn the Prince's Project."

18 "Conflict in the Gulf is Hurting Dubai," *The Economist* (November 15, 2018).

19 Matthew Martin, "Expats Go Home," Bloomberg (April 3, 2019), https://www.bloomberg.com/news/articles/2019–04–03/as-expats-leave-saudi-arabia-no-one-is-replacing-them-chart.

20 "Saudi King Extends Allowances as Biggest Budget ever is Announced," al Jazeera (December 18, 2018); and England and Kerr, "Saudi Arabia: How the Khashoggi Killing Threatens to Overturn the Prince's Project."

21 Karen E. Young, "Saudi Economic Reform Update: Saudization and Expat Exodus," Arab Gulf State Institute in Washington (February 28, 2018).

22 Vivian Nereim and Matthew Martin, "Saudis Raise Allowances for Some Royals after Purge," Bloomberg (February 1, 2018), https://www.bloomberg.com/news/articles/2018-02-01/saudis-are-said-to-raise-allowances-for-some-royals-after-purge. See also Karen E. Young, "The Difficult Promise of Economic Reform in the Gulf," Baker Institute for Public Policy, Rice University (September 2018), https://www.bakerinstitute.org/media/files/files/a9b497ad/cme-pub-carnegie-young-092618.pdf.

23 Cited in Kerr and Raval, "Saudi Prince's Flagship Plan Beset by Doubts After Khashoggi Death."

24 Karen E. Young, "The New Sino-Arab Gulf Visions of Economic Development," Lawfare (December 21, 2018), https://www.lawfareblog.com/master-developers-new-sino-arab-gulf-visions-economic-development.

25 Ecuador is a typical example of China gaining control of raw materials in a dependent political economy through a combination of loans, infrastructure projects and bribery. While most of these political economies are those enmeshed in the "Belt and Road Initiative," the case of Ecuador indicates that it is not only those that are negatively impacted. See Nicholas Casey and Clifford Krauss, "It Doesn't Matter if Ecuador Can Afford this Dam: China Still gets Paid," *New York Times* (December 24, 2018).

26 "2017–2018 Arab Opinion Index: Executive Summary," Doha: Arab Center for Research and Policy Studies (July 10, 2018).

27 David Pollock, "New Saudi Poll: Corruption a Major Concern, Divisions on Reforms and U.S. Ties," Washington Institute for Near East Policy (December 11, 2018).

28 Ibid.

29 Bilal Lotfi and Mohamed Karim, "Export Diversification and Economic Growth in Morocco: An Econometric Analysis," *Applied Economics and Finance* 4:6 (November 2017).

30 "Why Gulf Economies Struggle to Wean Themselves Off Oil."

31 Clement Henry Moore, *Politics in North Africa: Algeria, Morocco and Tunisia.* Boston: Little Brown, 1970.

32 "Statesman and Schemer," *The Economist* (March 30, 2019), pp. 25–32.

33 See https://data.worldbank.org/indicator/NE.TRD.GNFS.ZS?locations=ZQ.
34 Diwan, "The Arab Spring's Second Chance."
35 Maram Humaid, "Israel Meant to Kill More: Gaza Ten Years After Op Cast Lead," al Jazeera (December 27, 2018).
36 Nima Khorrami Assl, "Oman's Drive for Economic Diversification," *Sada*, Carnegie Endowment for International Peace (December 14, 2018).
37 See https://www.google.ca/publicdata/explore?ds=d5bncppjof8f9_&met_y=ny_gdp_pcap_cd&idim=country:TUN:MAR:DZA&hl=en&dl=en.
38 Zogby "Poll has Troubling News About State of Affairs in Tunisia and Egypt."
39 "Justice, Eventually: Unlike Other Arab Regimes, Tunisia's Remembers Old Crimes," *The Economist* (December 18, 2018).

CONCLUSION

1 World Bank, *MENA Economic Monitor* (October 2018), p. 45.

INDEX